Managing the Unknown

Why Fact-Finding Procedures Matter to Civil Justice

Managing the Unknown

WHY FACT FACT-FINDING PROCEDURES MATTER TO CIVIL JUSTICE

Nayha Acharya

UNIVERSITY OF TORONTO PRESS
Toronto Buffalo London

Managing the Unknown: Why Fact-Finding Procedures Matter to Civil Justice
© Nayha Acharya, 2026

Irwin Law
An imprint of University of Toronto Press
Toronto Buffalo London
utppublishing.com
Printed in Canada

ISBN 978-1-0498-0176-6 (EPUB)
ISBN 978-1-0498-0174-2 (PAPER)   ISBN 978-1-0498-0175-9 (PDF)

Library and Archives Canada Cataloguing in Publication

Title: Managing the unknown : why fact fact-finding procedures matter to civil justice / Nayha Acharya.
Names: Acharya, Nayha, author.
Description: Includes bibliographical references and index.
Identifiers: Canadiana (print) 20250327694 | Canadiana (ebook) 20250327716 | ISBN 9781049801742 (paper) | ISBN 9781049801759 (PDF) | ISBN 9781049801766 (EPUB)
Subjects: LCSH: Civil procedure — Canada. | LCSH: Evidence (Law) — Canada. | LCSH: Truth.
Classification: LCC KE8349 .A24 2026 | LCC KF8816.ZA2 .A24 2026 kfmod | DDC 347.71/5 — dc23

Cover design: Tamara Hawkins
Cover image: iStock.com/DNY59

The manufacturer's authorized representative in the European Union for product safety is Mare Nostrum Group B.V., Mauritskade 21D, 1091 GC Amsterdam, The Netherlands. Email: gpsr@mare-nostrum.co.uk.

We wish to acknowledge the land on which the University of Toronto Press operates. This land is the traditional territory of the Wendat, the Anishnaabeg, the Haudenosaunee, the Métis, and the Mississaugas of the Credit First Nation.

University of Toronto Press acknowledges the financial support of the Government of Canada and the Ontario Arts Council, an agency of the Government of Ontario, for its publishing activities.

For Murf

Summary Table of Contents

Detailed Table of Contents

Acknowledgements

My study in legal process is entirely a product of my interaction with Professor Ronalda Murphy, my first academic supervisor. She recognized this theoretical orientation in my thinking before I had the words to label it or comprehend it, and it was only her affirmation that encouraged me to pursue this work and academics generally. Her gentle and rigorous intellect guided me through the challenges and demands of theoretical thinking. This work is dedicated to her simply because it would not exist without her. Nor would the joy I get from my life in academia, especially lifting up my students as she did with me.

I am grateful also to all my other academic mentors, including Professors Richard Devlin, Vaughan Black, and Sheila Wildeman who have greatly helped me make this work as rigorous as I could.

Of course, many thanks go to my parents and late grandparents, who have a hand in everything I do, my mother-in-law for being a quiet champion, to my uncles and aunts for their affection, and my cousins who are my best friends.

And last, and indeed most significantly, my heart-filled thanks go to my husband, Ashwani, and our daughter, Kalyani, for surrounding me with their tremendous joy and passion for life.

Introduction

When a client comes to a lawyer with a civil matter, the first step is to seek answers to a crucial question — "what happened?" In most cases, that question of getting to know the facts underlying a legal claim is the cornerstone of the litigation. Yet, when I left law school, though I was comfortable arguing about legal principles based on a given set of facts, I did not have a clear understanding that civil litigation is so much about discerning, expressing, and arguing over the facts themselves, and doing so within a highly regulated process. From my time in legal practice, I came to understand that much of the lawyer's and judge's role revolves around fact-finding. Discoveries, which take up the bulk of civil litigation practice, is just that — a concerted inquiry into discovering what took place that gave rise to the litigation. Similarly, in civil trials our efforts are largely oriented toward displaying and convincing one another of what, in fact, really happened, because those factual questions are so often determinative of the legal outcome. For instance, if we can show that a doctor's negligence caused a patient's injury, the patient will be legally entitled to compensation. If we cannot show that the doctor's negligence in fact caused the patient's injury, the patient will be left uncompensated — the outcome depends on the facts that are found to be true, at least as far as the legal inquiry is concerned.

These questions of fact, which were the "givens" in law school hypothetical exams, are not givens at all. They are the crucial, arduous questions, full of doubt and ambiguity, that can make or break a legal claim. Unsurprisingly, then, a remarkable portion of our legal process is about putting a best effort into sorting through factual uncertainties.

Yet often, the uncertainty remains, and it is not only difficult, but impossible to say for certain what really happened. But the determination of a legal claim depends on making a certain and final decision about the facts. An exploration into how the legal system legitimately reconciles this inherent tension is the purpose of this book.

I have found this theme under-explored from theoretical perspectives, even though it is so central to civil litigation. In this book, I have offered an exploration into legal fact-finding by touring through some key relevant progressions and highlights in contemporary legal theory where big legal thinkers like Hart, Fuller, Habermas, Dworkin, and others, offer incisive insights into what the legal system is all about. I have found this approach and inquiry essential because knowing and being able to articulate why the legal system, though fraught with inherent imperfections, is nonetheless valuable and legitimate, is crucial to understanding our role as legal players, our ethical responsibilities, and offering principled reform efforts. It makes clear why being part of the legal system is socially valuable. I believe that everyone who is part of the legal process, and those who aspire to be, must deeply consider what the legal system is and should be aimed at. I hope this book will prove useful in that respect to students, lawyers, and judges, especially because of its focus on fact-finding.

Below, I have set out more thoroughly the concerns that I hope to address through the analysis that follows, and the approach that I have adopted. The book will be successful if it inspires your thinking (through either disagreement or agreement with what I set out) about what makes our legal system both imperfect yet valuable, and ultimately stimulates your reflection about how we may both improve it and uphold its values.

A. THE CONCERNS

As noted above, almost invariably, factual questions in legal cases involve guesswork, and recognizing that is the starting point of this book. The unavoidability of guesswork brings with it an inescapable risk of factual inaccuracy. The Canadian adjudicative system does not, because it cannot, promise factual accuracy.

Factual uncertainty permeates adjudication, whether the dispute centres on a tort, a contract, or a criminal matter. Consider a plaintiff who suffers an injury in a hit and run car accident. Based on whatever fragments of evidence they can gather, they bring a claim to the courts to have their right to be free from a negligently inflicted injury recognized. Given the uncertainty over whose negligence, if anyone's, caused their injury and how, the judge finds that the requisite factual elements of their claim are not established on the balance of probabilities standard of proof. The legal outcome is that there is no liability, and the plaintiff is left uncompensated, even though they suffered a legal wrong. On the converse, consider a case where medical evidence suggests that a defendant doctor *probably* (say, a 60 percent likelihood) caused an injury to their patient. If the patient brings a claim, the doctor could be held liable, despite the fair chance (40 percent chance in this example) that they did not cause the injury at all.

Similarly, consider a case where parties contracted for delivery of some equipment needed for the construction of a commercial property. Suppose that failure to deliver the equipment is clearly established, but the damages that flow from that breach, like prospective lost profits, are likely to be speculative. A judge will award damages based on the information available. If it turns out later that the lost profits were greater or less than the judicial award, then the compensation for breach of contract would be rendered inaccurate.

Even in the criminal context, where the standard of proof is heightened in favour of the accused, the risk of factual inaccuracy cannot be altogether escaped. And while the likelihood of factual error is less likely to adversely affect the accused person, the risk of false acquittal is amplified owing to the standard of proof in criminal matters: the elements of crimes must be established "beyond a reasonable doubt." For the sake of illustration, assume that this means the standard of proof is 95 percent. If the trier of fact concludes that they are anywhere from 0–94 percent sure that the accused committed the crime, then they must acquit the accused, even though there could be a high likelihood that the accused did commit the crime.

When material factual findings are inaccurate, the ultimate adjudicative outcome could fail to vindicate a legal right, or it could mistakenly impose legal obligations, like in the examples noted above. But because factual accuracy cannot be guaranteed in a plausible judicial system, there exists the possibility that factual determinations are inaccurate, yet legally valid. Being legally valid, those factual determinations are also authoritative in the simple sense that legally valid outcomes are considered to settle a matter, and are understood to be properly enforceable in the community on the basis of their legal validity.[1] In the chapters that follow, I will give jurisprudential attention to the question of why, and on what basis this is acceptable, which I hope will be seen as a contribution to explanations about the legitimacy of the Canadian adjudicative system.

It may be useful at this juncture to affirm that my focus on the validity of judicial fact-finding is just one aspect of adjudication. Factual findings are a crucial element of arriving at a judicial outcome, but there may be other relevant questions when it comes to assessing the validity of adjudicative outcomes, for instance, correct identification, articulation, interpretation, and application of the relevant laws that govern the dispute. Impropriety in any of these could render a judicial outcome invalid. For example, if a judge finds that causation is not established on the balance of probabilities, but nonetheless holds the defendant liable to the plaintiff, that outcome lacks legal validity because it misapplies the law to the legal facts.[2] If judges misinterpret legislated laws or precedents, that can be cause for a legal invalidity of their ultimate decision. Questions about how to assess whether judges have correctly interpreted and applied indeterminate laws occupy most discourses on valid and legitimate adjudication. But in most trial decisions, while the law is not at issue, the facts are very much in dispute. My focus is on

---

1 I note that significant work has been done to define exactly what it means for law to be authoritative, and what that entails both descriptively and normatively, in terms of the nature of the obligations that valid law can and should invoke. I revisit these themes in my jurisprudential discussions in chapter 1, and in more detail in chapter 2, outlining notions of legal validity and its relationship to authority in positivist traditions, focusing on H.L.A. Hart's jurisprudence and on Joseph Raz's theory, which centralizes and develops novel notions of legal authority and its implications. I also consider Jürgen Habermas and Lon Fuller's ideas about legal validity and authority in chapters 1 and 2. But the development of the argument I present depends on an uncontroversial notion: that legal validity brings authoritative implications, where authoritative implications are taken to mean that legally valid rules are understood to be the enforceable rules for a political community. This descriptive claim about the interrelation between legal validity and its implications of authority should sit comfortably with any legal theory.

2 Conceivably, there are instances where judges may have misapplied substantive legal principles in a given case. If the error of law is not caught prior to the expiration of an appeal period, the outcome can remain legally valid and relitigation barred. My point above is that in the usual course, a substantive error of law is cause to render a legal outcome invalid. The fact that even such substantive errors may maintain validity in order to protect the procedural rules of timely appeal constitutes a further endorsement of the idea presented in this chapter and this book generally: procedural propriety is a source of adjudicative validity and cannot be compromised.

this less discussed, though no less significant question of the validity and legitimacy of judicial determinations of "what happened."

Now consider the following: despite the potential inaccuracy of fact-finding in outcomes like those noted above, *they can remain legally valid*. That is because legal validity does not, because it cannot, depend on absolute factual certainty — it depends on likelihoods. And the legal validity of an outcome is important because being legally valid makes an outcome authoritative — compliance with it can and would be enforced. So, legal validity and legal authority go hand in hand. Therefore, legal validity (which implies legal authority) requires normative justification, or legitimacy. My effort in this book is to offer an answer for why and on what basis adjudicative fact-finding can be considered justifiably authoritative, or, legitimate despite potential risk of error.[3] It's a valuable exercise because when we have an answer for why something is legitimate, then we strive to protect that source of legitimacy and strengthen it further where necessary.

I would note here that the terminology that I adopt (legal validity versus legitimacy) can be easily mixed up, but in order for the arguments presented here to maintain their logical flow, they must be kept straight. Legal validity is about whether a legal outcome is acceptable from a purely legal perspective (that is, legal validity is not based on whether we like the outcome or that we can otherwise justify it). Legitimacy, on the other hand, is about whether something can be justified — it's a normative concept. If a legal outcome is legitimate, it means that it has justification. This still doesn't mean that we have to *like* the outcome, but it has some normative quality about it — it is somehow justifiable. This will be a running theme throughout this book which I will return to and reiterate throughout. Taking a look at adjudication through the lens of fact-finding highlights how important good legal procedures are, so this inquiry has opened an avenue for me to theorize how and why the right procedures lead to legitimate legal outcomes, particularly in the fact-finding context. This is the concept of procedural legitimacy, which is key in this book. Here is the basic point: consistent adherence to adjudicative procedures of fact-finding that ensure equal respect for

---

3   As a general abstraction, my inquiry into legitimacy asks for the basis on which adjudicative decrees are justifiably authoritative, in the sense of being binding and backed by force if necessary. As the book progresses, I will present further expansions of this general notion of legitimacy, and will canvass theorists' reflections on why legitimacy is significant and necessary in a theory of law, and especially on its relationship to legal validity.

litigants as autonomous agents are necessary conditions for legitimizing the authority afforded to adjudicative fact-finding. In the upcoming chapters, I seek to substantiate and defend a process-based approach to legal legitimacy and discuss why procedural legitimacy is important to recognize.

I want to be clear at the outset that procedural propriety of fact-finding is one, among other necessary conditions of legitimate adjudication. Other necessary conditions may include the propriety of the substantive laws, and appropriate judicial interpretation and application of those laws. I leave those concerns aside in order to focus on my primary purpose of highlighting the importance of procedural propriety as a crucial element of legitimate adjudicative fact-finding, and to demonstrate the significance of that claim in its own right.

Although the framework for procedurally legitimate fact-finding is applicable to adjudication generally, I maintain a special interest in civil disputes over negligently inflicted personal injuries. There are a couple of reasons for that. First, and perhaps least importantly, personal injury was a significant part of my law practice, and since my time in practice is the root of the inquiry presented in this book, the examples that occur most naturally to me are in that arena. Second, such disputes are notorious for difficulties associated with factual uncertainty. The issues that arise out of that problem provide fertile grounds for displaying the gravity of undervaluing procedural legitimacy in very practical terms.

B. SOME INTRODUCTORY COMMENTS ON PROCEDURE AND SUBSTANCE

My purpose in this work is to present and justify the claim that procedural propriety is essential to legitimate adjudicative fact-finding, and to outline the criteria that procedures must adhere to in order to uphold their justificatory demands. The proposal I offer has formal as well as substantive elements: it declares that legitimacy of fact-finding depends on consistent adherence to procedures (the formal aspect) when those procedures embody equal respect for legal subjects as free-acting agents (the substantive aspect). That requires that adjudicative procedures are genuinely oriented toward producing factually reliable and rational conclusions, and that they assure a full right of participation to affected parties. If they accomplish these things, legal procedures can be understood to maintain the foundational human dignity of those that are governed by them. As such, they can be trusted to produce outcomes whose authority may be respected, even though there is always risk of error and fallibility.

Developing and defending this proposal requires me to approach and consider the often blurry dichotomy between substance and procedure. Wherever relevant, I return to various aspects of this theme throughout the book. For now, I make the introductory comment that throughout my analysis, I draw a clear distinction between the rules that set out substantive legal rights, and the procedural rules around administration of those rights. Within the context of negligently inflicted injuries, this means that the tort law principle ensuring a right to compensation if a party is negligently injured constitutes a substantive rule; the rules associated with the adjudication of a claim for such compensation are procedural rules. In my focus area of fact-finding, this includes, for example, the rules dictating the applicable standards of proof, processes of adversarial presentation of evidence and argument, evidentiary doctrines stipulating that only relevant and non-privileged evidence is admissible, and doctrines pertaining to presentation of expert evidence.

C. MAPPING THE ANALYSIS

Below, I set out a very quick summary of the analysis that I will expand on in the chapters that follow. I have set out the questions that arise at each stage in the analysis and how I have tackled them. The introduction sets out basic foundational question of this book: why should we accept the authority of judicial fact-finding, given that it's not guaranteed to be accurate? In other words, it's not possible to say that we know exactly what happened with certainty, so there is an inevitable risk of error. So, on what basis is the authority of judicial fact-finding legitimate? My answer hinges on a notion of *procedural* legitimacy that bridges two unavoidable aspects of adjudication: evidentiary gaps leading to factual uncertainty/indeterminacy and the need for justifiably authoritative dispute resolution. I show how the notion of procedural legitimacy enables recognition that the civil litigation system, while inevitably imperfect, is nonetheless legitimate and acceptable. Of course, such a claim must be nuanced, and I have tried to demonstrate those nuances by situating the procedural legitimacy theory within exciting debates about what makes litigation procedures valuable, drawing on the work of Ronald Dworkin and Robert Bone, among others.

I note in chapter 1 that one aspect of the procedural legitimacy argument embodies the essence of formal justice and the rule of law — that everyone should be subjected to consistent rules non-arbitrarily. But stopping at this "germ of justice," as Hart has described it,[4] gives rise to critical questions: can consistent application of *any* procedural rules yield legitimate outcomes? What qualities must the procedural rules embody in order to justify their legitimizing role?

Taking on these questions is the aim of chapter 2. I begin by revisiting H.L.A. Hart's concept of legal validity and its implications, followed by a review of Joseph Raz's incisive additions to the positivist proposal. Hart's proposal can be considered a new starting point in contemporary positivism, and Raz's jurisprudence displays an arguably even stronger commitment to the central core of legal positivism. Positivist proposals are both helpful, and not. They are helpful because they contain insights that further a proceduralist orientation in that they place the validity of law in lawmaking procedures, but they also insist that legality, and the justification of legality are two separate things that do not have to occur together. That allows for something to be legally valid, and therefore authoritative, yet unjustified. Appreciating the root of the difficulty, which I attempt to demonstrate in my critique of Hart's and Raz's commitments, paves the road to overcoming them.

My review of Hart's and Raz's proposals serves as a more detailed argument in favour of the claims introduced in the previous chapter: first, that legal validity brings an implication of authority, and this requires legitimacy; second, that legal validity is best understood through a substantiated procedural declaration that *certain* procedures yield valid laws, and being products of that particular procedure, valid laws deserve, in a normative sense, their authoritative status. The procedural rules of determining facts must reflect those same qualities. When they do, their consistent application yields legitimately authoritative outcomes. But, what qualities must legal procedures possess in order to justifiably legitimize the outcomes that emerge from them?

To answer that, I draw on Lon Fuller's and Jürgen Habermas's insights because they both maintain that if a law is legal, it must also be justifiably authoritative. Another way to say that is that legal

---

4   H.L.A. Hart, *The Concept of Law*, 3d ed (Oxford: Oxford University Press, 2012) at 206 [Hart, *Concept of Law*].

validity and legitimacy occur simultaneously. Essentially, they conclude that if the process of creating a law demonstrates respect for legal subjects as autonomous agents who deserve non-arbitrary treatment, then the law that comes from those procedures is both legally valid and justifiable.

The following chapter uses that grounding notion of respect for autonomy to formulate the necessary qualities of legitimate fact-finding procedures: litigants can rationally accept adjudicative fact-finding on the basis of an application of a fact-finding process that genuinely respects them as free-acting agents. So, how can maintaining respect for litigants as autonomous agents be reflected in judicial fact-finding? I conclude that such fact-finding procedures need two categories of necessary features: factual reliability and participation rights. Judicial fact-finding should be factually reliable in the sense that the fact-finding process embodies a genuine effort toward achieving accurate factual determinations. Along with maintaining factual reliability, fact-finding procedures must include meaningful participation rights for affected parties. This chapter concludes with the assertion that when fact-finding procedures that reflect respect for litigants as rational agents are applied consistently, the fact-finding system is legitimate, and the authority of a judicial factual determination can be rationally accepted despite the risk of inaccuracy.

That's it for the substantive analysis. The concluding chapter will sum up the arguments offered in the previous chapters, reflect on the scope and limits of this book, and offer final reflections on the intended purpose of the book.

D. PRELIMINARY CHALLENGES AND LIMITATIONS

This project is my attempt at justifying an aspect of the legal system where its fallibility is very clear — the judicial inquiry into the facts that underpin a legal claim. An effort to provide a justificatory framework for fact-finding from the starting point of acknowledging that it cannot be perfect poses significant intuitive and analytical challenges. I have opted to navigate these challenges through jurisprudential inquiry, and this has led me to some of the deepest questions about law, its authority, its validity and, of course, its legitimacy. The breadth of thinking that has occurred in relation to these topics and their interrelations is awesome and daunting. In order to manage the scope of the project, I have had to constrain my discussions in a number of ways, which I explain further within the body of the book, but I make two broad comments here as to the scope of this project.

First, I have attempted to be diligent in maintaining my focus on adjudicative fact-finding, and refraining from any suggestion that my arguments here extend beyond the realm of fact-finding into adjudicative interpretation and application of law. At times, this has been difficult because I have drawn on thinking that goes far beyond fact-finding. I have tried to ensure clarity when I have extrapolated ideas from broader contexts and applied them to the realm of fact-finding. But I reiterate here that my comments throughout pertain only to what makes judicial fact-finding legitimate; that does not mean that I claim that legitimate fact-finding exclusively defines the legitimacy of the judicial outcome. I do hold, though, that if the factual findings are illegitimate, so is the judicial outcome, no matter how aptly a judge interprets and applies the law. I believe this position is wholly uncontroversial.

I have additionally constrained my inquiry to civil fact-finding, and I refer to the criminal context only tangentially. Though much of my analysis could apply in the criminal context, my discussion here should not be taken to be simply transferable there, because there are important differences between civil and criminal adjudication that I do not fully address here.

Finally, readers will find that throughout the book, I have often endorsed basic principles of Canadian fact-finding processes, including our balance of probabilities standard of proof, the adversarial nature of adjudication, and various evidentiary doctrines. But this should not be taken to mean that I began this project as an attempt to reinforce the status quo. My attempt has been to define justificatory principles that relate to fact-finding and consider how our system holds up against them. As it turns out, the Canadian fact-finding system has, *in its ideal form*, the requisite features of a legitimate process, but that does not mean that the Canadian fact-finding system operates perfectly and cannot be critiqued. My analysis is designed to make the justificatory features of a fact-finding system prominent and clear by articulating and defending them, and I do so through a critical analysis of various jurisprudential positions and philosophical ideas about the foundations of evidence doctrines and fact-finding processes which ultimately lead to the procedural legitimacy framework.

E. FINAL COMMENTS BEFORE GETTING STARTED

Working through the jurisprudential thinking of those who have theorized adjudication is intricate and has challenged me considerably. But the challenge has felt worthwhile and enjoyable because it took me into a deep inquiry into what, if anything, makes our judicial system justifiable. It has been a pleasure to put that inquiry onto paper with the intent of sharing it with interested students and legal players. I have tried to present the ideas of others as I have understood them accessibly and fairly, and to point out their pragmatic value throughout. I have attempted to make my logical steps clear and precise. But all that is presented here is, naturally, open to your dissection, critique, and disagreement. Opening a critical dialogue on the legitimacy of judicial fact-finding (and therefore the work of lawyers and judges) is what I perceive to be the value of this book.

I note finally that throughout the book, you will read that I have emphasized the need for consistent application of procedures that manifest respect for human dignity by recognizing individuals as autonomous, free agents. This is one expression of the foundational importance of the rule of law — good legal procedures must be applied consistently and equally to all to preserve legal legitimacy and ensure that the authority that the legal system and its actors assert is justified. Never in my lifetime has this needed more express articulation than now, as global authoritarianism is on the rise and it seems increasingly impossible to take democratic values for granted.

CHAPTER ONE

Setting the Stage for Procedural Legitimacy

INTRODUCTION

The overall goal of this book is to come to an understanding of what constitutes legitimate judicial fact-finding. In this chapter, I get started by setting out why the legitimacy framework that I defend and apply here is a procedural model. I have situated the claims and analyses presented within several relevant scholarly landscapes.

I'll start by posing a descriptive question — what constitutes valid fact-finding? My consideration of that question highlights the tension between the importance of authoritative and effective dispute resolution and the inevitability of factual uncertainty or indeterminacy in adjudication. This discussion yields my basic observation that *accurate* fact-finding is not a necessary pre-requisite for *valid* judicial fact-finding, and conversely, that procedural propriety is.

In my conception, the term "legally valid" denotes only the descriptive conclusion that when procedural integrity is maintained, an outcome has legal validity. Legal validity does not imply that an outcome is just or good — that is important and sometimes unsettling. Having legal validity does, however, come with an important implication: when an outcome is legally valid, it is authoritative in the sense that it is broadly acquiesced as final, binding, and even coercively enforceable. I contend that since law must be authoritative in that way in order to be

---

Earlier versions of Parts 1 and 3 of this chapter appear in Nayha Acharya, "Adjudicating Uncertain Facts: The Case for Procedural Legitimacy" (2018) 48 *Advocates Quarterly* 114.

meaningful at all, it must also be justified. That is, there must be a reason that legal validity means that a law is permissively authoritative and enforceable in the community. That justifying reason is what I refer to here as "legitimacy." It will be helpful to keep the terms validity and legitimacy straight from here onward.

Since it is legal validity itself that brings authoritative implications, I reason that whatever gives rise to legal validity must *also* underpin the justifiability of that outcome's authority. So, the reasoning goes that if legal validity makes judicial outcomes (and the underlying factual determinations) authoritative, and procedural propriety grounds the legal validity of the factual findings, then procedural propriety must be a necessary characteristic of their legitimacy as well. This leads to the conclusion that the framework for legitimate judicial fact-finding must have a fundamentally procedural character. Part 1 of this chapter concludes, therefore, with two observations: First, that valid adjudicative fact-finding *requires* normativity, or legitimacy, and second, that such legitimacy depends on the *processes* of resolving factual disputes — how was the evidence admitted, how was it evaluated, was the standard of proof appropriately employed, and so on.

In Part 2 of this chapter, I situate these two propositions within broader jurisprudential and philosophical discourses. First, the question of whether legal validity must be justified, or legitimate, is perhaps the most pervasive debate in contemporary legal theory, being one cornerstone of the disagreement between positivist and non-positivist traditions. I've provided a concentrated synopsis of some of the relevant positivist propositions, focusing on H.L.A. Hart's theory, juxtaposed with ideas contained in Ronald Dworkin's and Jürgen Habermas's theories, among others. The point is to show you the jurisprudential alignments that form the foundations of my commitment to process-based legitimacy of judicial fact-finding. This discussion sets the stage for the more in-depth jurisprudential analysis that comes in chapter 2.

From broad jurisprudential notions, I'll then move into the narrower context of fact-finding, outlining scholarly conversations that grapple directly with the problem of factual uncertainty in adjudication. I discuss my agreement and disagreement with various ideas about the harms that result from factual inaccuracies, and the role that procedures play in rectifying those harms. Through that discussion, I indicate my position on the normative value of procedural legitimacy in fact-finding: what are the limits of procedural legitimacy, and what must it achieve in order to ensure acceptable civil adjudication. Keep in mind that the goal of this first chapter is to set the stage for the rest. Here, the idea is to show you why the framework for legitimacy of fact-finding that I adopt is a procedural one; substantiating the requisite features of a legitimizing fact-finding process is the ultimate aim of the book, and primarily unfolds in the next chapters.

PART 1. UNDERSTANDING ADJUDICATIVE FACT-FINDING

A. Introducing the Fact-Finding Tension

Almost any successful legal action depends on establishing the relevant facts as defined by the governing legal principles. One of the primary tasks of the courts is to determine whether the facts that would give rise to a cause of action are established. In the context of a negligently inflicted injury, for instance, liability is established if the defendant owes the plaintiff a duty of care,[1] they breached their standard of care, and the breach caused the plaintiff's injury. The court is tasked with determining whether those facts are established. On the basis of the factual findings and subsequent application of legal principles, the court will determine whether the plaintiff is legally entitled to compensation. Quantifying the restoration that would compensate the plaintiff depends on further factual determinations — what losses they suffered as a result of the tortious injury; whether any pre-existing condition had an impact on the nature of their losses; what losses may occur in the future, and so on.[2] The value of accurate determination of the relevant factual circumstances is obvious. But the adjudicative process cannot guarantee accuracy in fact-finding — it is impossible to infallibly know what happened and what will happen.[3]

---

1   In some sense, the existence of a duty of care is not merely a question of fact: it presupposes a policy decision. Here, I do not presume a significant distinction between the question of the existence of a duty of care and the remaining factual elements that must be established for a finding of liability.

2   Kenneth Cooper-Stephenson & Iwan Saunders, *Personal Injury Damages in Canada*, 2d ed (Scarborough, ON: Carswell, 1996) at chapter 2: "Basic Principles" [Cooper-Stephenson & Saunders, *Personal Injury Damages*].

3   Jerome Frank captures this thought succinctly in his chapter title "Facts and Guesses," in *Courts on Trial: Myth and Reality in American Justice* (New Jersey: Princeton University Press, 1973) [Frank, *Courts on Trial*]. Later, he comments that, "Guessing legal rights, before litigation occurs, is, then, guessing what judges or juries will guess were the facts, and that is by

Evidentiary gaps and factual uncertainty have many causes. First, there is the practical issue that adjudicative claims arise out of events of the past, so determining what happened cannot simply be observed. Rather, it has to be inferred based on whatever fragments of evidence are available and presented to the court. The available evidence may be scarce to begin with, there may be a lack of competent witnesses in injury claims, and evidence may deteriorate over time.[4] Moreover, since adjudication requires relative efficiency to maintain its utility, waiting for additional evidence to become available may not be feasible.

In addition, sometimes the governing legal principles require the court to make factual inquiries that are inherently uncertain. This is particularly visible in injury litigation. For one, as Picard and Robertson note, relevant questions about physical injuries are often intrinsically uncertain: the "complexity of the human body and the uncertainties which still surround its nature . . . exacerbate the overwhelming task that the plaintiff often has in proving that the defendant's conduct was the factual cause of the injury."[5] These issues are highlighted in medical negligence cases, where it is often very difficult to determine whether the patient's inherent illness caused their losses, or the doctor's negligence caused the loss. And the uncertainties are not only limited to lack of knowledge about the human body. Some relevant inquiries are questions that simply have no certain answer. When assessing damages for injuries, for instance, determining

---

no means easy. Legal rights and duties are, then, often guessy, if-y" in Frank, *Courts on Trial* at 27.

4   In Walter Bloom & Harry Kalven, Public Law Perspectives on a Private Law Problem – Auto Compensation Plans" (1964) 31(4) *University of Chicago Law Review* 641 at 647, the authors note that some people have questioned the very viability of tort law for adjudicating injury claims arising out of motor vehicle accidents on the basis that evidentiary problems culminate such that the "actual trial involves an imperfect and ambiguous historical reconstruction of the event, making a mockery of the effort to apply so subtle a normative criterion to the conduct involved." Larry Laudan has made the same point in the context of criminal proceedings. Discussing the causes of evidentiary gaps in criminal trials, Laudan notes, "[the crime] is now in the past. What survive are traces of remnants of the crime. These include memories of the participants and eyewitnesses and physical evidence of the crime. . . . The police will come to find some, but rarely all, of these traces." Larry Laudan, *Truth, Error, and Criminal Law: An Essay in Legal Epistemology* (Cambridge, New York: Cambridge University Press, 2006) at 16.

5   Ellen I. Picard & Gerald B. Robertson, *Legal Liability of Doctors and Hospitals in Canada*, 4th ed (Scarborough, ON: Thomson Carswell, 2007) at 269.

prospective losses is obviously uncertain but must be determined since the full compensation principles apply irrespective of inherent uncertainty.[6]

Along with these practical issues, some legal principles prevent judicial access to relevant evidence in several ways. First, adversarial dispute resolution entitles parties to present evidence of their choice and binds decision-makers to make decisions based on the evidence presented. The adjudicator is generally not at liberty to collect their own relevant information.[7] This does not invariably contribute to the risk of inaccuracy, but it demonstrates that commitment to the adversarial process can outweigh the commitment to accuracy. Similarly, legal admissibility rules also restrict what might otherwise be relevant evidence in order to protect some other legal principle. For instance, evidence subject to legal privilege is not admissible, even if the privileged evidence would reduce the factual uncertainty.[8] Some legal principles reflect a commitment to an efficacious dispute resolution system by prioritizing the finality of outcomes, even in instances where factual uncertainties exist. Rules around introduction of fresh evidence on appeals are an example. Where a party wishes to introduce new evidence during an appeal of an action,[9]

---

6   See Cooper-Stephenson & Saunders, *Personal Injury Damages*, above note 3 at 150. See also Russel Brown, "The Possibility of 'Inference Causation': Inferring Cause-in-Fact and the Nature of Legal Certainty" (2010) 55 *McGill Law Journal* 1 (presenting his idea that causation is also an inherently uncertain factual question).

7   Michael Bayles makes this observation in "Principles for Legal Procedure" (1986) 5(1) *Law & Philosophy* 33 at 37: "Courts have limited investigative powers. At best, they can investigate matters relating to the specific case before them. They do not have the power to conduct a general investigation into, for example, business practices in an industry. In the common-law system, the burden of amassing and presenting evidence rests with the parties" [Bayles, "Principles for Legal Procedure"]. For additional commentary on this point, readers may see Larry Laudan, in *Truth, Error, and Criminal Law: An Essay in Legal Epistemology* (Cambridge University Press, 2006), which delves into the epistemological challenges in criminal trials, emphasizing the difficulties in reconstructing past events based on incomplete evidence. In addition, Frederick Schauer, in *Thinking Like a Lawyer: A New Introduction to Legal Reasoning* (Cambridge, MA: Harvard University Press, 2009), explores the constraints of legal reasoning, including the limitations imposed by procedural rules and evidentiary standards.

8   For a discussion of the evidentiary principles of privilege for example: David M. Paciocco, Palma Paciocco & Lee Stuesser, *The Law of Evidence*, 8th ed (Toronto: Irwin Law, 2019) at 7, and for a discussion focusing on procedural aspects of privilege principles, see Janet Walker & Lorne Sossin, *Civil Litigation* (Toronto: Irwin Law, 2010) at chapter 9.

9   *Mehedi v 2057161 Ontario Inc* 2015 ONCA 670 at 13. In *671122 Ontario Ltd v Sagaz Industries Canada Inc* 2001 SCC 59, the Supreme Court accepted (at paras 20 and 64), the test set

the onus is on the moving party to show that all the circumstances "justify making an exception to the fundamental rule that final judgments are exactly that, final." (Reference removed). In particular, the moving party must show that the new evidence could not have been put forward by the exercise of reasonable diligence at the original proceedings.

These comments indicate the principle that once a fair trial has occurred, the outcome is legitimately final and ought to be respected as such. While there may be justifiable reasons to re-open legal actions and even factual determinations, the efficacy of the adjudicative process would be significantly compromised if it was not the norm to accept judicial outcomes, including the underpinning factual findings, as final, even though the evidence presented to the court cannot be guaranteed to be complete.

In short, adjudication occurs in conditions of inevitable factual uncertainty, and this condition must be balanced against the need for an effective dispute resolution system. Accurate appraisal of the facts is necessary to ensure that the resolution of disputes accords with substantive legal principles. If adjudicative decision-makers were consistently inaccurate in their fact-finding, their subsequent application of the legal principles would be based on errors, and protection of substantive rights would be impossible. As Robert Summers puts it, "without findings of fact that generally accord with truth, the underlying policy goals or norms of the law could not be served."[10] The importance of accuracy in fact-finding is undeniable, yet it is impossible to guarantee that all adjudicative dispute resolution will invariably be factually accurate. Even so, in order to be a meaningful system of administration of law,

---

out in *Scott v Cook* [1970] 2 OR 769 (SC), for presentation of fresh evidence on appeal: First, would the evidence, if presented at trial, probably have changed the result? Second, could the evidence have been obtained before trial by the exercise of reasonable diligence?

10   Robert Summers, "Formal Legal Truth and Substantive Truth in Fact-Finding – Their Justified Divergence in Some Particular Cases" (1999) 18 *Law & Philosophy* 497 at 498 [Summers, "Formal Legal Truth"]. Alex Stein makes a similar remark in *Foundations of Evidence Law* (Oxford, New York: Oxford University Press, 2005) at 2: "accuracy in fact-finding is a logical pre-requisite to proper administration of the controlling substantive law"; and at 10: "Accuracy in fact-finding . . . is a straightforward understandable objective of the law. Getting the facts right is a prerequisite to proper determination of the litigated entitlements and liabilities."

the adjudicative system must provide legally valid outcomes that constitute final, authoritative resolutions to legal disputes. On what basis, then, are adjudicative factual determinations legally valid? The first step to answering that question is to discern how the tension between factual uncertainty and the need for final and binding resolution of disputes is handled.

B. Valid Fact-Finding: Resolving the Fact-Finding Tension Through Process

The tension between the need for a resolution to a legal dispute and the reality that factual accuracy cannot be guaranteed is reconciled by enabling facts to be found on a "less than certain" standard of proof.[11] In civil cases, facts are proven on the balance of probabilities.[12] If it is more likely than not that the defendant's negligence caused the plaintiff's injury, for instance, then causation is taken to be a legal certainty — it is established as a "legal fact."[13] In this way, factual uncertainty morphs into legal certainty — relevant factual conditions are legally established, and the governing law is applied to those facts, resulting in a certain legal outcome — one that is authoritative and enforceable.[14]

---

11   I have presented a similar preliminary derivation of procedural legitimacy in Nayha Acharya, "Law's Treatment of Science: From Idealization to Understanding" (2013) 36 *Dalhousie Law Journal* 1.

12   For the most recent commentary from the Supreme Court of Canada on the civil standard of proof, see *FH v McDougal* 2008 SCC 53 at para 40, where the Court opines, "Like the House of Lords, I think it is time to say, once and for all in Canada, that there is only one civil standard of proof at common law and that is proof on a balance of probabilities." My argument here does not require a discussion of why the balance of probabilities standard of proof is acceptable. The crucial point here is that fact-finding occurs on some standard of proof that is less than certainty. As a result, there is inevitable potential for legally valid, yet inaccurate outcomes. My argument here depends only on the existence of a risk of inaccuracy implicit in adjudicative fact-finding. How much risk is tolerable is an important question, but that discussion is not required for the development of the argument at this stage.

13   I use the term "legal facts" to denote facts that are established for the purpose of making a legal determination, whether or not the facts are actually true.

14   Of course, judicial outcomes can be appealed, but that does not diminish the authoritative nature of adjudicative outcomes. This is especially true in the fact-finding context, because appellate courts afford the highest degree of deference to the trial judge's fact-finding. This was most recently reaffirmed in *Benhaim v St-Germain* 2016 SCC 48 at paras 36–39. The majority of the Supreme Court of Canada noted that:

Legal fact-finding, therefore, contemplates the chance that an event found as a legal "fact" may not be a fact in reality. Still, the applicable legal rules will be applied on the basis that the legal facts are true.[15] This creates the potential for situations where, for example, a plaintiff is negligently injured, but the available evidence is insufficient to meet the standard of proof for a requisite factual element, so despite the violation of the plaintiff's legal rights, the defendant will not be liable to compensate them. Or, evidence may suggest that a defendant's negligence was more likely than not the cause of a plaintiff's harm, so liability is established, but there remains a significant risk that the defendant's negligence was not, in fact, the cause of the harm at all. In civil cases, through our system of fact-finding on a balance of probabilities standard of proof, we tolerate up to a 50 percent risk of such factually erroneous outcomes.

The implication that can be drawn from our method of fact-finding is that the validity of factual determinations is not contingent on their accuracy. Rather, that we accept the validity of a

---

The standard of review is . . . palpable and overriding error for findings of fact and inferences of fact . . .

Stratas J.A. described the deferential standard as follows in *South Yukon Forest Corp. v R*, 2012 FCA 165 at para 46:

Palpable and overriding error is a highly deferential standard of review . . . . "Palpable" means an error that is obvious. "Overriding" means an error that goes to the very core of the outcome of the case. When arguing palpable and overriding error, it is not enough to pull at leaves and branches and leave the tree standing. The entire tree must fall.

For more case-specific comments as to the deference owed to the trial judge's fact-finding in *Benhaim v St-Germain*, see paras 71–81.

Another stark testament to the recognition of the authoritative status of a valid judicial outcome is that civil trial decisions remain, by default, enforceable even pending appeal. See for example: Rule 90.41 of *The Nova Scotia Civil Procedure Rules* and R 63 of the Ontario *Rules of Court*, which expressly hold that filing an appeal does not automate a stay of proceedings of the trial decision being appealed. Rule 14.48 of the *Alberta Rules of Court*, Alta Reg 124/2010 and R 9 of the *British Columbia Rules of Court*, similarly hold that a court order would be required in order to stay the enforcement of a trial decision pending an appeal.

15   See Summers, "Formal Legal Truth," above note 10, for an explanation of the potential instances where "truth" and "formal truth" (which distinction I refer to as "facts" versus "legal facts") diverge by the very design of the legal system, and the rationales for that divergence. In this paper, Summers concludes that "the concept of 'formal' legal truth, in those cases in which it diverges from substantive truth, is not necessarily something to be disparaged at all," paving the road to my inquiry into the requisite features that make "formal legal truth" legitimate.

determination of fact when it results from appropriate adherence to adjudicative procedures. Despite their potential incongruence with factual reality, the hypothetical outcomes noted above are acceptable because of their procedural propriety. That is, when parties present evidence in accordance with adversarial procedures, and when the trier of fact relies on properly admitted evidence and weighs that evidence against the requisite standard of proof, the factual finding, along with the ultimate legal outcome, is acceptable, even if we do not know whether it is accurate, and sometimes, even if we know it is inaccurate.

Conversely, a legal outcome would be considered invalid in the event that the process of fact-finding is compromised. If, for instance, the trier of fact relies on inadmissible evidence, or misconstrues the applicable standard of proof, their factual determination would not be considered valid. That is true even if the factual finding is ultimately accurate. For instance, if a judge erroneously applies the criminal "beyond reasonable doubt" standard of proof in a civil claim for compensation for a negligently inflicted injury, the factual finding they arrive at may be accurate, but the outcome cannot be considered valid due to the procedural error of applying the wrong standard of proof.

So far, I have arrived at two observations about the validity of a judicial determination of fact. First, that fact-finding is valid on the basis of procedural propriety, and second, the converse, that a factual finding may be invalid on the basis of procedural impropriety. That is, outcomes that bear a risk of inaccuracy can be acceptable on the basis that fact-finding procedures were adhered to. And a factual finding can be unacceptable on the basis that the procedures of fact-finding were not adhered to, even if that factual determination is accurate. Here is the crux of these observations: in our legal system, the validity of judicial fact-finding does not depend on the ultimate accuracy of each determination; it depends on its procedural propriety.

Canadian courts have recognized and affirmed the significance of procedural propriety through their express resistance to tampering with the established principles of legal fact-finding in the face of perceived unfairness caused by factual uncertainty. This commitment has been especially visible in the personal injury context, where medical and scientific uncertainty over causation results in a perception of undue evidentiary disadvantage for plaintiffs.[16] In *Snell v Farrell* for instance, medical evidence was inconclusive as to whether a doctor's negligence during an eye surgery caused the plaintiff's subsequent eye injury.[17] The plaintiff argued that since the surgeon's negligence caused a material increase in the *risk* of her eye injury, the onus should shift to the surgeon to show that his negligence did *not* cause the injury.[18] The Supreme Court of Canada rejected the "material increase in risk" and onus reversal approach to establishing the causal link. Instead, the Court advocated a "robust and pragmatic" approach to the traditional "but for" analysis to establish causation, with a reminder that scientific precision is not a prerequisite to satisfying the "but for" causal test on the balance of probabilities standard of proof.[19]

In *Clements v Clements*,[20] the Supreme Court was tasked with making a liability determination where a plaintiff was severely injured in a motorcycle accident. Evidence was inconclusive as to whether the driver's negligence caused the passenger plaintiff's injuries. Affirming its discussion in *Snell*, the Supreme Court explained that "[t]he law of negligence has never required proof of scientific causation . . . . If scientific evidence of causation is not required, as *Snell* makes plain, it is difficult to see how its absence can be raised as a basis for ousting the usual 'but for' test."[21] Thus the trial judge's insistence on scientific proof to satisfy the requisite balance of probabilities standard of proof for causation

---

16   I discuss judicial use of scientific evidence and adjudicative accommodation of causal uncertainty from a procedural legitimacy perspective more comprehensively in chapter 4. At this point my purpose is limited to pointing out judicial commitment to the value of procedural propriety in injury litigation scenarios.

17   *Snell v Farrell* [1990] SCJ No 73. The plaintiff had undergone a cataract surgery. During the surgery, it became known that the anaesthetic had caused some bleeding behind the plaintiff's eye. Still, the surgeon continued the surgery, and this decision was found to be negligent. Later, the plaintiff lost sight in the eye. The medical experts, however, were unable to provide conclusive evidence that the surgeon's negligent decision to continue the surgery caused the plaintiff's blindness.

18   This approach was adopted by the House of Lords in *McGhee v National Coal Board* [1972] 3 All ER 1008 (HL) and the Supreme Court of Canada was urged to adopt this reasoning in *Snell v Farrell, ibid.*

19   See *Snell v Farrell*, above note 17, generally, and at para 29.

20   *Clements v Clements* 2012 SCC 32. The Supreme Court's caution that scientific precision is not required for valid legal fact-finding has been recently reiterated in *British Columbia Workers Compensation Appeal Tribunal v Fraser Health Authority* 2016 SCC 25. See especially, paras 32 and 38.

21   *Ibid* at para 38.

was found to be in error.[22] This was most recently affirmed yet again in *Benhaim v St-Germain*, where the Court held, "Simply put, scientific causation and factual causation for legal purposes are two different things. Factual causation for legal purposes is a matter for the trier of fact, not for the expert witnesses, to decide."[23]

In these opinions, the Supreme Court of Canada has provided a clear endorsement of the concept that despite the conditions of uncertainty and associated risk of inaccuracy, the adjudicative process and the outcomes it produces maintain legal validity through consistent observance to its own procedures. Undeniably, the judicial inquiry into the relevant facts is significantly restricted and factual accuracy cannot be guaranteed. It follows that the legal validity of factual determinations and subsequent judicial outcomes cannot be contingent on factual accuracy. This conclusion implicitly highlights the role of procedural propriety in grounding legal validity: despite the unavoidable risk of inaccuracy, judicial decisions maintain legal validity through procedural propriety. But it's important to keep in mind here and throughout that this is not the same as saying that striving for factual accuracy is not relevant or essential to a legitimate legal system.[24]

The conclusion that legal validity depends on the proper application of legal procedures is a descriptive one, but there are important normative implications contained within it. Those implications exist because when judicial outcomes are legally valid, they are authoritative in the sense that outcomes are acquiesced by the litigants and the society more generally as non-optional, and permissibly enforceable.[25]

---

22   *Ibid* at para 49: "As discussed above, the cases consistently hold that scientific precision is not necessary to a conclusion that 'but for' causation is established on a balance of probabilities. It follows that the trial judge erred in insisting on scientific precision in the evidence as a condition of finding 'but for' causation."

23   *Benhaim v St-Germain* 2016 SCC 48 at para 47 [references removed].

24   I elaborate the relationship between seeking truth and maintaining adjudicative legitimacy below and in chapter 3. Here, my purpose is to show the significance of process-based approach to adjudicative legitimacy by recognizing the implications that can be drawn from the impossibility of guaranteeing factual, or substantive, accuracy. At this juncture, I offer the uncontroversial acknowledgement that an adjudicative system of fact-finding that does not seek to find out the truth at all could hardly be regarded as a fact-finding system, let alone a legitimate one.

25   As Joseph Raz provides, "[l]aw is a structure of authority, and central to its functioning is the interplay between legislators and other authorities on one side, and the courts, which are entrusted with delivering authoritative interpretations of its norms, on the other side. Judicial interpretations are authoritative in being binding on the litigants, whether they

If not, adjudicative outcomes would have no utility. Being authoritative in this way, I contend, judicial outcomes, including their factual determinations, require justification, which serves as a reason for *why* legally valid outcomes are permissibly authoritative and *why* litigants and community members can agree to that. I refer to that justificatory reason as legitimacy.[26]

I reason that since legal validity implicates legal authority, and since legal authority must be justified, or, legitimate, then whatever gives rise to legal validity must *simultaneously* give rise to legitimacy as well.[27] On that basis, I hold that not only is the validity of judicial fact-finding grounded in procedural propriety, but that its legitimacy is too. Here it is in one sentence: a procedurally proper outcome is legally valid, and as such it is authoritative — that authority has to be justified.

One upshot of this conclusion is that just as factually inaccurate outcomes can be legally valid, they can also be legitimate, because neither their validity nor their legitimacy can depend on their accuracy. Concluding that a factually inaccurate outcome is nonetheless

---

are correct or not," in Joseph Raz, "Interpretation: Pluralism and Innovation," in Joseph Raz, *Between Authority and Interpretation: On the Theory of Law and Practical Reason* (Oxford: Oxford University Press, 2009) at 320 [Raz, *Between Authority and Interpretation*]. I note that holding that judicial outcomes are authoritative does not mean that every individual in a society will always accept the authority of every, or even any judicial outcome. But to the extent that, as a society, we accept the validity of the Canadian political system and its outcomes, so we also generally speaking, accept that judicial outcomes are authoritative. I also note that the concept of authority and its relation to law and legal legitimacy can be complex. I take up questions of legal authority and its relation to legitimacy with particular reference to Raz's theory (which, as evidenced in the above quotation, extensively theorizes law as authority) in more detail in chapter 2. Here, I rely only on the uncontroversial descriptive reality that when a rule, including a judicial outcome, is found to have legal validity, that outcome is final and binding on the litigants.

26　As I explain further in chapter 2, this understanding of legitimacy resonates with Jürgen Habermas's approach when he contends that legal norms must "*deserve* legal obedience. Such legitimacy," he holds, "should allow a law-abiding behavior that, based on respect for the law, involves more than sheer compliance." (Emphasis in the original.) Jürgen Habermas, *Between Facts and Norms: Contributions to a Discourse Theory of Law and Democracy*, (Cambridge, MA: MIT Press, 1996) at 198 [Habermas, *Between Facts and Norms*].

27　Compare this with Dan Priel, "The Place of Legitimacy in Legal Theory" (2011) 57 *McGill Law Journal* 1 at 6 who suggests that while normativity and legitimacy are related, they address two different issues: "the question of normativity asks, 'how are legal obligations possible?' whereas the political question of legitimacy asks 'what political conditions need to be in place for law to bind those subject to it?'" In my conception, these questions are inseparable, as I argue further below, drawing especially on the legal theories of Lon Fuller and Jürgen Habermas.

legitimate is really uncomfortable, and that discomfort leads people away from accepting procedural legitimacy. How can an outcome that is factually wrong possibly still merit its authority, and how can there be a reason to accept such an outcome? I take up this question in more detail below, but it warrants some mention now.

In the case of criminal convictions that are put into doubt by subsequently available evidence, ministerial reviews to rectify potential wrongful convictions are necessary and wholly warranted. And granting motions to allow for introduction of fresh evidence on appeal in appropriate circumstances is also justifiable, as discussed above. However, a generalized commitment that factual inaccuracy can delegitimize an adjudicative outcome and revoke the acceptability of its authority is logically unsustainable.

Since the requisite factual elements are not decided on a standard of certainty, there is always a risk that the factual findings are inaccurate. Nearly all injury claims will bear a risk of some factual error. If potential inaccuracy could delegitimize a judicial outcome, there would be no basis for considering judicial dispute resolution authoritative, final, and binding (which it must be in order to be effective), because there is almost invariably a risk of factual error. This recognition clears the way for the claim that both the validity and the legitimacy of adjudicative outcomes must be sourced in the virtues of the process that gave rise to that outcome. But again, don't make the mistake of thinking that this means that accuracy isn't relevant at all — it is, and in later chapters I will show how it manifests as a procedural virtue.

But for the argument to unfold clearly, we need to go one step at a time. I have presented the propositions that (1) valid judicial fact-finding must be legitimate, and (2) such legitimacy is grounded in the process of arriving at a judicial outcome rather than the accuracy of the outcome itself, as observations. In order for the normative aspects of these propositions to hold, they can, and must, be considered through broader jurisprudential lenses. The assertion that legal validity and legitimacy must be intertwined in the context of fact-finding maps onto one of the most divisive debates in the philosophy of law: is the existence of valid law contingent on its justification? This question, often framed in terms of whether there is a necessary connection between law and morality, is the fulcrum of debates between positivists and their critics. Moreover, among those who conclude that legal validity requires legitimacy, there are varying conceptions of what the criteria for legitimacy can and should be. For instance, should legitimacy be grounded in certain substantive ideals, like equality or autonomy? Should legitimacy be grounded in formal or process values? Or some combination? Reviewing some of the major milestones of these debates enables me to situate my claims about legitimate fact-finding within a jurisprudential framework, and facilitates an uncovering of the underlying assumptions and implications of those claims.

In chapter 2, I take up these jurisprudential questions in greater detail in order to defend and substantiate the concept of procedural legitimacy with respect to judicial fact-finding. Here, I provide a synopsis of some jurisprudential and philosophical concepts that are relevant to the two propositions about fact-finding that I have posed above. Through this overview, I demonstrate which lines of reasoning I align with, foreshadowing and setting the groundwork for my deeper jurisprudential analyses in chapter 2. The following sections are a journey through some major highlights of contemporary legal theory, and I hope I have presented the ideas with the right balance of being comprehensive but succinct and pointed for this stage in the analysis.

PART 2. LEGAL VALIDITY AND LEGITIMACY: FINDING A PLACE AMONG MAJOR POSITIVIST AND NON-POSITIVIST PERSPECTIVES

The cornerstones of a positivist conception of law is what is sometimes referred to as the separation thesis, which holds that law and its justification are, and must be, distinct. John Austin delivered this message in 1832 in the lectures resulting in *The Province of Jurisprudence* as follows:[28]

> The existence of law is one thing; its merit or demerit another. Whether it be or be not is one enquiry; whether it be or be not conformable to an assumed standard, is a different enquiry. A law, which actually exists, is a law, though we happen to dislike it, or though it vary from the text, by which we regulate our approbation and disapprobation.

While modern positivism has seen significant development since Austin, the general commitment to the separation of the questions "is it law?" and the evaluative question of whether it is a good law remains

---

28   John Austin, *The Province of Jurisprudence Determined* (1832), excerpts reprinted in Keith Culver (ed), *Readings in the Philosophy of Law*, 2d ed (Broadview Press, 2007) at 92.

the defining feature of modern positivism.[29] H.L.A. Hart, who is usually seen as one of the most significant proponents of contemporary positivism, holds that it is "in no sense a necessary truth that laws reproduce or satisfy certain demands of morality."[30]

In Hart's famous conceptualization, law is seen as a system of two levels of rules.[31] The primary rules are the substantive rules that govern the conduct of citizens. For instance, the rule that a person who is negligently injured by another person has a right to compensation is a primary rule in Canadian society. Such a primary rule can be created, altered, and, importantly, recognized as a legally valid rule in a society through secondary rules. The most important of the secondary rules is the rule of recognition. The officials in a society refer to a rule of recognition in order to determine whether or not a rule has legal validity. For instance, officials in Canadian society could recognize the validity of a rule on the basis that it was passed by Parliament. Whatever criteria a society uses to determine whether a rule is authoritative on the basis of its legal validity within a community is called the secondary rule of recognition.[32] The legal validity of the rule is discernible by reference to the rule of recognition alone, so "what is law and what is not is a matter of social fact."[33] This concept contains within it the separation thesis — legal validity is discernible by reference to the rule of recognition, whatever it may be. In other words, a rule's validity depends only on whether it accords with the rule of recognition, and not by reference to any evaluative or justificatory standard. As such, inefficient, silly, or unjustifiable rules can be valid laws, so long as they accord with the community's rule of recognition.[34]

---

29   In chapter 2, I undertake a much more detailed look at the positivist separation thesis, and particularly how the thesis unfolds in Hart's and Joseph Raz's legal theories.

30   H.L.A. Hart, *The Concept of Law*, 3d ed (Oxford: Oxford University Press, 2012) at 185–86 [Hart, *The Concept of Law*].

31   *Ibid.*

32   *Ibid* at 92–95.

33   Joseph Raz, *Authority of Law: Essays on Law and Morality* (Oxford: Oxford University Press, 2009) at 37 [Raz, *Authority of Law*].

34   It is important not to overstate the thesis. There are those, particularly those advancing what has come to be known as "soft" or "inclusive" positivism, who note that in some legal systems the merits of a law may be recognized as necessary for legal validity to attach to a rule, so long as the conditions that define "merits" are themselves recognized as legal principles. Hart himself explicitly allows for this possibility in Hart, *The Concept of Law*, above note 30 at 204. For one of the most significant explanations of this version of positivism, see Jules Coleman, "Negative and Positive Positivism" (1982) 11 *Journal of Legal Studies* 139.

The positivist tradition of studying law through a separation between law and the evaluation of the justifiability of law is in tension with my view that the legal validity of a factual determination must be justified. Yet there are two significant undercurrents in my conception of legal validity and its derivation that align with the positivist tradition. First, positivists hold that validity of law is not necessarily contingent on any particular quality of the substance of the law itself. Even a law that is unacceptable in substance may nonetheless have legal validity, so long as the secondary rule of recognition is satisfied. This notion finds a parallel in my understanding of factual determinations, whose validity also does not depend on the correctness of the outcome. An incorrect factual determination may nonetheless have legal validity. In both conceptions, therefore, the validity of a legal outcome does not depend on the substantive quality/nature of the outcome itself; it depends on where that particular outcome came from.

The second positivist-like undercurrent in my approach relates to one of the reasons for why the separation thesis is an important methodology for understanding law: certainty. Hart holds that existence of the secondary rule of recognition is a remedy to uncertainty that results when a society (and its governing rules) become increasingly complicated.[35] Since legal validity depends only on adherence to the relevant rule of recognition, laws are, at least in theory, universally discernible by reference to that rule of recognition.[36] This is important from the perspective of maintaining a society that is meaningfully ordered by law. If legal subjects could constantly question the validity of law on the basis of its merit, then legal validity would have no certainty, and law could provide no stability.[37] This commitment to certainty is paralleled in my approach to legal fact-finding. When the procedures of fact-finding

---

Other proponents include Mathew Kramer, "How Morality Can Enter the Law" (2000) 6 *Legal Theory* 83; David Lyons, "Principles, Positivism and Legal Theory" (1977) 87(2) *Yale Law Journal* 415. Still, the unifying feature of theorists in the positivist tradition is the thesis that: "In any legal system, whether a given norm is legally valid, and hence whether it forms part of the law of that system, depends on its sources, not on its merits." John Gardner, "Legal Positivism: 5 ½ Myths" (2001) 46 *The American Journal of Jurisprudence* 199 at 199. Gardner holds that despite the many unique aspects of various positivist propositions, this is a common ground among those that can fall within the positivist label.

35   Hart, *The Concept of Law*, above note 30 at 94–95.

36   *Ibid.*

37   Hart comments on this danger in H.L.A Hart, "Positivism and the Separation of Law and Morals" (1958) 71(4) *Harvard Law Review* 593 at 598 [Hart, "Separation of Law and Morals"].

are adhered to, the resultant outcome is valid, and any further arguments as to the accuracy of the factual question are no longer relevant.[38] As such, judicial decisions maintain certainty — when they are produced through adherence to the applicable procedures, they are valid and authoritative for everyone concerned, even if one believes that the outcome is factually inaccurate. This is necessary, as I noted above, in order for the adjudicative process to be effective, and its outcomes meaningful.

In sum, the notion of process-based validity of factual determinations aligns with some positivist conceptions of legal *validity*, yet the positivist crux of separating validity and legitimacy is a key point of divergence. The positivist approach to understanding law is not oriented toward providing an answer for why a legally valid rule *deserves* to be authoritative for a given community within its concept of law.[39] As such, it cannot further my goal of providing an answer for why, and on what basis, judicial fact-finding should be acceptable in our community. In other words, the positivist conception can provide a framework to say *that* a particular rule is a valid law and therefore authoritative, but its purpose is not to provide any framework for *why* the validity and authority of law should be accepted.

---

38   Subject to successful motions for introduction of fresh evidence on appeal, as noted above.

39   Holding that the positivist approach is not oriented toward providing an explanation of law's normative features suggests a *methodological* commitment among positivists. As Stephen Perry explains:

> The more plausible way to understand the methodological claim is that Hart is simply setting out to describe the conceptual scheme that we apply to certain of our own social practices . . . . On this view, Hart is simply describing the content of the relevant concepts and the relationships between them, whatever that content and those relationships turn out to be . . . . The idea is to describe and elucidate our conceptual scheme from the outside, as it were. In that way the theorist can remain neutral with respect to such questions as whether the social practice in question is justified, valuable, in need of reform, and so forth. He or she can simply describe what is there.

(Stephen Perry, "Hart's Methodological Positivism" (1998) Faculty Scholarship. Paper 1136, online: http://scholarship.law.upenn.edu/faculty_scholarship/1136 at 440.) A similar methodological commitment is evident in Joseph Raz's approach, which I discuss further in chapter 2. Roughly, Raz understands law as a system of rules that *claims* legitimate authority. The laws are justified when they actually have legitimate authority, but whether or not the authority is legitimate does not influence the question whether the system of rules claims such authority as a descriptive matter, and as such, classifies as law. See Raz, *Authority and Interpretation*, above note 25 at 104, 111. And Joseph Raz, *Ethics in the Public Domain* (Oxford: Clarendon Press, 1994) at 215: "Though a legal system may not have legitimate authority, or though its legitimate authority may not be as extensive as it claims, every legal system claims that it possesses legitimate authority" [Raz, *Ethics in the Public Domain*].

The positivist commitment to the separation of legal validity and the justification for legal validity has been challenged from a variety of angles. Ronald Dworkin launched a prominent contemporary critique, which I briefly outline here.[40] I caution, though, that it is far beyond my scope to provide a full summary and critique of Dworkin's jurisprudence and the voluminous scholarship that it has generated. What I offer below is a presentation of some of Dworkin's commitments that are particularly relevant to my purpose of situating my own discussion within various ideas about the relationship between legal validity and legitimacy, and the criteria for legitimacy offered by those scholars (including Dworkin, in my understanding) who demand legitimacy for legal validity.

A central feature of Dworkin's critique is that the positivist tradition cannot explain how judges resolve legal indeterminacy in "hard cases" where laws are ambiguous or have multiple potential interpretations. He points out that when judges must determine what the law is, they do turn to moral principles to justify their interpretation, particularly when there is more than one viable interpretation. Accordingly, Dworkin argues, recognizing the legal validity of a rule *does* depend on justificatory and evaluative principles, including extra-legal principles of justice and fairness, contrary to the positivist tradition.[41] When judges are

---

40   The debates and exchanges between Hart and Dworkin have generated significant scholarship. For a sampling, see, Scott Shapiro, "On Hart's Way Out" in *Hart's Postscript: Essays on the Postscript to the Concept of Law*, J. Coleman (ed) (Oxford University Press, 2001); Kenneth Himma, "H. L. A. Hart and the Practical Difference Thesis" (2000) 6 *Legal Theory* 43; Steven Burton, "Ronald Dworkin and Legal Positivism" (1987) 73 *Iowa Law Review* 1.

41   As Scott Shapiro explains in "Hart-Dworkin Debate: A Short Guide for the Perplexed" (2007) University of Michigan Law School Public Law and Legal Theory Working Paper Series, Paper 77) at 14:

> According to Dworkin, therefore, the Pedigree Thesis [referring to the idea that a rule's legal validity is determined by referring to the secondary rule which gives rise to it] must be rejected for two reasons. First, legal principles are sometimes binding on judges simply because of their intrinsic moral properties and not because of their pedigree. Second, even when these principles are binding in virtue of their pedigree, it is not possible to formulate a stable rule that picks out a principle based on its degree of institutional support.

Dworkin's own formulation in *Taking Rights Seriously* (London: Ducksworth, 1977) at 22 is as follows:

> I want to make a general attack on positivism, and I shall use H.L.A. Hart's version as a target, when a particular target is needed. My strategy will be organized around the fact that when lawyers reason or dispute about legal rights and obligations, particularly in those hard cases when our problems with these concepts seem most acute,

called on to determine the legal validity of competing interpretations of a rule, they must grasp the interpretation that best comports with justice and fairness, which Dworkin calls the principle of integrity.[42] Doing so enables the judge to determine the valid interpretation of the law, *and* justifies that interpretation. Accordingly, unlike the positivist tradition, for Dworkin, legal validity and legitimacy are intertwined.[43]

For Dworkin, determining legal validity occurs through constructive interpretation.[44] This interpretive process has two stages: a

---

they make use of standards that do not function as rules, but operate differently as principles, policies, and other sorts of standards. Positivism, I shall argue, is a model of and for a system of rules, and its central notion of a single fundamental test for law forces us to miss the important role of these standards that are not rules . . . . I call a "policy" that kind of standard that sets out a goal to be reached, generally an improvement in some economic, political, or social feature of the community . . . . I call a "principle" a standard that is to be observed, not because it will advance or secure an economic, political, or social situation deemed desirable, but because it is a requirement of justice or fairness or some other dimension of morality.

Note that Dworkin's critique has been met with numerous responses from positivists. For example, Genaro Carrio, *Legal Principles and Legal Positivism* (Buenos Aires: Abeldo-Perrot, 1971) at 25, argues that the extra-legal principles that Dworkin refers to do indeed have a legal pedigree, because they are principles that judges have used in the past to guide their interpretation. Compare with Joseph Raz, "Postscript to "Legal Principles and the Limits of Law" in *Ronald Dworkin and Contemporary Jurisprudence*, Marshall Cohen (ed) (Totowa, NJ: Rowman & Allanheld, 1983), arguing that the fact that judges apply moral principles does not mean that these principles are legal in nature. Others have argued along the lines that Dworkin is inaccurate in his assumption that positivism prohibits moral questions from being part of the criteria for legal validity. See for example, Philip Soper, "Legal Theory and the Obligations of a Judge: The Hart/Dworkin Dispute" (1977) *Michigan Law Review* 75 at 473; David Lyons, "Principles, Positivism and Legal Theory" (1977) *Yale Law Journal* 87 at 415; Wilfred Waluchow, *Inclusive Legal Positivism* (Oxford: Clarendon Press, 1994).

42   Ronald Dworkin, *Law's Empire* (Cambridge, MA: Harvard University Press, 1986) at 225: "The adjudicative principle of integrity instructs judges to identify legal rights and duties, so far as possible, on the assumption that they were created by a single author – the community personified – expressing a coherent conception of justice and fairness" [Dworkin, *Law's Empire.*]

43   Dyzenhaus gives a similar reading of Dworkin, stating, "Whatever answer the theory gives to the legal question posed by the case is the 'right answer', the answer that the judge is under a legal and moral duty to give. Dworkin's position is thus plausibly understood as claiming that the authority of law (as he would put it, law's ability to justify coercion) is grounded by that moral theory." David Dyzenhaus, "Dworkin and Unjust Law" in Will Waluchow & Stefan Sciaraffa (eds), *The Legacy of Ronald Dworkin* (New York: Oxford University Press, 2016) at 133.

44   Dworkin introduces the concept of constructive interpretation as follows: "Roughly, constructive interpretation is a matter of imposing purpose on an object or practice in order to make of it the best possible example of the form or genre to which it is taken to belong." In Dworkin, *Law's Empire*, above note 42 at 52.

test of "fit" and then an interpretive justification.[45] In the first step, a judge must consider which interpretation of a law fits within the existing legal landscape. A simplified example can help make this more tangible: consider a personal injury case where a negligently injured plaintiff claims compensation for the wages that they lost as a result of being unable to work due to their injuries. This claim fits simply into the existing tort law landscape, which calls for returning negligently injured parties to the position they would have been in absent the injuries. This includes compensation for lost earnings. The judicial inquiry into the legal validity of the plaintiff's claim for lost wages can end there.

The "fit" aspect of Dworkin's theory is complex, but it can, I suggest, safely be interpreted as a vigorous commitment to formal justice: when ascertaining whether a rule has legal validity, judges should consider law as an integrated whole which contains a unifying notion of what is fair and just, and fresh cases should be treated in accordance with that unifying notion. That ensures that community members are subject to a consistent and coherent concept of justice and fairness, whatever that concept may be in substance. This resonates with Dworkin's well-known commitment that the law must treat subjects with equal concern and respect. In Dworkin's words, the first stage of interpretation[46]

> asks judges to assume, so far as this is possible, that the law is structured by a coherent set of principles about justice and fairness and procedural due process and it asks them to enforce these in the fresh cases that come before them, so that each person's situation is fair and just according to the same standards.

But Dworkin's interpretive theory does not end there. Suppose that the plaintiff argues that they should also be compensated for the potential future earnings that they may lose in the event that they require further debilitating medical treatment after the trial is over. This claim may not fit as neatly into the existing body of tort law. The judge will

---

45   *Ibid* at 65–66: "First, there must be a 'preinterpretive' stage in which the rules and standards taken to provide the tentative content of the practices are identified .... Second, there must be an interpretive stage at which the interpreter settles on some general justification for the main elements of the practice identified at the preinterpretive stage. This will consist of an argument why a practice of that general shape is worth pursuing, if it is."

46   *Ibid* at 243.

likely find that the existing law may support two or more interpretations of when and whether potential future losses are compensable. Therefore, whether the plaintiff has a legal right to the potential future losses that they claim is open to interpretation.

These types of "hard" cases lead to the second step of Dworkin's interpretive analysis: the justification step. This step requires that judges decide which interpretation of the law is best by making an explicitly moral judgment that justifies their conclusion. That is, a judge must decide which interpretation best reflects abstract principles of justice and fairness.[47] For Dworkin, then, rules have legal validity when they best reflect certain moral principles that can justify that validity. In his words:[48]

> Hard cases arise, for any judge, when his threshold test [i.e., the fit test] does not discriminate between two or more interpretations of some statute or line of cases. Then he must choose between eligible interpretations by asking which shows the community's structure of institutions and decisions – its public standards as a whole – in a better light from the standpoint of political morality. His own moral and political convictions are now directly engaged.

Although it is easiest to understand the fit and justification stages of Dworkin's analysis as distinct, Dworkin explains the two stages as closely intertwined. For instance, he notes that[49]

> questions of fit arise at this [second] stage of interpretation as well, because even when an interpretation survives the threshold requirement, any infelicities of fit will count against it . . . in the general balance of political virtues.

This indicates that for Dworkin both stages of the analysis of legal validity involve justificatory components, and that coherence, which is the characterizing feature of the "fit" analysis, is a relevant justificatory virtue. Dworkin's turn toward indicating that there are interconnections between legal validity and its justification lend support to my notion that legal validity must be legitimate. But can Dworkin's jurisprudential ideas about the nature of legal validity usefully inform my consideration of the narrow context of valid fact-finding? And if so, to what extent?

---

47 *Ibid* at 249 and 250.
48 *Ibid.*
49 *Ibid* at 256.

As noted, there are aspects of Dworkin's theory of legal validity that have a formal character. The fit analysis seems to contain within it a general commitment to treating litigants equally and fairly by ensuring that a coherent set of legal principles, including procedural principles, applies to everyone.[50] These principles, for Dworkin, tell at least part of the story of how legal validity is justified. This aspect of his theory can translate into the fact-finding context, and can bolster the procedural legitimacy claim that I am aiming to present — guaranteeing that litigants are subjected to the same set of coherent processes of fact-finding can play a role in justifying the validity of factual determinations, because it ensures that litigants are treated equally and fairly.

But, there are also difficulties with applying Dworkin's theory to build a framework for legitimacy of legal fact-finding. The primary problem (for my purposes) arises because part of the test for legal validity in Dworkin's theory is grounded in the substantive merits of the judicial result. That is, a particular interpretation of the law is considered "right" on the basis that it best expresses the community's moral principles of justice and fairness. The judge's duty is to arrive at this "right" or "best" result.[51] Ultimately, upon arriving at the best interpretation of the law, the judge will make a ruling that will signal to one party that their viewpoint is wrong, or at least, not the best interpretation, and an authoritative ruling will be rendered. The legal validity of the judge's decision, as well as the justification for its authority, is grounded in the moral principles that are reflected in the result. This implies that the losing party's moral position is either irrelevant or wrong.

This implication seems problematically destabilizing in modern pluralistic societies because it does not embrace the reality of deeply held moral disagreements.[52] Estlund's comments on the issue of plural-

---

50   See for instance Dworkin, *Law's Empire*, above note 42 at 176–86, describing that the political integrity principle is one of coherence at both the legislative level (where legislators try to make the law coherent) and at the adjudicative level (where judges try to give coherent interpretations).

51   For Dworkin's comments on the "right answer" thesis and his response to critics of it, see Ronald Dworkin, "No Right Answer?" in *Law, Morality, and Society: Essays in Honour of H.L.A Hart*, P.M.S. Hacker & Joseph Raz (eds) (Oxford: Clarendon Press, 1977).

52   Jeremy Waldron has given a parallel critique grounded in pluralism with respect to Dworkin's claim that appears in *Freedom's Law: The Moral Reading of the American Constitution* (Oxford: Oxford University Press, 1997) at 34, that developing and choosing standards that would apply to institutions that make decisions about democratic rights should be results driven. Dworkin writes, "I see no alternative but to use a result-driven rather than a

ism and impact on "correctness" based theories of legitimacy are, to me, convincing, and express the concerns precisely (albeit in a democratic theory context), so they are worth reproducing here:[53]

> One thing to notice about a correctness theory of legitimacy is that in a diverse community there is bound to be little agreement on whether a decision is legitimate, since there will be little agreement about whether it meets the independent standard, say, justice. If the decision is made by majority rule, and voters address the question whether the proposal would be independently correct, then at least a majority will accept its correctness. However nearly half of the voters might deny its correctness, and on a correctness theory, they would in turn deny the legitimacy of the decision – deny that it warrants state action and/or places them under any obligation to comply. Brute disagreement of this kind raises pragmatic questions about how to maintain stability. A morally deeper worry stems from the fact that much of the disagreement might be reasonable, or in our more generic term, qualified. First, there might be qualified disagreement on what counts as just. Second, even if there is an account of justice that is beyond qualified objection, I assume there will be qualified disagreement in many cases about what actual decisions and institutions meet the agreeable principles of justice. If so, correctness theories of legitimacy, those that say that a law is legitimate simply because it meets the independent standards of justice, will not have a justification that is acceptable to all qualified points of view. Correctness theories cannot meet the qualified acceptability requirement. I take this to be conclusive against them.

---

procedure-driven standard . . . . The best institutional structure is the one best calculated to produce the best answers to the essentially moral question of what the democratic conditions actually are, and to secure stable compliance with those conditions." In response, Waldron points out that a results-driven approach cannot fully account for moral disagreements: "Using a results-driven approach, different citizens will attempt to design the constitution on a different basis . . . . How can they together design a political framework to structure and accommodate the political and ideological differences between them?" (Jeremy Waldron, *Law and Disagreement* (Oxford: Oxford University Press, 1999 at 294–95).

53 David Estlund, *Democratic Authority: A Philosophical Framework* (Princeton, NJ: Princeton University Press, 2008) at 99 [Estlund, *Democratic Authority*]. Estlund's comments are especially important today, where there is an alarming trend toward derogation of democratic values, rise in authoritarianism, and disinterest in pluralistic thinking among those in power.

Dworkin's theory does not seem to go far enough to respond to the question of why someone should accept the authority of a judicial outcome even if they deeply and cogently disagree with it in substance. In my view, if there is to be an answer to that question, then it must be located within the acceptability of the process that leads to the particular outcome.[54] But Dworkin's theory suggests that laws are recognized, and simultaneously justified, on the basis of the substantive merits of their judicial interpretation, largely ignoring the argumentative process that ultimately gives rise to the judicial decision.[55] The result is an exclusive emphasis on the judge's interpretation yielding

---

54　This is suggestive of Stuart Hampshire's contention that "within different moralities, liberal and conservative, the fairness of the actual outcome of a conflict will be evaluated differently, even though both sides recognize the fairness of the adversarial processes. Outcomes are by their nature open to dispute, but procedures need not be." (Quoted in Joshua Cohen, "Pluralism and Proceduralism" (1994) 69 *Chicago-Kent Law Review* 589 [Cohen, "Pluralism and Proceduralism"] and Stuart Hampshire, *Liberalism: The New Twist* (1993) *New York Review of Books* at 44.

The implications of pluralism on legal theory is, as it must be, a prominent theme in modern jurisprudence. It is far too large a question to fully canvass at this juncture, especially given that I intend to maintain a focus here on the utility of Dworkin's approach for the development of a framework for legitimate fact-finding. (For a sample of commentaries that focus on the problems posed by pluralism, see for example, Jack Winter, "Justice for Hedgehogs, Conceptual Authenticity for Foxes: Ronald Dworkin on Value Conflicts" (2016) 22(4) *Res Publica* 463; Avery Plaw, "Why Monist Critiques Feed Value Pluralism: Ronald Dworkin's Critique of Isaiah Berlin" (2004) 30(1) *Social Theory and Practice* 105; Martha Minow & Joseph William Singer, "In Favour of Foxes: Pluralism as Fact and Aid to the Pursuit of Justice" (2010) 90 *Boston University Law Review* 903.) I recognize the controversy in the claim that committing to the correctness of a particular outcome is difficult or impossible due to pluralism, yet agreeing on particular procedures remains possible. (See Joshua Cohen's important discussion in Cohen "Proceduralism and Pluralism," above note 54.) As will become evident below and in chapter 2, drawing on Jürgen Habermas's legal theory, I hold that the best response to finding a place for legitimacy within legal systems in pluralistic societies is to locate that legitimacy in the realm of processes rather than in the correctness of outcomes. Roughly, this is possible so long as the relevant processes *reflect* the pluralism of the society by ensuring that all opinions and viewpoints are given due importance. Such a process would require a fundamental commitment to certain substantive values, including equality and autonomy, and some may consider those commitments to be impossible to reconcile while duly noting a pluralistic context. But following that line of reasoning would suggest that a feasible theory of legitimacy is not possible in modern societies, and I disagree.

55　This may seem surprising, considering that Dworkin opens *Law's Empire* arguing that law is special in character because it is argumentative. (Dworkin, *Laws Empire*, above note 42 at 13.) Dworkin's point there is to show that an understanding of law as a "plain fact" is flawed because it does not account for legal disagreements about what the law is, notwithstanding that law is argumentative in nature. (see Dworkin, *Law's Empire*, above note 42 at 4–13).

a particular result and corresponding de-emphasis on the legitimizing virtues that may inhere in the adjudicative process.[56]

This poses obvious problems when trying to extrapolate principles from Dworkin's theory into the context of fact-finding. In the world of factual indeterminacy, neither the validity nor the legitimacy of an outcome can depend on the "rightness" or accuracy of the outcome because that cannot be guaranteed.[57] In that context, as I have noted above, both the validity and the legitimacy of fact-finding must be grounded in process. Accordingly, while I agree with Dworkin's notion that legal validity is intertwined with legitimacy, and that the formal commitments to consistent and coherent treatment of litigants is an integral aspect of that legitimacy, the lack of emphasis on the structural process of decision-making which involves arguments and evidence presentation from both sides in Dworkin's theory limits its utility as a jurisprudential orientation that can *of itself* ground a framework for procedurally legitimate fact-finding, though it provides some very significant contributions, as I return to further below.

I turn, then, to theorists who have emphasized procedural/formal aspects of law and examined the relationship of those elements to notions of legal validity and legitimacy. Jeremy Waldron has presented an insightful commentary on the formal concept of the rule of law and its role in maintaining legal validity. To begin, he explains the rule of law as follows:[58]

> The Rule of Law is a multi-faceted ideal. Most conceptions of this ideal, however, give central place to a requirement that people in positions of

---

56 Jürgen Habermas, *Between Facts and Norms*, above note 26 at 225: "The critique of Dworkin's solipsistic theory of law must begin…in the shape of a theory of legal argumentation, ground the procedural principles that henceforth bear the brunt of the ideal demands previously directed at Hercules."

57 Dworkin has discussed the problem of factual indeterminacy in a less known piece called "Principle, Policy, and Procedure" in *A Matter of Principle* (Cambridge, MA: Harvard University Press, 1985) [Dworkin, "Principle, Policy, and Procedure"]. There, he proposes two procedural rights in relation to factual indeterminacy. I discuss his ideas in that respect below, and offer critique that largely parallels my brief comments on Dworkin's theory of legal validity provided above.

58 Jeremy Waldron, "The Concept and the Rule of Law" (2008) 43(1) *Georgia Law Review* 1 at 6 [Waldron, "Rule of Law"]. This, as Waldron notes at 6, is in keeping with Ronald A. Cass's comments in *The Rule of Law in America* (Baltimore, London: The John Hopkins University Press, 2001) at 17: "A central element of the rule of law, constraining from external authority, . . . helps assure that the processes of government, rather than the predilections of the individual decisionmaker, govern."

authority should exercise their power within a constraining framework of public norms, rather than on the basis of their own preferences, their own ideology, or their own individual sense of right and wrong.

The rule of law, Waldron explains above, can be understood as a framework that legitimizes legal authority. I have suggested above that legitimacy is necessary for adjudicative factual determinations, which ultimately underpin judicial outcomes, because of the authoritative implications that are necessarily parceled within those outcomes. Accordingly, considering (1) whether the rule of law is a requisite feature of legal validity as well as legitimacy, and (2) why, and on what basis, the rule of law can play its legitimizing role, are relevant questions for my inquiry into legitimate fact-finding. I note, though, that it is beyond my scope to engage fully with the rule of law discourse, and what I offer below draws largely from Waldron's work on the rule of law, given his alignment with my thinking, as I point out below.

The rule of law has two broad dimensions. The first highlights the formal characteristics of laws: a system of law that adheres to the rule of law has laws that are predictable and certain, and officials apply and enforce rules that have legal validity, and *only* those rules.[59] As Waldron notes, that conception of the rule of law is paralleled in what Lon Fuller describes as the *Internal Morality of Law*.[60] He sets out the formal features that law must have — laws must be general in nature, they should be clear, ascertainable by the public, and consistent with one another; they should apply prospectively and not retroactively, they should be relatively stable, and there should be congruence between what the laws are and their application.[61] Adherence to these principles constrains lawmakers' authority, and ensures that laws govern, not human beings.

The idea of the rule of law is also used to denote ideals of natural justice or due process in the administrative law context.[62] That principle

---

59   *Ibid.*

60   *Ibid* at 7: "A conception of the Rule of Law like the one just outlined emphasizes the virtues that Lon Fuller discussed in The Morality of Law: the prominence of general norms as a basis of governance; the clarity, publicity, stability, consistency, and prospectivity of those norms; and congruence between the law on the books and the way in which public order is actually administered."

61   Lon Fuller, *Morality of Law* (New Haven and London: Yale University Press, 1964) [Fuller, *Morality of Law*]. See also my discussion in chapter 2, Part 2.

62   The notion of the rule of law that was popularized by A.V. Dicey in *Introduction to the Study of the Law of the Constitution* (1885) focused more squarely on this administrative aspect of

is violated when officials fail to administer the law in accordance with the relevant procedural safeguards. For example, in the fact-finding context, if a judge uses the criminal standard of proof to determine whether a doctor caused a patient's injury in an action in negligence, a violation of due process should be asserted. Similarly, if a party is disallowed from calling an expert witness of their choice (assuming that the expert is qualified to give relevant evidence), that constitutes a violation of due process as well.

For me, the relevant disagreements that arise as to what the rule of law denotes go to the precise value(s) that the rule of law protects, what the normative value of the rule of law is, and to what extent, if at all, the rule of law is relevant to a concept of legal validity.[63] Waldron articulates these questions this way:[64]

> Suppose for a moment that the Rule of Law does represent a more or less coherent political ideal. How central should this be to our understanding of law itself? What is the relation between the Rule of Law and the specialized work that modern analytic philosophers devote to the concept of law, and to the precise delineation of legal judgment from moral judgment and legal validity from moral truth?

For Fuller, the eight formal principles that he outlines are the constituent features of law itself. For him, therefore, the idea of the rule of law is intertwined within the concept of legal validity. Absent the eight formal principles that constitute law's internal morality, a legally valid rule does not arise. This indicates that for Fuller, law requires adherence to a certain internal morality, or internal justification scheme, in order to be valid law, and that internal morality is a product of law's formal features.[65] I discuss Fuller's concepts in far greater detail in chapter 2,

---

the rule of law. See also Richard Fallon, "'The Rule of Law' as a Concept in Constitutional Discourse" (1977) 97 *Columbia Law Review* 1 at 18–19.

63 For a discussion around the development of the concept of the rule of law and confusion around what it means, see Brian Tamanaha, "On the Rule of Law: History, Politics, Theory" (Cambridge: Cambridge University Press, 2004). See also Brian Z. Tamanaha "Functions of the Rule of Law" (2021) Scholarship@WashULaw 318, online: https://openscholarship.wustl.edu/law_scholarship/318.

64 Waldron, "Rule of Law," above note 58 at 10.

65 Fuller, *Morality of Law*, above note 61 at 96–97: "What I have called the internal morality of law is in this sense a procedural version of natural law . . . . The term 'procedural' is, however, broadly appropriate as indicating that we are concerned, not with the substantive aims of legal rules, but with the ways in which a system of rules for governing human

including a discussion on why he refers to the formal principles that he articulates as "morality." For now, my purpose is to point out my alignment with his notions that legal validity requires justification, so validity and legitimacy are inextricably connected, and that this connection occurs within law's formal features as opposed to within its substantive content.[66]

Unsurprisingly, theorists of the positivist tradition disagree with Fuller's notion that adherence to the internal morality of law principles is a prerequisite for the existence of valid law. Hart, for instance, referred to Fuller's principles as simply concepts of "efficacy," which do not warrant the label of moral principles; accordingly, those principles may be useful in ascertaining the effectiveness of a legal system, but not its existence.[67] Joseph Raz has offered a different response, recognizing the rule of law as a virtue-laden concept, but in keeping with positivist tradition of separating law from any evaluation of that law, he holds that whether the rule of law is upheld in a legal system or not has no bearing on legal validity. Contrasting his position with Lon Fuller's, Raz notes that "the principles of the rule of law which [Fuller] enumerated are essential for the existence of law [in Fuller's view]. . . . I have been treating the rule of law as an idea, as a standard to which the law ought to conform but which it can and sometimes does violate most radically and systemically."[68] He goes on to argue that "the Rule of Law is a negative virtue . . . the evil which is avoided is evil which could only have been caused by the law itself."[69] That is, a legal system that does not uphold the rule of law may be a bad or evil legal system, but it can still be a legal system, in contrast to Fuller's position.

---

conduct must be constructed and administered if it is to be efficacious and at the same time remain what it purports to be." I refer to this, and provide further commentary on Fuller's internal morality principles in chapter 2, Part 2.

66   As Dyzenhaus puts it, "Roughly, Fuller wished to focus debate about the legitimacy of the law on the process whereby decisions with the force of law are produced rather than on the content of the decisions." (David Dyzenhaus, "The Legitimacy of Legality" (1996) 46 *University of Toronto Law Journal* 129 at 130.

67   See H.L.A. Hart, "Book Review of *Morality of Law* by Lon Fuller" (1964–1965) 78 *Harvard Law Review* 1281.

68   Joseph Raz, "The Rule of Law and its Virtue" in Raz, *Authority of Law*, above note 33 at 223.

69   *Ibid* at 224.

Jeremy Waldron has critically referred to this viewpoint as "casual positivism."[70] He notes, "Not every system of command and control that calls itself a legal system *is* a legal system. We need to scrutinize it a little – to see how it works – before we bestow this term."[71] In other words, for Waldron, a legal system has to *deserve* to be a legal system, and in parallel, a law has to deserve legal validity.[72]

Waldron's comments about the rule of law in relation to adjudicative bodies are the most relevant for my project. First, he notes that although Hart and Raz seem to suggest that some sort of administrative bodies, like courts, that have the authority to determine legal disputes and apply the valid legal norms of a society are a necessary feature of law, neither of them make any suggestions about the "mode of operation or procedure" of the administrative bodies to which they refer.[73] As a result, "Star Chamber ex parte proceedings – without any sort of hearing"[74] would satisfy the requirement of an administrative body in the positivist view of law. For Waldron, however, *how* administrative decisions are made matters to whether an administrative system ought to be understood as a legal system:[75]

> [T]he essential idea is much more than merely functional – applying norms to individual cases. Most importantly, it is procedural: the operation of a court involves a way of proceeding that offers to those who are immediately concerned an opportunity to make submissions and present evidence, such evidence being presented in an orderly fashion according to strict rules of relevance and oriented to the norms whose application is in question. The mode of presentation may vary, but the existence of such an opportunity does not . . . . Throughout the process, both sides are treated respectfully and above all listened to by a tribunal that is bound to attend to the evidence presented and respond to the submissions that are made in the reasons that are given for its eventual decision.

---

70   Waldron, "Rule of Law," above note 58 at 13.

71   *Ibid* at 13–14.

72   *Ibid.*

73   *Ibid* at 22.

74   *Ibid* at 21. Of course, that type of administrative system could be criticized, but the positivist tradition maintains that such evaluations are irrelevant to the conception of a legal system. All that is relevant is that there exists a body that has the power to make authoritative decisions about legal disputes and application of law. I make further arguments about the limitations of this conception of law in my discussions of Hart's and Raz's theories in chapter 2.

75   *Ibid* at 23.

Waldron notes that none of these features of the administrative process is emphasized in positivist conceptions of law, yet all of them "should be regarded as an essential aspect of our working conception of law."[76] Waldron's viewpoints are aligned with both of the propositions that I outlined above. First, he finds the positivist conception of law lacking because it is empty of any commitment to why a legal system deserves its status as valid law. This supports my contention that legal validity requires legitimacy, and my parallel insistence that adjudicative determinations of fact must deserve their legal validity in the sense that there must be some reason why one can acquiesce to their authority. Second, Waldron's complaint that positivist legal theories do not set out any essential features of processes by which law should be administered indicates that for him, certain procedural features are prerequisite for a legitimately valid legal system. I echo this sentiment in my complaint of lack of attention to the process of adjudicating legal claims in Dworkin's approach to legal legitimacy presented above, and in my general claim that legally valid fact-finding must emerge from legitimizing fact-finding processes.

My alignment with viewpoints that insist that legal validity requires legitimacy, and that legitimacy is properly placed in law's formal features (as in Fuller's and Waldron's theoretical commitments noted above), along with the points of divergence from Dworkin's approach, have led me to what I hold to be one of the richest procedural theories: the discourse theory offered by German philosopher, Jürgen Habermas.[77]

I noted above that Dworkin's theory may have difficulties accounting for the legitimate disagreements that animate the political field in pluralistic societies; in contrast, the notion of plurality seems to permeate Habermas's legal theory. This, as I explain further below, makes Habermas's ideas more easily transferable to my context of factual determinations than Dworkin's theory, while maintaining the important commitments to equal and fair treatment that pervade Dworkin's legal philosophy. Habermas's concepts also, as I explain further in chapter 2, further substantiate some of the shared ideas that thematically link him with thinkers like Fuller and Waldron.

Habermas explains that in modern societies, there is no overarching agreement on the ideals of morality or the related question of what

---

76   *Ibid* at 24.

77   Habermas, *Between Facts and Norms*, above note 26.

constitutes substantively just or good laws. Many individuals, he notes, may genuinely disagree on whether a law aligns with their notions of what is just.[78] Nonetheless, the law is, and must be, authoritative for everyone in the society.[79] Habermas notes that while a law's authority can be coercively enforced to ensure compliance, stable integrated societies require that people must have a *reason* to respect the law's authority, even if they disagree with that law in substance. That reason is law's legitimacy. "Such legitimacy," Habermas explains (and as I have noted above), "should allow law abiding behaviour that, based on respect for the law, involves more than sheer compliance."[80] Accordingly, for Habermas, the stability of modern societies demands that law be authoritative, and that its authority be legitimate. Therefore, legal validity and its legitimacy must be intertwined. Importantly, that legitimacy, Habermas holds, cannot be a product of the law's substance, because the law is authoritative even for those that disagree with the law. Accordingly, he proposes that:[81]

> Legality can produce legitimacy only to the extent that the legal order reflexively responds to the need for justification that originates from the positivization of law and responds in such a manner that legal discourses are institutionalized in ways made pervious to moral argumentation.

Interpreting this quotation, Dyzenhaus observes, "Habermas's own account of the legitimacy of law looks to the form of law to establish a connection between law and morality."[82] In other words, the justification of legal outcomes comes from the *process* through which the law emerges. This gives rise to Habermas's notion of rational discourse as a

---

78   See generally Jürgen Habermas, *Between Facts and Norms*, above note 26 at the introduction; and at 200: "In a pluralistic society in which various belief systems compete with each other, recourse to a prevailing ethos . . . does not offer a convincing basis for legal discourse." A further discussion of Habermas's notions of law and legitimacy is undertaken in chapter 2.

79   Though it is not necessarily true that everyone (including individuals and marginalized subgroups) subjectively regard the law as having equal authority, nor any moral authority.

80   Jürgen Habermas, *Between Facts and Norms*, above note 26 at 197–98.

81   Jürgen Habermas, "Law and Morality" (Tanner Lectures on Human Values, delivered at Harvard University, 1 and 2 October 1986) at 243–44. In this lecture, Habermas argues at 220 for the thesis that "legality can derive its legitimacy only from a procedural rationality with moral impact. The key to this is an interlocking of two types of procedures: processes of moral argumentation get institutionalized by means of legal procedures."

82   David Dyzenhaus, *Legality and Legitimacy: Carl Schmitt, Hans Kelsen, and Hermann Heller in Weimar* (Toronto: Oxford University Press, 1997) at 239.

theory of law: where law emerges through a process that embodies the principles of rational discourse, whereby affected parties are ensured an equal right to freely and meaningfully voice their viewpoints and arguments, which may include whatever traditions or moral convictions they may have, there is a justifiable reason, grounded in that process, to recognize the emergent law as having legitimate authority. In my reading, the assurance of freedom and equality in the argumentative process is, in Habermas's theory, the legitimizing feature of the law.[83] Since the justifying features of law arise from of the process of law-making, the law, in Habermas's theory, refrains from grounding its authority on the law's substantive moral content; rather, the legitimacy of its authority is on the basis that those affected are treated fairly in the process of legal decision-making.[84]

This idea of rational discourse is paralleled in the adjudicative context. Where the fundamental features of a rational discourse are reflected in the adjudicative process, those outcomes also have legitimacy. Applied in the fact-finding context, where the process of fact-finding enables free and equal ability to make arguments and present evidence as to the relevant facts, the authority of a valid legal fact-finding becomes legitimate, while simultaneously allowing for the inevitable acceptance of the possibility that it might be factually inaccurate.[85]

In chapter 2, I engage more deeply with Hart's and Raz's jurisprudence, representing positivist legal theories, and Fuller's and Habermas's theories, representing theories of law that I describe as "thinly substantiated procedural models" for law and its legitimacy. At this stage, my purpose is to position my approach within a broader jurisprudential landscape. My ultimate focus, though, is on judicial fact-finding, one of the most arduous yet under-theorized aspects of judicial work. The jurisprudential notions that I have presented above form the deepest grounding for my ultimate goal of building a procedural legitimacy framework that can be used to assess the propriety

---

83   This is elaborated further in chapter 2.

84   Compare with Estlund's brief account of Habermas's theory in *Democratic Authority*, above note 53 at 88–90, suggesting that legitimacy of a legal outcome, in Habermas's theory, is grounded in the fact that it "*could* have been produced by ideal deliberative procedures," not that it actually was. If that is true, Estlund suggests, Habermas's theory of legitimacy is dependent on the merit of the outcome, and not on the particular procedures that gave rise to the outcome. I do not find this reading of Habermas to be accurate. A more detailed account of my interpretation of Habermas's theory is presented in chapter 2.

85   The longer form of this argument appears in chapter 2, Part 2B.

of fact-finding processes. That requires proceeding now more squarely into the fact-finding context, which I introduce below.

Transitioning the broad jurisprudential principles that I canvass above (and which will be more fully unfolded in chapter 2) into the context of fact-finding involves engaging in challenging and foundational debates about evidence doctrine and other procedural doctrines relating to factual determinations.

The procedural legitimacy proposal that I am advancing stems from the observation that the authority of a factual finding is not (because it cannot be) dependent on the factual accuracy of the finding itself. This results in an unavoidable possibility of a factually inaccurate judicial finding that, nonetheless, has justifiable authority. But for some, being factually inaccurate is one way that an outcome can be unjust. An injured plaintiff who does not receive compensation due to factual error, for instance, can be thought to suffer an injustice. Those who believe this would raise the question of how it is possible that an unjust outcome, in the sense of its being factually inaccurate, can possibly merit its authority.[86] Below, I take up the question of the injustice that may be associated with factual inaccuracies, and how I perceive the procedural legitimacy proposal's response. I do so by providing an explanation of various viewpoints relevant to this question, and situating my own commitments, which will ground my conception of procedurally legitimate fact-finding, in relation to them.

I start with Robert Bone's proposal in "Procedure, Participation, Rights."[87] There, he suggests that the answer to the adjudicative tension caused by factual uncertainty can be found through a re-conceptualization of "injustice" in relation to inaccurate factual determinations. His response is premised on a commingling of substantive rights and procedural rights.[88] He suggests that the processes of administration and enforcement of laws deliberately limit the substantive rights for which the laws provide. In the torts context, for

---

86   Hock Lai Ho, *Philosophy of Evidence Law: Justice in the Search for Truth* (Oxford, New York: Oxford University Press, 2008) at 65 suggests, for instance: "That someone has had a fair trial may justify our insistence that she accepts an adverse verdict in the absence of reason to doubt the court's finding. But we are not entitled to maintain that stance towards her once we realize that some crucial part of the material findings was false; we now have to acknowledge that there was a miscarriage of justice" [Ho, *Philosophy of Evidence Law*].

87   Robert G. Bone, "Procedure, Participation, Rights" (2010) 90 *Boston University Law Review* 1011 [Bone, "Procedure, Participation, Rights"].

88   *Ibid* at 1022.

instance, while a plaintiff has a substantive right to compensation for negligently inflicted injury, that right is contingent on the procedures of adjudicating the plaintiff's claim. That process of adjudication includes a risk of factual error. This line of reasoning prompts the following comments from Bone, illustrating how the interpretation of the interplay between substance and procedure can affect the existence of a harm:[89]

> Has a moral harm occurred if the plaintiff is unable to sue successfully because of judicially-imposed procedural limits? The answer depends on the best interpretation of what the legislature did when it created the substantive right. One possible interpretation is that the legislature meant to adopt a substantive right conditioned on appropriate procedural implementation. If this interpretation is correct, then the right to compensation has an error risk already built in, so it is difficult to see how moral harm can occur when that risk materializes and a deserving plaintiff loses.

Accordingly, Bone advises that when an outcome is either deliberately factually erroneous, or is a result of procedural impropriety, it may be appropriate to consider the outcome to be an injustice, but where there is an innocent factual error, in the sense that all the appropriate procedures were adhered to but a factually erroneous outcome was rendered, there is no obvious injustice.[90]

As Bone cautions, there is no doubt that depending on a procedure-substance divide is "notoriously problematic."[91] Dworkin makes the point too: "the sharp distinction between substance and procedure is arbitrary from a normative standpoint. . . . [A]ny descriptive theory that relies so heavily on that distinction, even if factually accurate, cannot be a deep theory about the nature of adjudication."[92]

Bearing in mind these cautions, it is useful to acknowledge that there are substantive aspects to procedural rules and procedural aspects of substantive rules. For instance, the degree of conviction that a standard of proof requires (e.g., balance of probabilities or reasonable doubt require different degrees of conviction) is a substantive aspect of the process of

---

89   *Ibid.* Note that the phrase "moral harm" that Bone employs here is borrowed from Dworkin, and is synonymous with the term "injustice factor," as I discuss further below.

90   Bone, "Procedure, Participation, Rights," above note 87 at 1021–2.

91   *Ibid.*

92   Ronald Dworkin, "Principle, Policy, and Procedure," above note 57 at 77.

fact-finding. Still, in my view, it is descriptively accurate and analytically helpful to draw a distinction between the rights protected by tort laws and the process of fact-finding during adjudication of those rights.

The principles of tort law dictate that members of our society have rights against one another for injuries caused by a party who owed us a duty of care and who breached the standard of care owed.[93] These principles translate into the factual elements that must be established for a finding of liability when a dispute over that right occurs. As pointed out earlier, our process of fact-finding requires a 50 percent or greater chance of the relevant event to be established. But that does not mean that the *substantive* question at stake for a liability determination is whether there was a greater than 50 percent chance of causation, or any other required factual element. The *process* of proof demands at least a 50 percent chance of causation, but that does not influence the nature of the rights we have against one another in principle. Liability for negligent injury exists, in principle, when there is a duty of care, not the chance of a duty of care; when there is a breach of the standard of care owed, not the chance thereof; when an injury was caused by the defendant's negligence, not when an injury was potentially caused by his negligence. Those chances are relevant in the context of the process of proof; they are not relevant in terms of the substantive rights at stake. Conflating the rights protected in legal principles and the process of proving relevant facts to adjudicate disputes involving those rights is unsustainable because that would change the nature of the right to be free from negligent injury altogether. We have rights against each other in relation to negligently inflicted injuries, not the *chances* of injuries, even though those chances may be relevant as part of the process of administering those rights.[94]

Treating substantive rights and the processes of making factual determinations for the purpose of resolving disputes about those rights as inextricable enables, for Bone, a denial of the injustice that occurs when

---

93   Here, I am adopting the rights-based interpretation of tort law that can be defined as characteristic of Ernest Weinrib. See generally, Ernest Weinrib, *The Idea of Private Law* (Cambridge, MA: Harvard University Press, 1995).

94   Robert Stevens, *Torts and Rights* (Oxford: Oxford University Press, 2007) at 43 points out, "the rights we have against everyone else are in relation to the outcome of injury, not its risk of occurring in the future." And see *Barker v Corus UK Ltd* [2006] 2 AC 572 at 579 (HL), Lord Hoffmann (House of Lords): "[t]he standard rule is that it is not enough to show that the defendant's conduct increased the likelihood of damages being suffered . . . . It must be proved on a balance of probabilities that the defendant's conduct did cause the damages."

a person who is entitled to compensation in principle is refused compensation due to factual error. For me, this denial constitutes an avoidance of the uncomfortable reality that an adjudicative outcome that denies compensation when it is deserved in principle *does* bear an injustice, in the sense that a litigant's legal right was not vindicated, even if there was no error in the process of adjudication, so the outcome is legally valid. Similarly, if an adjudicative outcome erroneously holds a party liable due to factual error, an injustice *does* occur, even absent procedural error. As Ho puts it, "the person against whom a verdict is wrongly given is the victim of an injustice; it misses an essential force of her grievance to dismiss her plight as a mere misfortune."[95] And as Dworkin holds, that injustice factor exists whether or not it ever comes to light that a factual error occurred, and even if the error was wholly innocent.[96] In this respect, I agree with Ho and Dworkin: factual errors do result in a certain type of injustice, when injustice is understood as the failure to uphold a legal right.[97] And, importantly, it is the inevitability of that possibility that gives rise to the normative work accomplished by the procedural legitimacy framework that I develop here and in upcoming chapters.

Bone's idea of conceptually commingling substantive rights with the procedural rules of adjudication, which contemplate risk of inaccuracy, de-problematizes factual uncertainty. It implies, in my understanding, that procedural correctness is synonymous with justice (provided that the procedures themselves are acceptable) because it denies the

---

95 Ho, *Philosophy of Evidence Law*, above note 86 at 65.

96 Dworkin, "Principle, Policy, and Procedure," above note 57 at 81.

97 This is not to say that factual inaccuracy is the only way that an adjudicative outcome can be rendered unjust. Even outcomes where the factual determinations were perfectly accurate may nonetheless be unjust. For instance, if a judge misapprehends the law, and thereby applies the wrong legal principle to an accurate set of facts, that outcome can be said to be unjust. Injustice can also occur when, for instance, a judge accurately determines that a fugitive slave is legally property of some owner and decides, in accordance with the law, that the slave must be returned to the owner. Here, one may argue that factual inaccuracy may have generated a more just result. But it is not the factual inaccuracy that would generate a more just response; the more just response would be generated because the factual inaccuracy would cause an unjust law to go unapplied. Injustice can occur as a result of unjust legal principles, even absent factual inaccuracy. But given the centrality of the legitimacy of factual determinations in this project, my focus is on the type of injustice that occurs through factual inaccuracy, not the injustices that occur due to unjust substantive laws or judicial misapprehension of the laws. Those circumstances do lead to improper adjudicative outcomes, even if the underlying fact-finding was accurate. Addressing those types of outcomes, and the injustice associated with them, is not central to the procedural legitimacy framework for legitimate fact-finding that I am developing.

injustice that occurs when a factual error results from correct adherence to the relevant procedural rules. Bone's approach parallels my purpose of demonstrating the significance of procedural propriety to some extent, but it is not the view I am presenting because it masks the true normative work that procedural propriety accomplishes.

Procedural integrity, in my proposal, grounds adjudicative *legitimacy,* which is the normative grounding for the authority of judicial outcomes. This concept of legitimacy must not be confused with a guarantee of justice; rather, the normative work that it achieves is maintaining the integrity of a fallible judicial system that must tolerate a gap between perfect justice (which requires, among other things, factual accuracy) and legitimate adjudicative outcomes (which cannot depend on factual accuracy). As Frank Michelman explains, there is nothing inherently problematic with having a gap between justice and legitimacy: [98]

> There is nothing wrong or untoward about allowing in this way for the possibility of legitimacy in a governmental system whose performance observably fails to measure up to justice. *For what purpose, after all, do we employ the term "legitimate," if not to convey the complex judgment that a governmental system in the dock, so to speak, for its clear shortfalls from justice continues nevertheless to merit loyalty.* On the other hand, the justice-legitimacy gap normally strikes us as something we have little choice but to accept in a partially fallen world, not as something we positively cherish.

In parallel to Michelman's comments above, we have little choice but to accept that a plaintiff who is entitled to win their claim in principle may not win at trial due to factual error. We may consider that

---

98   Frank I. Michelman, "Justice as Fairness, Legitimacy, and the Question of Judicial Review: A Comment" (2004) 72 *Fordham Law Review* 1407 at 1414 [emphasis added] [Michelman, "Justice as Fairness, Legitimacy"]. For similar guidance on the distinction between legitimacy and justice, see Wilfried Hinsch, "Legitimacy and Justice" in Jorg Khunelt (ed), *Political Legitimization Without Morality?* (Nurnberg, Germany: Springer, 2008) at 45. Echoing the sentiments presented above, Hinsch discussing the laws of constitutional democracies, notes that "political legislation may in many cases be put legitimately into effect, against which reasonable objections can be raised, at least on the part of some citizens." Making the case for procedural legitimization, he goes on to say, "such controversial decisions cannot be fully justified on the basis of substantive argument alone but only by appealing to the fact that they are the result of a fact decision-making process."

an injustice. Nonetheless, that adjudicative outcome must still be legitimate in order for its authority to be defensible. As Lawrence Solum explains:

> When we know the outcome to be unjust, the justice of the outcome cannot be the source of its legitimacy. This conceptual point has a crucial corollary: only just procedures can confer legitimate authority on incorrect outcomes.[99]

To Solum's point, I add the qualifier that whether we "know the outcome to be unjust," is not significant because it is possible that we will never know whether or not a legal fact is true. For instance, where there is a difficulty in establishing causation of an injury due to medical uncertainty, it may never be possible to know for certain whether the defendant's error really did cause the plaintiff's injury, or some other medical condition caused it. By accepting probabilistic fact-finding, we embrace indeterminacy and the associated risk of inaccuracy and logical consistency requires that we must also be ready to accept the materialization of that risk, whether or not we know it has materialized. It is the *potential* for factually inaccurate outcomes that are nonetheless valid and legitimate, that leads to the claim that the legitimacy of adjudicative factual determinations cannot depend on factual accuracy, and are, rather, contingent on procedural merits.

Accordingly, legitimacy bears a hefty normative burden: it gives us the reason that we can assert that a litigant should accept the authority of a valid law, even if they believe or even know it to be factually erroneous. Given the significance of legitimacy, its essential features must be neither over-inclusive nor under-inclusive.[100] The standard of legitimacy has to be practical — something that the legal system can actually achieve. Of course, factual accuracy cannot be absolutely guaranteed in an

---

99 Lawrence Solum, "Procedural Justice" 78 *Southern California Law Review* 181 at 267–68 [Solum, "Procedural Justice"]. And at 278, he states: "The exercise of adjudicative power to bind an individual must be legitimate for the adjudication to be authoritative and, hence, to create content-independent obligations of political morality, to obey judicial decrees, and to respect the finality of judgments."

100 Michelman, "Justice as Fairness, Legitimacy," above note 99 at 1419. The same notion is evident in Habermas's thinking presented above. He suggests that a criterion for legitimacy that depends on substantive moral justification would be overly stringent because the law cannot be guaranteed to have a substantive quality that will be acceptable to every individual's moral sentiments. Law's legitimacy must be achievable.

efficacious dispute resolution system. This means that adjudicative legitimacy cannot depend on the factual accuracy of outcomes; that, in turn, implicates the role of process in maintaining the legitimacy of authoritative judicial outcomes that unavoidably bear a risk of inaccuracy. The normative burden of maintaining legitimate adjudication, in light of factual uncertainty, must be borne by procedural propriety.

This leads, of course, to a number of questions. Most broadly, "on what basis can the fact-finding procedures play their legitimizing role?" Surely it cannot be the case that just any procedures will do. A flip of a coin, for instance, or an otherwise arbitrary fact-finding procedure, could not capture the rich normative foundations that one must demand of procedural legitimacy. Responses can be grouped into two categories: instrumental approaches and non-instrumental approaches.[101] Instrumental approaches are those viewpoints that perceive adjudicative procedures as a means to achieve particular ends. When such approaches are adopted, efforts to provide principles of procedure are oriented toward effective achievement of some outcome. In the fact-finding context, the accuracy of the outcome is the central concern. Non-instrumental viewpoints are held by those who perceive adjudication as a process of dispute resolution and for whom adjudicative procedures have (or should have) some inherent or intrinsic value that is independent of the outcome itself. In order to provide additional background for my discussion in upcoming chapters, I provide an introduction to some pertinent aspects of various instrumental and non-instrumental viewpoints in relation to fact-finding, and situate myself among them.

---

101   These categories are referred to differently by different people. For example, Michael Bayles uses the "instrumental" and "non-instrumental" terminology that I adopt here in "Principles for Legal Procedure," above note 8; Robert Bone opts for "outcome-oriented" and "process-oriented" in "Rethinking the 'Day in Court' Ideal and Non-party Preclusion" (1992) 67 *New York University Law Review* 193; Richard B. Saphire uses "substantive" and "inherent" in "Specifying Due Process Values: Toward a More Responsive Approach to Procedural Protection" (1978) 127 *University of Pennsylvania Law Review* 111. Adopting the instrumental and non-instrumental categorization has enabled the most conceptual clarity for me, so I have adopted it here.

PART 3. SITUATING THE ARGUMENT AMONG INSTRUMENTAL AND NON-INSTRUMENTAL APPROACHES

Those who hold instrumental viewpoints of adjudication and, particularly adjudicative fact-finding, centralize the relationship between procedure and outcome accuracy. Acknowledging that accuracy cannot be guaranteed, instrumentalists attempt to determine which procedures justifiably manage the risk of inaccuracy by weighing the cost of errors associated with inaccuracy (like the harms associated with a false conviction or a false acquittal in the criminal context, or an inaccurate finding of liability, or inaccurate dismissal of a claim in a civil suit), with the costs of achieving better accuracy, generally assuming that higher accuracy comes at a higher cost.[102] Posner's economic analysis of law, for instance, refers to this as the balance between "the cost of erroneous judicial decisions" and "the cost of operating the procedural system."[103] Capturing the central tenet of such cost-balancing based analyses, Kaplow holds that:[104]

> [A]ccuracy is a central concern with regard to a wide range of legal rules. One might go so far as to say that a large portion of the rules of civil, criminal and administrative procedure and rules of evidence involve an effort to strike a balance between accuracy and legal cost.

Accordingly, evaluation of adjudicative fact-finding procedures occurs on the basis of whether rules that increase legal costs for the sake of accuracy, and vice versa, are desirable by determining the various harms associated with inaccuracy and comparing it to the costs that come with decreasing the risk of such inaccuracy, making them fundamentally utilitarian models. To give a simplified example, an economic analysis of adjudication may hold that the harm associated with a wrongful

---

102 As Louis Kaplow notes in "The Value of Accuracy in Adjudication" (1994) 23 *Journal of Legal Studies* 307 at 307, it is usually assumed that higher accuracy comes with higher economic cost, and that assumption seems sound [Kaplow, "Value of Accuracy"]. See also Richard Posner, "An Economic Approach to the Law of Evidence" (1999) 51(6) *Stanford Law Review* 1477; Richard A. Posner, "An Economic Approach to Legal Procedure and Judicial Administration" (1973) 2 *Journal of Legal Studies* 399; Richard A. Posner, *Economic Analysis of Law*, 2d ed (Boston: Little, Brown and Co, 1977) at 429; Gordon Tullock, *Trials on Trial* (New York: Columbia University Press, 1980) at 5–6.

103 Richard Posner, *Economic Analysis of Law*, 8th ed (New York: Aspen Publishers, 2011) at 757.

104 Kaplow, "Value of Accuracy," above note 103 at 307–8.

conviction is greater than the harm associated with an inaccurate civil claim. This difference in harm would justify the more onerous criminal standard of proof beyond a reasonable doubt compared with the less onerous balance of probabilities standard of proof in the civil context.

Ronald Dworkin has provided one of the most intricate and compelling explanations of why such utilitarian models cannot tell the full story of managing factual accuracy. He explains that these models do not duly account for individual rights protected by substantive law, and offers a theory of managing factual uncertainty that provides two procedural rights that correspond to the rights set out by the substantive law. Still, his approach remains fundamentally instrumental, and is, in my view, exemplary of instrumental approaches.[105] Therefore, I have found it appropriate to set out his approach in some detail below. This enables me to highlight the lessons that it can contribute to the version of procedural legitimacy that I ultimately propose, as well as the points of divergence between my approach and those that are exclusively instrumental.

In *Principle, Policy, Procedure*,[106] Dworkin considers whether a society that provides its subjects with certain rights can be considered "morally consistent" if it administers those rights through a process that compromises accuracy for the sake of the societal benefit of less costly legal procedures. For instance, if we have substantive rights to not be convicted of a crime if innocent, should we also have a right to the most accurate procedures available to determine our innocence? Similarly, in the civil context, tort law provides us with a legal entitlement to be compensated if we suffer a negligently inflicted injury, so should we also have corresponding procedural rights to accurate determination of whether we suffered an injury, and the extent of its damage?[107] In taking up these questions, Dworkin analyzes whether a utilitarian cost-benefit

---

105 Michael Bayles refers to Dworkin's approach as "'multi-value instrumentalism', that is, an approach that evaluates procedures by seeking to maximize several values," in "Principles for Procedure," above note 6 at 45.

106 Ronald Dworkin, "Principle, Policy, Procedure" in *A Matter of Principle* (Cambridge, MA: Harvard University Press, 1985).

107 Stated in a criminal law context, Dworkin asks, "Does it flow, from the fact that each citizen has a right not to be convicted if innocent, that he has a right to the most accurate procedures possible to test his guilt or innocence, no matter how expensive these procedures might be to the community as a whole?," Dworkin, "Principle, Policy, and Procedure," above note 57 at 72.

analysis can adequately respond to the dilemma posed by the practical inability of guaranteeing factual accuracy in the adjudicative process. Dworkin starts by introducing what he calls the "cost-efficient society" as follows: [108]

> This society . . . designs criminal procedures, including rules of evidence, by measuring the estimated suffering of those who would be mistakenly convicted if a particular rule were chosen, but would be acquitted if a higher standard of accuracy were established, against the benefits to others that will follow from choosing that rule instead of a higher standard.

In one respect, Dworkin explains, there is some consistency between the substantive right to not be convicted if innocent and the criminal procedure rules, because although factual errors are permissible, factual errors would not be acceptable if they are deliberate. That is, a person who is known to be innocent cannot be convicted.[109] This society, Dworkin explains, "accepts the risk of innocent mistakes about guilt or innocence in order to save public funds for other uses, but will not permit deliberate lies for the same purpose."[110] But this, for Dworkin, is not enough.

Dworkin's account for why it is not enough begins with a clarification of the nature of the harm that occurs when a factually inaccurate adjudicative outcome is rendered. He explains the impact of inaccuracy by introducing the concept of the "injustice factor" or "moral harm." The injustice factor arises wherever a substantive right, like the right to be free from conviction if innocent or the right to compensation for a negligently inflicted injury, is not vindicated due to factual error:[111]

> Someone who is held in tort for damage caused by negligently driving, when in fact he was not behind the wheel, or someone who is unable to pursue a genuine claim for damage to reputation because she is unable to discover the name of the person who slandered her . . . has suffered an injustice.

---

108   *Ibid* at 79.
109   *Ibid.*
110   *Ibid* at 80.
111   *Ibid* at 92. This is consistent with my comments above.

This harm arises whether the inaccurate outcome was an innocent mistake or deliberate (though there is greater harm when deliberate inaccuracy occurs).[112] It is an objective harm: it makes no difference whether anyone, including the victim of the injustice factor knows about it, accepts it, or has any concern whatsoever for it.[113] It exists in addition to the bare harm that comes with an inaccurate outcome — frustration, irritation, even anger or outrage.[114] Dworkin explains that because of its objective quality, the injustice factor cannot be accounted for in a utilitarian cost-benefit analysis because a utilitarian analysis can only capture a manifest harm that is subjectively experienced.[115]

For Dworkin, the existence of the injustice factor grounds the requirement for procedural rights of accuracy. Being rights, these procedural guarantees would trump collective concerns, taking them outside a purely utilitarian justification scheme. That is, certain procedural rights cannot be compromised on the basis of weighing the societal cost of more stringent fact-finding procedures, like less efficient adjudication, against the injustice suffered in the event of inaccuracy. This is because the injustice caused by inaccuracy may not be "suffered" at all, but it exists nonetheless.[116]

Although Dworkin argues that some procedural rights of accuracy in complement to substantive rights are a necessary aspect of an acceptable adjudicative system, he does not advocate the overly onerous guarantee of the most accurate possible adjudicative procedures. A society that absolutely prioritizes adjudicative accuracy, Dworkin explains, would be unable to "devote public funds to amenities like improvements to the highway system, for example, so long as any further expense on the criminal process could improve its accuracy. "Our

---

112   *Ibid.*

113   *Ibid* at 80: "[The 'injustice factor'] is an objective notion which assumes that someone suffers a special injury when treated unjustly, whether he knows or cares about it, but does not suffer that injury when he is not treated unjustly, even though he believes he is and does care."

114   *Ibid.*

115   For Dworkin's more detailed explanation of this point, see generally *ibid* at 81–84. At 81, Dworkin demonstrates why a society that fixes its adjudicative fact-finding procedures through a utilitarian calculus makes no place for the injustice factor, which exists even when "no one knows or suspects it, and even when — perhaps especially when — very few people very much care."

116   *Ibid.*

own society," Dworkin notes, "does not observe that stricture, and most people would think it too severe."[117]

In furtherance of finding a middle ground between no right to accuracy, and an absolute right to accuracy, Dworkin calls for adherence to two principles of "fair play" that correspond to his general commitment to ensuring a legal system that maintains integrity through assurance of equal concern and respect for legal subjects.[118] These two principles of fair play manifest in Dworkin's proposal as two procedural rights that involve ensuring a coherent scheme for the distribution of the risk of factual errors, and consistent adherence to that scheme.[119]

First, everyone has a right to be subjected to only those procedures that assign the correct level of importance to the injustice factor that may occur as a result of those procedures.[120] Dworkin refers to this as a "background and a legislative right," in the sense that the drafters of the rules of adjudicative procedure must set rules that correctly identify the potential of the injustice factor, and its harm.[121] The "correctness" of such a procedural rule depends on whether it accords with the general scheme of risk tolerance in a society. This procedural right calls for a legal system to maintain an internal integrity in terms of its theory of risk distribution. Consider, for example, a procedural rule that calls for a balance of probabilities standard of proof when adjudicating negligently inflicted injuries. If a court or legislator then introduced a procedural rule that reduced the standard of proof to a

---

117 *Ibid* at 84.

118 *Ibid*:

  I propose the following two principles of fair play in government. First, any political decision must treat all citizens as equals, that is, as equally entitled to concern and respect.... Second, if a political decision is taken and announced that respects equality as demanded by the first principle, then a later enforcement of that decision is not a fresh political decision that must also be equal in its impact in that way. The second principle appeals to the fairness of abiding by open commitments when adopted – the fairness, for example, of abiding by the result of a coin toss when both parties reasonably agreed to the toss.

119 The two rights that Dworkin provides are paralleled in his broader theory of integrity: "We have two principles of political integrity: a legislative principle, which asks lawmakers to try to make the total set of laws morally coherent, and an adjudicative principle, which instructs that the law be seen as coherent in that way, so far as possible." Dworkin, *Law's Empire*, above note 42 at 176.

120 Dworkin, "Principle, Policy, and Procedure," above note 57 at 89 in the criminal context, and at 93 for the application in the civil context.

121 *Ibid* at 93: "Everyone has the right that the legislature fix civil procedures that correctly assess the risk and importance of moral harm, and this right holds against the courts when these institutions act in an explicitly legislative manner."

de minimus standard if the claim is against a doctor, then a defendant doctor may argue that such a rule violates their first procedural right, because it does not cohere with the broader risk allocation scheme within the society.

Second, Dworkin suggests that people are entitled "to procedures consistent with the community's own evaluation of moral harm embedded in the law as a whole."[122] This is a right of equal and consistent treatment. "It holds the community to a consistent enforcement of its theory of moral harm, but does not demand that it replace the theory with a different one."[123] Dworkin explains this as a "legal right. It holds, that is, against courts in their adjudicative capacity."[124] This is the application aspect of Dworkin's rights.[125] When a litigant asserts this right, they do not question the substance of the procedural rules, but they demand a consistent application of them. They could assert this right when, for instance, their expert evidence is improperly deemed inadmissible, or if the trier of fact fails to properly assess the reliability of expert evidence, or when the wrong standard of proof is applied. In such cases, the litigant does not claim that the admissibility rules or the standards of proof are improper; rather, they demand that they be subjected to those procedural rules consistently as an equal member of society.

These rights, Dworkin concludes, "provide a middle ground between the denial of all procedural rights and the acceptance of a grand right to supreme accuracy."[126] I find the concept of the injustice factor associated with factual inaccuracy — even when that inaccuracy is innocent — helpful and accurate. And the move to introduce procedural rights on the basis of the inability to guarantee factual accuracy is in keeping with my theme of highlighting the significance of procedural propriety. In addition, through the idea that adherence to procedural rights enables and maintains equal concern and respect for litigants, Dworkin's theory provides at least some grounding for the idea that

---

122   *Ibid* at 89.

123   *Ibid* at 90.

124   *Ibid* at 93.

125   *Ibid*: "It is a legal right to the consistent application of that theory of moral harm that figures in the best justification of settled legal practice."

126   *Ibid*. Dworkin explains his aim in "Principle, Policy, and Procedure," above note 57, as seeing "whether a middle ground can be found between the impractical idea of maximum accuracy and the submersive denial of all procedural rights" at 77.

procedural integrity can provide legitimacy to the authority of factual determinations that arise through a fact-finding system that accepts some risk of inaccuracy.

But there are unaddressed tensions in Dworkin's proposal that stem, I suggest, from his fundamentally instrumental approach to adjudication. Since his central focus is the potential inaccuracy of the ultimate factual determination, the procedural rights that he advocates are exclusively oriented toward fair management of the risk of that inaccuracy. In my view, this approach fails to assign enough normative value to adjudicative procedures in their own right, independent of any relationship to outcome accuracy. While Dworkin's procedural rights provide helpful guidance, and can play a crucial role in the procedural legitimacy proposal, they cannot suffice on their own to ground the legitimacy of adjudicative fact-finding. That is, Dworkin's procedural rights may be necessary conditions of legitimate judicial fact-finding procedures, but they are underinclusive.

The problem with Dworkin's proposal becomes evident when one tries to reconcile the tension between the rights provided by the sub-stantive law (like the right to be compensated if negligently injured) and procedural rights. The procedural rights he articulates are necessarily somewhere between "the extravagant and nihilistic"[127] — a society cannot reasonably assure its citizens of a right to the most accurate possible fact-finding procedures and still maintain expeditious or cost-effective dispute resolution.[128] Accordingly, Dworkin's procedural rights guarantee fair distribution of the risk of factual error that duly notes the harm that accompanies inaccuracy.[129] Being risk distribution rights, these procedural guarantees contemplate the potential for fac-tual inaccuracy. Should that risk manifest, the injustice factor would exist, because that moral harm arises even in instances of innocent errors. Therefore, in my reading, within Dworkin's proposal, it is

---

127   Dworkin, "Principle, Policy, and Procedure," above note 57 at 78.

128   *Ibid.*

129   Dworkin provides an intricate conceptual argument for why a right to the most accurate possible procedures is not required for an acceptable adjudicative system beyond the practical problem of the impact of such a commitment on societal resources. His comments in that respect are not significant for my critique here, because here I depend only on the uncontroversial fact that Dworkin does not, of course, advocate for the most accurate possible procedures. I return to his argument more extensively in chapter 3 to demonstrate how it can be construed as an endorsement of some aspects of my ultimate procedural legitimacy proposal.

possible that a litigant's procedural rights are fully respected but their substantive rights were not vindicated due to manifestation of the risk of factual error. That is, the injustice factor associated with factual inaccuracy can occur even if the procedural rights that Dworkin advocates are fully respected.

Dworkin seems to be suggesting that adherence to the procedural rights would justify a system that must accommodate potential injustice arising from inaccuracy. Presumably, the procedural rights can bear that justificatory role because they ensure that litigants are treated equally and non-arbitrarily in conditions of inevitable uncertainty. If this is a correct reading, then Dworkin's argument is that the acceptability of judicial fact-finding depends on maintenance of procedural rights, since even outcomes that bear a potential injustice of factual error can be accepted on the basis of adherence to the procedural rights. The logical extension of this argument is that it is not the vindication of the substantive right that gives legitimacy to the outcome — rather, that legitimacy comes from vindication of the procedural rights. That means that the legitimacy of *accurate* judicial factual decisions must *also* depend on observance of procedural rights.

Suppose, for instance, that a judge applies the criminal standard of proof in a civil case. The outcome that they render is factually accurate, but clearly the procedural rights have been violated. Presumably, this outcome is unacceptable in Dworkin's proposal because of the procedural rights violation, even though the outcome is accurate. Holding otherwise would be to hold that if an outcome is factually accurate, a violation of procedural rights becomes irrelevant, and factual accuracy could be pursued at the expense of the procedural rights on the basis that the ends justify the means.

Accordingly, in order for a procedural theory of legitimate fact-finding to be workable, procedural guarantees must ground the acceptability of *all* factual determinations, whether those determinations are ultimately accurate or inaccurate. As such, a procedural theory for legitimate factual determinations must be able to accomplish two things: it must provide a reason to accept factually inaccurate outcomes (which Dworkin's rights arguably can do); but it must also give us a clear, principled reason to reject factually accurate outcomes where a procedural compromise has occurred. The procedural rights that Dworkin articulates, while helpful, cannot fully accommodate the second requirement. That is because his procedural rights provide for the assurance of consistent and coherent treatment only in terms of managing risk of outcome inaccuracy. This restricts the extent of their promise of providing equal concern and respect, as illustrated in the following two examples.

Suppose it is decided that Canadians who are visible minorities will not be permitted to present their own evidence in civil actions, and instead all evidence will be selected and presented on their behalf, as competently as possible, by White representatives. All judicial fact-finding will occur on the basis of the evidence put forth by the White representatives. In such a system, both of Dworkin's procedural rights could be satisfied because the applicable principles in relation to fact-finding and risk of error may be perfectly coherent and applied consistently. Yet it is unacceptable to claim that a fact-finding process that prevents visible minority individuals from participating fully in decision-making can be legitimate.[130] That is true even if there is no difference in the chances of obtaining an accurate outcome between a system that permits everyone to participate and one that does not. In other words, we would not have a good enough reason to expect any minority person (or any person) to accept the legitimacy of a judicial outcome when the outcome arises through a process that excludes their participation, whether or not the outcome is factually accurate, and even if Dworkin's procedural rights are honoured.

Now suppose that a society decides that in instances where evidence indicates that there is a 50/50 chance that a fact is true or not true, it will break the tie through a coin toss. For example, imagine that a patient suffers some medical detriment after being treated negligently by a doctor, but that medical consequence was just as likely to happen even absent the doctor's negligence. In that claim, there is a 50/50 chance that the doctor's conduct caused the injury. Under current Canadian rules of tort litigation, we would conclude that the plaintiff has not satisfied their burden of proof, so the claim must be dismissed. But suppose that in a hypothetical society, such 50/50 situations are broken by a coin toss. If the coin lands on its head, the plaintiff wins the case, and if it lands on its tail, the defendant wins. That coin-toss process simply distributes the risk of inaccuracy equally between two

---

130 Compare to Owen Fiss, "The Allure of Individualism" (1993) 78 *Iowa Law Review* 965, where he argues that having a full representation of one's interests could satisfy a demand for participation in an adjudicative procedure. I take this up further in chapter 3.

parties, and it can be applied consistently wherever there are 50/50 situations. It could satisfy Dworkin's procedural rights. Yet there is something deeply problematic about a coin toss deciding a legal right, because it is arbitrary decision-making, even though it arguably has no impact on the chances of getting the outcome right in the 50/50 cases.

The procedures in both of these examples seem to maintain the important requirement that litigants should be treated equally and coherently within the system of management of inaccuracy that exists in a given society, but they fail to truly treat litigants with equal concern and respect. This is more obvious in the first example, because removing a class of legal subjects from a decision-making process that will result in an authoritative outcome is clearly outrageous. In the second example, although the litigants are treated equally, it would seem that they are treated with equal *dis*respect, because they are bound to a decision that results from an arbitrary fact-finding process. The key point is that even if Dworkin's coherence and consistency requirements are respected, and even if the ultimate outcome produced is accurate, such processes are not equipped to provide for legitimate decision-making.

I reiterate that Dworkin's procedural rights, as they relate to ensuring equal, coherent treatment in terms of managing the risk of inaccuracy are entirely in keeping with the procedural legitimacy theme that I am developing. In chapter 3, I discuss their precise role in a procedural legitimacy framework further. But since the procedural rights that Dworkin advocates are exclusively concerned with fair management of the risk of inaccuracy, they fail to take into account other intrinsic values of the process of arriving at a factual conclusion, irrespective of the impact of the procedures on outcome accuracy. And those intrinsic procedural values are important, because as I have noted above, the process must legitimize all judicial fact-finding, even accurate fact-finding. In order to discharge this normative burden, the fact-finding procedures must embody values that are independent of outcome accuracy, in addition to the fair management of potential inaccuracy, as Dworkin's proposal provides. Robert Summers has stated the point precisely as follows:[131]

[G]ood result efficacy is not the only kind of value a process can have *as a process*. . . . [A] process may also be good insofar as it

---

131   Robert Summers, "Evaluating and Improving Legal Process – A Plea for 'Process Values'"
in *The Jurisprudence of Law's Form and Substance (Collected Essays in Law)* (Brookfield, VT: Ashgate Publishing Ltd, 2000) at 115–16.

implements or serves "process values" such as participatory govern-ance and humanness. These forms of goodness are attributable to what occurs, or does not occur, in the course of a process. They are thus process-oriented, rather than results-oriented.

This conclusion prompts a turn to non-instrumental approaches to judi-cial decision-making, and particularly fact-finding. Evident in the above two examples, for me, processes that disallow participation, and that are in some way irrational or arbitrary, are unacceptable because they fail to display due respect for legal subjects. Grounding process values in notions of dignity and respect for the agency of litigants is well known. Jerry Mashaw is usually credited with advancing an influential dignitary theory of law.[132] Others have pointed to numerous values that ought to be considered valuable aspects of procedures. Bayles, for instance, points to a number of principles suggesting that processes should maintain values of peacefulness, voluntariness, meaningful participation, fairness through equal treatment, intelligibility of procedures, timeliness, and finality.[133] Others have focused on autonomy, and have often concluded that par-ticipation, in some form, is a key feature of acceptable legal procedures, grounded in those values.[134] Participation rights have also been lauded from the perspective of their role in positively influencing a litigant's subject-ive satisfaction with the outcome, even when unfavourable.[135] Lawrence

132　See Jerry Mashaw, "The Quest for a Dignitary Theory" (1981) 61 *Boston University Law Review* at 902–4. See Waldron, "Rule of Law," above note 58 for comments on the theme of dignity that permeates the value implicit in the rule of law. See also Jeremy Waldron, "How Law Protects Dignity" (2012) 71 *Cambridge Law Journal* 200.

133　Bayles, "Principles for Legal Procedure," above note 7 at 53–56. See also Summers, "A Plea for 'Process Values,'" above note 131.

134　For example, Robert Bone, "Statistical Adjudication: Rights, Justice, and Utility in a World of Process Scarcity" (1993) 46 *Vanderbilt Law Review* 561 at 619 notes: "ideal in American adjudication is linked to a process-oriented view of adjudicative participation that values participation for its own sake. Participation is important because it gives individuals a chance to make their own litigation choices"; Martin H. Redish & Nathan D. Larsen, "Class Actions, Litigant Autonomy, and the Foundations of Procedural Due Process" (2007) 95 *California Law Review* 1573 at 1578, make note of "a foundational belief in the value of allowing individuals to make fundamental choices about the judicial protection of their own legally authorized rights."

135　Tom Tyler's work in this respect is well known. See for instance, Tom Tyler, "The Psycho-logical Consequences of Judicial Procedures: Implications for Civil Commitment Hearings" (1992) 46 *Southern Methodist University Law Review* 433; Tom Tyler, "What is Procedural Jus-tice?: Criteria used by Citizens to Assess the Fairness of Legal Procedures" (1988) 22 *Law & Society Review* 103, 106; see also Stephen LaTour, "Determinants of Participant and Observer Satisfaction with Adversary and Inquisitorial Modes of Adjudication" (1978) 36 *Journal of*

Solum has concluded that while the need for participation cannot be reduced to any one particular value like dignity or autonomy, participation is a requisite feature of legitimate adjudicative decision-making.[136]

Notably, Jürgen Habermas has linked the need for participation to rational decision-making. In his theory, a law is rationally acceptable when it is a product of a rational discourse process. Rational discourse requires equal and free exchange of information and reasons, and a commitment on the part of participants that the force of reason alone will motivate the outcome. When those features are present in the decision-making process, the emergent law can be said to be rationally acceptable, irrespective of its ultimate substantive content. This demand for rationality would not be satisfied in a coin-toss procedure or other such arbitrary procedure, nor would it be satisfied absent meaningful participation.[137]

My aim for offering a framework of procedural legitimacy for judicial fact-finding depends on determining which values should be represented in fact-finding processes, and to propose principles that can guide questions about how those values should relate to one another and how they can manifest in fact-finding rules. That is the work of the next two chapters. My answer to those questions will be grounded in jurisprudential scholarship tackling legal legitimacy generally, and will be informed by the insights of those who have considered fact-finding processes specifically, including both instrumental and non-instrumental approaches.

The differences between instrumental and non-instrumental approaches to adjudication map directly onto the tension inherent in adjudicative fact-finding that I presented at the beginning of the chapter: on one hand, part of the purpose of the adjudicative process must be to arrive at the "truth" in the sense of ascertaining what facts occurred that ultimately gave rise to the legal claim. If a fact-finding procedure was more often wrong than right, then claiming its legitimacy would be difficult. Instrumental approaches rightly emphasize that fact-finding

---

Personality & Social Psychology 1531. See also Frank Michelman, "Formal and Associational Aims in Procedural Due Process" (1977) 18 *Due Process: NOMOS* 126 for the (non-empirical) comment that the intrinsic value of participation may be, in part, the psychological value that it affords to the individual.

136   I take up this point further in chapter 3.

137   It is worth mentioning here that participation is also sometimes argued from an instrumental standpoint. From such points of view, participation is necessary because it improves outcome accuracy. I take this up further in chapter 3.

processes must be oriented toward achieving a truthful outcome. This orientation toward correctness of outcome is the key feature of David Estlund's development of a theory of "epistemic proceduralism" in the analogous context of democratic decision-making. Making the point that epistemic correctness matters to legitimacy by reference to jury trials, Estlund remarks:[138]

> The jury trial would not have this moral force [i.e., the legitimate authority] if it did not have its considerable epistemic virtues. The elaborate process of evidence, testimony, cross-examination, adversarial equality, and collective deliberation by a jury all contribute to the ability – certainly very imperfect – of trials to convict people only if they are guilty, and not to set too many criminals free. If it did not have this tendency, if it somehow randomly decided who goes punished and who goes free, it is hard to see why vigilantes or jailers should pay it much heed. So its epistemic value is a crucial part of the story. Owing partly to its epistemic value, its decisions are (within limits) morally binding even when they are incorrect.

I agree with the sentiments in the above quotation: epistemic value is crucial, but it is important to emphasize that it only tells part of the story. Along with having a fact-finding role, adjudication, including adjudication of factual disagreements, is also rightly understood as a process of resolving disputes efficiently and fairly.[139] Non-instrumental approaches remind us that the process of resolving disputes must be principled, irrespective of the ultimate outcome. Both of these aspects of adjudication must maintain relevance within a theory of legitimate fact-finding. For instance, a fact-finding system that has

---

138 Estlund, *Democratic Authority*, above note 53 at 8. Estlund's more general thesis is that "Democratic procedures are legitimate and authoritative because they are produced by a procedure with a tendency to make correct decisions. It is not an infallible procedure, and there might be more accurate procedures. But democracy is better than random and is epistemically the best among those that are generally acceptable in the way that political legitimacy requires." As I note above, the epistemic qualities of fact-finding procedures are crucial, and I reiterate this point in chapter 3. But those epistemic features must be supplemented with other non-instrumental procedural features in a robust theory of legitimate fact-finding. That is because such a theory must be able to provide a framework to assess when epistemic values can be compromised in pursuit of other values, and to what extent. I take up this crucial central question in chapter 2.

139 As Michael Bayles puts it, "Two general purposes are inherent in the above concept of adjudication - resolving disputes and finding the 'truth.'" Bayles, "Principles for Legal Procedure," above note 7 at 39.

no demonstrable interest in truly ascertaining facts (like an arbitrary coin-toss process) cannot be redeemed by even the most robust participation rights. Simultaneously, without a commitment to principled dispute resolution, even the search for truth can become unfair and illegitimate.

Accordingly, the procedural legitimacy model that I intend to offer is situated in between the models of procedural justice that John Rawls famously describes as "imperfect procedural justice" and "pure procedural justice."[140] Imperfect procedural justice holds that there is a procedure-independent criterion for justice, and, the procedure cannot guarantee that outcome. In the context of fact-finding, that model would hold that factual accuracy is the relevant procedure-independent criterion. A pure procedural model holds that there is no procedure-independent criterion to assess outcomes, and that procedure guarantees correct outcomes.[141]

But for me, acknowledging the importance of factual accuracy is crucial, but factual accuracy is not an appropriate criterion to assess the legitimacy of the outcomes of judicial procedures *because* factual accuracy cannot be guaranteed. The model I would propose should be considered imperfect in the sense that factual accuracy cannot be guaranteed, while also being a substantiated version of pure procedural justice which requires that the significance of factual accuracy, along with other important values, be reflected in the procedures of fact-finding in order to achieve legitimate outcomes. This aligns with Habermas's contention where he suggests (albeit in the context of majority rule in the democratic process) that its legitimacy is derived from an "'imperfect,' but 'pure' procedural rationality."[142]

Dworkin's theory (an exemplar of instrumental approaches) provides an important starting point for understanding a basis on which outcomes that bear a risk of factual inaccuracy may, nonetheless, merit their authority by calling for a principled method of managing the risk

---

140 John Rawls, *A Theory of Justice* (rev ed) (Cambridge, MA: Harvard University Press, 1977, 1999) at 73–78.

141 *Ibid.*

142 Jürgen Habermas, "Reply to Symposium Participants Benjamin N Cardozo School of Law" (1995–1996) 17 *Cardozo Law Review* 1477 at 1494–5. For more on Habermas and Rawls, see James Cledhill, "Procedure in Substance and Substance in Procedure: Reframing the Rawls-Habermas Debate" in J.G. Finlayson & F. Freyenhagen (eds), *Habermas and Rawls: Disputing the Political* (New York: Routledge, 2011).

of factual error through consistent and coherent treatment of litigants. Still, there are gaps in his approach that could lead to unfair dispute resolution. Non-instrumental approaches that insist that procedures have inherent virtues that must be maintained can help to fill those gaps. A theory that combines both approaches is best suited to provide a justifying framework for authoritative judicial determinations of fact, whether those factual determinations are accurate or inaccurate. Such a theory would enable answers to the following questions:

1. Why, and on what basis can the authority of factual findings be legitimate despite being (or potentially being) inaccurate?
2. Why, and on what basis, should accurate outcomes be considered illegitimate due to procedural compromises?

A theory of procedural legitimacy that can answer both of these questions is equipped to provide a framework that can be used to assess the propriety of fact-finding procedures, including assessing when, and to what extent epistemic concerns can be compromised in pursuit of other values.[143] In upcoming chapters, I will draw on the insights of the various scholarly viewpoints presented here, and provide more detailed endorsements and critiques of them, culminating in my suggestion of a framework for procedural legitimacy in a fact-finding context that can provide grounding for these questions.

CONCLUSION AND NEXT STEPS

This chapter has been aimed at showing that valid and legitimate judicial fact-finding depends on a rich conception of procedural propriety. My first goal in this chapter was to demonstrate, through a description of judicial fact-finding, that the validity of factual determinations depends on procedural propriety. Then I proposed that valid factual determinations must also be legitimate because of the authoritative implications that come with legal validity. I then situated that conclusion within jurisprudential debates on intermingling legal validity and legitimacy. All of that indicated that I am aligned with those anti-positivist theorists who hold that legal validity requires in-built justification, and that such justification is a procedural virtue.

----

143   As I noted in Part 1, the legal system has rules that clearly prioritize values besides outcome accuracy.

Where do we go from here? In chapter 2, I will provide more detailed accounts of my alignment and divergence from positivist traditions through a more in-depth analysis of H.L.A. Hart's and Joseph Raz's theories. By the end of chapter 2, I will indicate the lessons that may be learned from turning to Lon Fuller's and Jürgen Habermas's proceduralist theses, particularly in terms of what substantive values legal procedures ought to manifest (and why) in order to play their legitimizing role. There, I'll show that Habermas and Fuller both argue that procedures must treat legal subjects as intrinsically equal, autonomous agents. Law-making procedures that fail in that respect cannot accomplish the normative work assigned to them. I'll use this jurisprudential foundation to substantiate the notion of procedural legitimacy in the specific context of fact-finding.

After the jurisprudential comments in this chapter, I turned to outlining discourses situated more squarely within the context of judicial accommodation of factual uncertainty to show that there are different viewpoints relevant to how fact-finding procedures should be assessed. That discussion informs the ultimate goal of showing how procedural legitimacy should manifest within fact-finding procedures in the civil litigation context, such that those procedures can fulfill their normative purpose of maintaining the legitimacy of factual determinations. This foreshadows my analysis in chapter 3, where I discuss how the necessary values of equality and autonomy can and must be expressed through rational fact-finding processes. By the end of chapter 3, I offer a substantiated notion of procedural legitimacy through engagement with the topics introduced here, including: why and to what extent does accuracy of outcome matter to procedural legitimacy, and how must it be relevant in the procedural legitimacy framework? What principles should guide the distribution of the risk of inaccuracy among litigants? How and why does participation matter, and how should it be reflected in legitimate fact-finding processes?

CHAPTER TWO

The Jurisprudential Inquiry into Law and Legitimacy

INTRODUCTION

In chapter 1, I introduced the idea that since valid judicial outcomes are final, binding, and enforceable, their validity requires normative justification, or legitimacy. Legitimacy must be contingent on procedural propriety, given that outcomes cannot be guaranteed to be factually accurate. This claim was situated within a jurisprudential landscape, outlining some major theoretical ideas about the nature of legal validity and its relationship to legitimacy.[1]

I noted in chapter 1 that one aspect of the procedural legitimacy argument embodies the essence of formal justice — that everyone should be subjected to the consistent rules non-arbitrarily. But stopping at this "germ of justice," as Hart has described it,[2] gives rise to critical questions: can consistent application of *any* procedural rules yield legitimate outcomes? What qualities must the procedural rules embody in order to justify their legitimizing role? In this chapter, the aim is to expand on some of the jurisprudential themes presented in the previous chapter to answer these questions.

I begin by revisiting H.L.A. Hart's concept of legal validity and its implications, followed by a review of Joseph Raz's incisive additions to the positivist proposal. Hart's proposal represents the beginning of

---

1   Note that in this chapter, as in chapter 1, the terms *legal validity*, *status as law*, and *legality* are used interchangeably to connote the positivistic idea of formal legal validity.

2   H.L.A. Hart, *The Concept of Law*, 3d ed (Oxford: Oxford University Press, 2012) at 206 [Hart, *Concept of Law*].

contemporary positivism, and Raz's jurisprudence displays an argu-ably even stronger commitment to the central core of legal positiv-ism, as I explain further below. As I suggested in chapter 1, positivist accounts contain insights that further a proceduralist jurisprudential orientation, but their foundational insistence on maintaining a sever-ance between legal validity and its justification displays the deficits of a form-based notion of legal validity that has no in-built normativity. These shortcomings translate as problems with a purely procedural notion of legitimate adjudicative fact-finding. Getting at the root of this difficulty paves the road to overcoming them.

The review below of Hart's and Raz's proposals serves as a more detailed argument in favour of the claims introduced in chapter 1: first, that legal validity brings an implication of authority, and this requires legitimacy; second, that legal validity is best understood through a substantiated procedural declaration that *certain* procedures yield valid laws, and being products of that particular procedure, valid laws deserve, in a normative sense, their authoritative status. The proced-ural rules of determining facts must reflect those same substantive qualities. When they do, their consistent application yields legitimately authoritative outcomes. The second half of this chapter is oriented toward delineating the substantive qualities that legal procedures must possess in order to justifiably legitimize the outcomes that emerge from them.

In that effort, I draw on Lon Fuller's and Jürgen Habermas's insights. Both maintain a rich notion of legality that normatively accounts for the authoritative implications that come with it. Most importantly for my purpose, both authors affirm the theme presented in chapter 1, that legal validity and legitimacy must occur simultaneously. That leads both to maintaining a fundamentally proceduralist paradigm. I'll show below that Fuller's and Habermas's ideas about law are thematically linked through the idea that the process of law-making must demon-strate respect for legal subjects as autonomous agents who deserve non-arbitrary treatment. When that respect for autonomy is present in law-making procedures, *then* the emergent law is legitimate. That conclusion marks the end of this chapter.

In chapter 3, I'll use the grounding notion of respect for auton-omy to formulate the necessary substantive qualities of legitimate fact-finding procedures. For now, let us focus on broad jurisprudential notions of law generally.

PART 1. THE POSITIVIST APPROACH TO LEGAL VALIDITY: HART AND RAZ

A. The Legal Theory of H.L.A. Hart

(1) Legal Validity and Its Implications

Hart's positivism emerged at a time when positivist thinking was still influenced by writers such as Jeremy Bentham (1748–1832) and John Austin (1790–1859), who presented law as a command of a sovereign. Hart, however, while maintaining the positivist creed of separating the question of what law is and what it ought to be, presented a new positivism — one that did not depend on interpreting law as a command. Rather, Hart's positivism, presented in the book *The Concept of Law*,[3] introduced the idea of law as a system of primary and secondary rules, and stands as the starting point of contemporary positivist thinking. His explanation for how a rudimentary system of rules transforms into a legal system in complex societies reveals his conception of how societal rules gain status as law, that is, how those rules gain validity as law or legal validity.

According to Hart, very simple societies are governed by rules developed through habitual conduct of members of the group. These rules dictate acceptable behaviour for the members.[4] As societies become more complicated, however, governance through such rules alone becomes defective for three reasons. The first defect is uncertainty. As the complexity of a society begins to increase, there are likely to be ambiguities as to what the rules actually are, but there may not yet be a system in place to settle the doubts.[5] Second, the rules of a society are relatively stagnant, because they are the product of habitual conduct. Changes to them are necessarily very gradual. This threatens to prevent the society from accommodating changing circumstances without losing stability.[6] Third, as societies become larger and more sophisticated, enforcement of the rules becomes difficult. In rudimentary societies,

---

3   *Ibid.*

4   *Ibid* at 91–92.

5   *Ibid* at 92: "Hence if doubts arise as to what the rules are or as to the precise scope of some given rule, there will be no procedure for settling this doubt . . . . This defect in the simple social structure of primary rules we may call its *uncertainty*."

6   *Ibid*: "A second defect is the *static* character of the rules. The only mode of change in the rules known to such a society will be the slow process of growth, whereby courses of conduct once thought optional become first habitual or usual, and then obligatory."

obedience to the rules is maintained through social pressure. In more complex societies, this becomes infeasible.[7]

These defects are accommodated, Hart explains, by adding secondary rules to complement the primary rules of a society. The primary rules impose duties and confer powers. These are the substantive rules of behaviour that govern simple societies. For instance, the tort law principle that negligently injured people should be fully compensated by the person who caused the injury constitutes a primary rule in our society. Secondary rules are procedural. They "specify the ways in which the primary rules may be conclusively ascertained, introduced, eliminated, varied, and the fact of their violation conclusively determined."[8] In doing so, the secondary rules remedy the defects that would occur as a society exclusively governed by primary rules becomes more complex.[9]

The uncertainty defect is remedied through secondary rules of recognition, which specify what features a rule must have in order to be recognized as a valid rule of the society.[10] In our society, for instance, we recognize rules that have passed through legislative procedures as valid rules. We also recognize the legal validity of judicial decrees that have emerged out of adjudicative processes. We do not, however, recognize rules that are dictated by a religious institution as valid laws. The fact that a rule has emerged from parliamentary or judicial processes are included in our rules of recognition, but religious endorsement is not a rule of recognition in our society. But in societies where there is no separation between state and religion, religious endorsement can be a rule of recognition.

The remedy for stagnancy is another set of secondary rules called the rules of change. These define the procedure to be followed in legislating laws, and specify who has the authority to make changes to the rules.[11] Sections 91 and 92 of the Constitution of Canada, which delineate the areas of provincial and federal law-making authority, are

---

7　*Ibid* at 92–93: "The third defect of this simple form of social life is the *inefficiency* of the diffuse social pressure by which the rules are maintained."

8　*Ibid* at 94.

9　*Ibid*: "[W]hile primary rules are concerned with the actions that individuals must or must not do, these secondary rules are all concerned with the primary rules themselves. They specify the ways in which the primary rules may be conclusively ascertained, introduced, eliminated, varied, and the fact of their violation conclusively determined."

10　*Ibid* at 94–95.

11　*Ibid* at 95–96.

examples of "rules of change" in our society.[12] Third, the inefficiency of relying on diffuse social pressure to enforce rules is corrected through secondary rules that empower "individuals to make authoritative determinations of the question whether, on a particular occasion, a primary rule has been broken."[13] These are the rules of adjudication. "Besides identifying the individuals who are to adjudicate," Hart explains, "such rules will also define the procedure to be followed."[14] In Canada, for instance, all the provinces have enactments that set out the procedures to be followed in provincial courts.[15] These rules of court processes are examples of Hart's rules of adjudication. So are the rules governing proof of facts in a tortious injury claim, such as admissibility of evidence, and the relevant standard of proof.

Along with conferring decision-making power on judges, the rules of adjudication give authoritative status to judicial decisions. Since a judge has to decide whether a rule has been broken, they also have to decide whether a rule *exists*.[16] Consequently, a judge must be equipped to make authoritative statements about what the law is and which rules are valid laws. In turn, this necessitates rules of recognition so that judges can determine whether a rule has legal validity according to some acceptable standard.[17]

For Hart, once secondary rules are introduced, a society has a concept of legal validity.[18] Only those primary rules that have adhered to secondary rules of recognition, change, and adjudication are legally valid laws. This basic model explains how primary rules attain their status as law, but leaves open the question of where secondary rules derive their legal status. Hart explains that there is an upward chain of rules of recognition, ending with the "ultimate rule of recognition."

---

12   *Constitution Act, 1982*, being Schedule B to the *Canada Act 1982* (UK), 1982, c 11.

13   Hart, *Concept of Law*, above note 2 at 96.

14   *Ibid* at 97.

15   For example, British Columbia *Supreme Court Rules*, BC Reg 221/90; *Alberta Rules of Court*, Alta Reg 390/1968; Ontario *Rules of Civil Procedure*, RRO 1990, Reg 194; *Nova Scotia Civil Procedure Rules*.

16   Hart, *Concept of Law*, above note 2 at 97.

17   *Ibid* at 97: "Indeed a system which has rules of adjudication is necessarily also committed to a rule of recognition of an elementary and imperfect sort. This is so because, if courts are empowered to make authoritative determinations of the fact that a rule has been broken, these cannot avoid being taken as authoritative determinations of what the rules are."

18   *Ibid* at 103: "We can indeed simply say that the statement that a particular rule is valid means that it satisfies all the criteria provided by the rule of recognition."

All the secondary rules are subordinate to one supreme criterion contained in the ultimate rule of recognition. If the validity of a secondary rule is at issue (for instance, someone might question the authority of an administrative tribunal to make a certain decision, thus challenging the validity of the power-conferring secondary rule) then the validity of the secondary rule is tested by moving further up the chain of rules of recognition. Eventually, the inquiry will reach a stopping point, which is the ultimate rule of recognition. For England, Hart describes this ultimate rule of recognition as, "what the Queen in Parliament enacts is law." There is no further rule that can be referred to in order to assess the legal validity of this ultimate rule of recognition.[19] The question of legal validity ends with this rule, and any question of the derivation of the legal status of the ultimate rule is outside the scope of determining whether a rule has legal status.[20]

It is this system of primary and secondary rules, Hart asserts, that "deserves, if anything does, to be called the foundations of a legal system."[21] There is evidence that a legal system exists when the population generally obeys legally valid laws, and when officials (like legislators and judges) actively accept and adhere to secondary rules that yield valid laws:

> There are two minimum conditions necessary and sufficient for the existence of a legal system. On the one hand, those rules of behaviour which are valid according to the system's ultimate criteria of legal validity must be generally obeyed, and, on the other hand, its rules of recognition specifying the criteria of legal validity and its rules

---

19   *Ibid* at 107: "Finally, when the validity of a statute has been queried and assessed by reference to the rule that what the Queen in Parliament enacts is law, we are brought to a stop in inquiries concerning validity."

20   *Ibid*. Hart's concept of the ultimate rule of recognition may appear simple enough on its surface, but it has proven difficult to apply in contexts outside of 1960s Britain. Assessments of Hart's theory on the basis of difficulties around the ultimate rule of recognition are beyond my scope, but see, for example, Scott Shapiro, "What is the Rule of Recognition (And Does it Exist)?" (2009) Yale Law School, Public Law and Legal Theory Research paper Series no. 181, and Kent Greenawalt, "The Rule of Recognition and the Constitution" (1987) 85 *Michigan Law Review* 621. Both authors examine the opposition to Hart's concept of an ultimate rule of recognition and provide insightful commentaries on the difficulty of precisely defining Hart's doctrine of the rule of recognition, and therefore applying it in other jurisdictions.

21   Hart, *Concept of Law*, above note 2 at 100.

of change and adjudication must be effectively accepted as common public standards of official behaviour by its officials.[22]

The development of the primary and secondary rules concept, and the two necessary conditions of a legal system, together indicate both the derivation of legal validity and its implications in Hart's analysis. The status of both primary and secondary rules is derived through adherence to secondary rules. Having that status as law infuses a rule with its authoritative quality: valid laws dictate the acceptable behaviour for community members and legal officials, demonstrated by general obedience to primary laws, and acceptance of secondary rules by officials. The status as law, for Hart, implies that a rule is authoritative within a community, and so application and enforcement of that rule is considered justifiable on the basis of its legal validity. That inference can be drawn from Hart's conclusion that judges must be equipped with the secondary rules of recognition so that only the rules that have valid status as law are treated as authoritative — only such rules can authoritatively dictate behaviour, govern legal relationships, and be justifiably applied and enforced in the society. In other words, a judge would be unjustified in applying a rule that does not comply with the secondary rules of recognition and thereby gain legal validity. That suggests that legal validity enables officials to justifiably treat laws as authoritative, in the sense that the laws can be applied to resolve disputes with finality, and can be enforced in the society.[23]

Hart's description of valid law is clearly analogous to how I have described the derivation of valid legal facts in chapter 1. For both, adherence to some formal requirements results in legal validity, and having legal validity brings authoritative implications. As Hart explains, being a valid law implicates that the rule will be generally obeyed, and applied and enforced by officials; similarly, being a valid legal fact implicates that judges are justified in relying on that fact to arrive at an authoritative legal outcome — one that is final, binding, and enforceable. In this form, both claims assert that adherence to procedural rules culminates

---

22   *Ibid* at 116.

23   See also Frederick Schauer, *The Force of Law* (Cambridge, MA: Harvard University Press, 2015) for a powerful argument that law's coercive power is essential to its function and authority. Schauer emphasizes that legal compliance often results from the credible threat of sanctions, not just generalized acceptance of norms. This quality of valid law matters when developing a theorization of what law is.

in valid, authoritative legal outcomes (laws or legal facts), but neither substantiates the claim by explaining *why* adherence to secondary or procedural rules justifiably infuses the resultant law or legal fact with the authoritative implications that come with legal validity.

As introduced in chapter 1, the authoritative implications that are parceled within legal validity demand normative justification.[24] But Hart's concept of law does not provide any. Under Hart's theory, so long as the rule adheres to some secondary rule, it gains status as law, irrespective of the quality of the law itself. The merit of the secondary rules is not relevant to their validity, because their validity is derived from adherence to superior secondary rules that are themselves unsubstantiated, in the sense that within Hart's theory, there is no stipulation about what secondary rules ought to be.[25] That being the case, a government could enact a rule that is improper in substance, that accords with the secondary rules in place, and that rule will have status as law. For instance, laws preventing homosexual marriage may be considered immoral by some community members, but they have had legal validity in Canadian society in the past due to their adherence to secondary rules of recognition. The legal validity of such laws was not compromised by any perceived or actual immorality. The same goes for procedural laws. A legal system could have iniquitous procedural laws that have legal validity due to their adherence to superior secondary rules. A valid legal system could exist where, for instance, a rule is passed by the government (thereby satisfying the secondary rules) that only White community members were qualified to be witnesses in courts could be a valid adjudicative procedure, given its adherence to the secondary rules of recognition that exist and apply. Owing to its legal validity, a judge has reason to apply that rule in the course of making a judicial ruling.[26]

---

24   This claim, as well as anti-positivist responses, are discussed at some length in chapter 1.

25   Hart, *Concept of Law*, above note 2 at 107–8, and at 185–86: "Here we shall take Legal Positivism to mean the simple contention that it is in no sense a necessary truth that laws produce or satisfy a necessary truth, that laws produce or satisfy certain demands of morality, though in fact they have often done so."

26   I note that Hart tells us that officials, including judges, must actively accept the secondary rules, but he does not provide any reason for what would make a secondary rule legitimately acceptable. Evil officials of an evil regime could ground their acceptance of secondary rules on any self-serving motive. For the same argument, see Hannah Arendt, *Eichmann in Jerusalem: A Report on the Banality of Evil* (New York: Viking Press, 1963).

This leads back to the fundamental criticism of notions of formal justice that any proceduralist account of legality must contend with — can consistent adherence to such laws be said to yield legitimate adjudicative outcomes, just because they have legal validity? Since valid laws can, in Hart's theory, have any substantive character, and since he gives no further explanation for why valid laws nonetheless warrant their status as law, his theory, as I have noted in chapter 1, is not oriented toward offering a justifiable answer to this critical question.

The express commitment to maintaining a separation between legal validity and the justification for that legality is defended in Hart's writing. In "Positivism and the Separation of Law and Morals,"[27] and in *The Concept of Law*, Hart defends the viewpoint that having legal validity is not, and must not be, dependent on a rule's adherence to some concept of what law ought to be. This is called the "separation thesis," referring to the famous theoretical cornerstone of positivism-disjoining legal validity, or the descriptive question of "what *is* law?" (i.e., what is valid law?) from the value-ridden question of "what *should be* the law?" (i.e., what is legitimate law?). As Brian Bix has clearly articulated:

> The rule of recognition expresses, or symbolizes, the basic tenet of legal positivism: that there are conventional criteria, agreed upon by officials, for determining which rules are and which are not part of the legal system; this in turn points to the separation of the identification of the law from its moral evaluation, and the separation of statements about what the law is from statements about what it should be.[28]

As I discussed in chapter 1, the separation thesis is in direct opposition to the claim that legal validity and legitimacy must occur simultaneously because of the authoritative implications that inhere in a rule that has status as law. Accordingly, it is worthwhile to consider and evaluate, in more detail, the positivist insistence on their separation. There are two categories of concerns that support Hart's commitment to separating legal validity and its justification: societal stability and theoretical shortcoming. First, if law and the moral defensibility of law (or the law's legitimacy) were inseparable, Hart advises, then any

---

27   H.L.A Hart, "Positivism and the Separation of Law and Morals" (1957) 71(4) *Harvard Law Review* 593 [Hart, "Separation of Law and Morals"].

28   Brian Bix, *Jurisprudence: Theory and Context*, 3d ed (London: Sweet & Maxwell, 2003) at 41.

citizen could conclude that a law does not resonate with their morality, so it is not law, so it is not authoritative.[29] That results in the danger "that law and its authority may be dissolved in man's conceptions of what law ought to be."[30] What is law would not be universally discernible, resulting in instability. Societal stability depends on a citizen's ability to recognize authoritative law without resorting to their individual moral sentiments.

Along with that practical concern, Hart explains that combining law and morality requires adopting a narrow theoretical concept of law that would exclude all rules that displayed all the other qualities of being law, but were iniquitous. The broader definition, where all rules that adhere to the "formal tests of a system of primary and secondary rules" even if some of these offend morality, is preferable, Hart suggests, because it enables both a recognition and study of abuse of law, which the narrower definition would preclude.[31] For instance, as I explain below, for Hart, it would be better to understand the Nazi regime as constituting valid, though immoral law, rather than suggesting that it was not a legal regime at all and precluding those laws from study *as laws*. Hart concludes that practical and theoretical concerns are best addressed by a theory that enables a determination of what rules have status as law in a society, and to state the moral worth of those laws as a distinct declaration, enabling the statement, "this is law, but it is too iniquitous to be applied or obeyed."[32]

Hart's invitation to recognize the possibility of valid laws that are too improper to be obeyed unfolds in his discussion of the anti-positivist sentiments that arose post-Nazi Germany. The Nazi regime, where evils were carried out under the auspices of valid law, resulted in increased conviction that legal validity should be contingent on substantive morality. The issue was brought to the forefront when determining what ought to be done with individuals who had committed immoral acts that were endorsed, or at least, were not contrary to German law at the time. Judges often reasoned, Hart explains, that Nazi laws could

---

29   The separation thesis is often described as a separation between law and morality. Morality can be understood as the basis on which law can be justified. In the terminology that I have adopted, law's morality constitutes what I refer to as law's legitimacy.

30   Hart, "Separation of Law and Morals," above note 27 at 598.

31   Hart, *Concept of Law*, above note 2 at 209.

32   *Ibid* at 208.

be considered illegal due to their moral failure. In that sense, the evil acts endorsed by Nazi rules did not properly bear the status as law at all. Accordingly, people who engaged in evil acts could not escape punishment under the new legal regime by citing the legality of their acts under the Nazi regime. For many, this was a welcome and celebrated defeat of the positivist separation thesis.[33]

While Hart recognized the worthwhile cause of lawfully punishing individuals who committed evils during the Nazi regime, for him, the judicial solution led to the improper result of calling something that was factually law, "not law." For Hart, the criticism of the thesis that what is posited as law is, in fact, law, "depended upon an enormous overvaluation of the importance of the bare fact that a rule may be said to be a valid rule of law, as if once declared, was conclusive of the final moral question: "ought this rule of law to be obeyed.""[34] What should have been recognized, Hart suggests, is that a valid law can exist in fact, but can also be too immoral to be obeyed and applied.[35] The better solution to the post-Nazi Germany problem, for Hart, would have been to accept that there were evil laws during the Nazi regime, and introduce laws in the new regime that permit retroactive punishment, given that many laws during Nazi rule were too evil to be obeyed. Since the new law would comply with the existing rules of recognition, they would have legal validity. For Hart, although

---

33   Hart, "Separation of Law and Morals," above note 27 at 615–18. Besides Lon Fuller's opposition to Hart's view on this topic discussed later in this chapter, Gustav Radbruch is famous for having "switched camps," from positivism to natural law after bearing witness to Nazi rule (but compare with Thomas Mertens, "Radbruch and Hart on the Grudge Informer: A Reconsideration" (2002) 15 *Ratio Juris* 186). See also, Frederick Schauer, "Positivism as Pariah," in *The Autonomy of Law Essays on Legal Positivism*, Robert George (ed) (Oxford: Clarendon Press, 1996) at 32 questioning the "caricature of positivism as an amoral mandate to unquestioning obedience," as may have been assumed after the Nazi Germany experience or American Fugitive Slave Laws, among others.

34   Hart, "Separation of Law and Morals," above note 27 at 618.

35   See David Dyzenhaus, "Dworkin and Unjust Laws" in Wil Waluchow & Stefan Sciaraffa (eds), *The Legacy of Ronald Dworkin* (Oxford: Oxford University Press, 2016) [Dyzenhaus, "Dworkin and Unjust Laws"] for a discussion of the distinction between the perspective of the citizen, who obeys or disobeys laws and the judge, or other official, who applies or refuses to apply laws. As Dyzenhaus explains, Hart suggests in "Separation of Law and Morals" that immoral laws ought not to be obeyed, but does not hold that they must not be applied by judges. In *Concept of Law*, above note 2, Hart's position is adjusted. There, he formulates his position as "This is law; but it is too iniquitous to be *applied* or obeyed" at 208 [emphasis added].

retroactivity in law is clearly undesirable, this solution is a lesser evil than declaring that what was in fact valid law was not law at all.[36]

Through this line of reasoning, Hart suggests that the possibility of valid though — intolerably immoral laws is de-problematized by calling for recognition that there is no obligation to recognize the law as authoritative solely on the basis that it is a valid law. This is implicit in Hart's assertions that a law can be too iniquitous to be obeyed and applied, because if that is the case, then the obligation to obey and apply law depends on external criteria of morality rather than legal validity alone. This, however, results in an internal tension in Hart's theory. On the one hand, the theory asserts that a rule that is legally valid (i.e., a law) is authoritative — it will be applied and enforced by officials. But having status as law does not imply that a law's authoritative quality is warranted, because that depends on some criteria of morality, which is necessarily external to the definition of law. If a law fails to live up to that external standard, then it is unworthy of its authoritative status, and according to Hart, it is in fact *not* authoritative; it is too evil to be obeyed or applied.[37]

The result is that while the state of the law is discernible without any resort to external moral criteria, citizens need not feel obligated to obey law *just* because it is law, and officials need not feel bound to apply law *just* by virtue of its legal validity, because whether a law should be obeyed or applied ultimately depends on moral considerations of whether a law is "too evil," which is external to the question of what the law is, as a descriptive matter. This is problematic, because it means that Hart's theory contains two conclusions that pull in opposite directions: that valid law *is*, by its very nature as law, applicable and enforceable and therefore authoritative for community members; at the same time, it is also not, by its nature alone, necessarily authoritative.[38]

---

36 *Ibid.*

37 Here, I agree with Dyzenhaus's explanation of the tension within Hart's theory: "The deep issue here is the question of the role of authority in Hart's conception of law. If a central feature of law that any philosophy of law has to explain is law's authority, legal positivism is faced with the puzzle of unjust law. If the commands of the powerful are incapable of sustaining a claim to be exercised with right on those subject to their power, the commands lack authority, and therefore lose any claim to legal status." Dyzenhaus, "Dworkin and Unjust Laws," above note 35 at 146.

38 As I elaborate further below, this point is Fuller's fundamental complaint against Hart's theory. See Lon Fuller, "Positivism and the Fidelity of Law – A Reply to Professor Hart" (1958) 71 *Harvard Law Review* 630. It is one of the central features of the positivist versus

Before elaborating on this difficulty and my response to it, I turn to a discussion of Joseph Raz's theory. Raz has demonstrated a resilient and arguably even stronger commitment to the separation thesis than Hart. While Hart seems to have adopted an "inclusive" version of legal positivism, accepting that a community can delineate moral criteria as the secondary rules that give rise to legal validity,[39] Raz has advocated "exclusive" legal positivism, suggesting that moral criteria cannot be necessary and sufficient conditions for legal validity. This position, coupled with the fact that Raz's jurisprudence is focused on the relationship between law and authority, make a critical study of his thinking valuable because my central focus is also the relationship between legal validity, the authority that accompanies it, and the justifiability of that authority which I refer to as legitimacy.

His contributions contain too much breadth and intricacy to summarize briefly, but I have stated my understanding of Raz's jurisprudence below, bearing in mind my goal of demonstrating that the difficulty noted in Hart's approach above is paralleled in Raz's model of legal validity as well. After discussing Raz's stand, I will provide my diagnosis for the problem encountered in both theories, and explain why the positivist approaches advanced by Hart and Raz do not further the goal of delineating the demands of legitimate adjudicative fact-finding. The solution, I suggest, is turning to a substantiated proceduralist model for legal validity that contains an in-built justification for the authoritative implication that accompanies legal validity. This conclusion marks the close of Section A of this chapter,

---

natural law/anti-positivist debate, as well as a key aspect of debates about the tenability of exclusive versus inclusive legal positivism. See, for instance, contemporary natural law theorist John Finnis, "The Incoherence of Legal Positivism" (2000) 75 *Notre Dame Law Review* 1613 for his defence of the claim that "positivism's attempts to explain the law's authority are doomed to fail" at 1608. And see Jules Coleman, "Authority and Reason" in Robert George (ed), *The Autonomy of Law: Essays on Legal Positivism* (Oxford: Clarendon Press, 1996) for a defence of a form of inclusive legal positivism called incorporationism on the basis that the normative justification of the authority of law is not accounted for in exclusive legal positivism [Coleman, "Authority and Reason"].

39 Responding to Ronald Dworkin's criticism, Hart notes in his Postscript in *The Concept of Law*, above note 2: "I expressly state both in this book and in my earlier article on 'Positivism and the Separation of Law and Morals' that in some systems of law, as in the United States, the ultimate criteria of legal validity might explicitly incorporate besides pedigree, principles of justice or substantive moral values, and these may form the content of legal constitutional restraints" at 247.

and prompts my turn to Fuller's and Habermas's jurisprudence in Section B.

B. The Legal Theory of Joseph Raz

(1) Legal Validity and Its Implications

Raz's concept of law as a system of rules is similar to Hart's, but hinges more expressly on law as an authoritative structure.[40] For Raz, political communities are societies that authoritatively decide how their members should act. Rules that are endorsed by the political community, evidenced by the relevant actions of legal institutions, have status as law.[41] This is what Raz refers to as the "sources thesis": what the law is (i.e., the existence and content of law) is fully determined by its social sources — the law-conferring institutions in the society.[42]

A rule that comes from the appropriate source in a given society gains status as law. Gaining status as law marks a "decisive moment" where a standard of behaviour becomes authoritative for the community — at that moment, any debate as to whether that rule is authoritative is settled.[43] That authoritative quality becomes the reason that community members act in accordance with a legal directive:

---

40 Demonstrating his alignment with Hart's theory, Raz summarizes his position on the validity of law in Joseph Raz, *Authority of Law* (Oxford: Oxford University Press, 2009) at 150 [Raz, *Authority of Law*] as follows:

> The legal validity of a rule is established not by arguments concerning its value and justification but rather by showing that it conforms to tests of validity laid down by some other rules of the system which can be called rules of recognition. These tests normally concern the way the rule was enacted or laid down by a judicial authority. The legal validity of rules of recognition is determined in a similar way except for the validity of the ultimate rule of recognition which is a matter of social fact, namely those ultimate rules of recognition are binding which are actually practiced and followed by the courts.

> At footnote 10: "I am here following Hart's doctrine of the rule of recognition in a slightly modified form."

41 Joseph Raz, *Between Authority and Interpretation: On the Theory of Law and Practical Reason* (New York: Oxford University Press, 2009) at 101 [Raz, *Authority and Interpretation*].

42 For a detailed discussion of the social thesis which Raz dubs the "sources thesis," see Raz, *Authority of Law*, above note 40 at 37–52.

43 Raz, *Authority and Interpretation*, above note 41 at 109:

> The authoritative laying down of standards is the decisive moment in the legal process not merely because in it new reasons are created. It is the decisive moment because those new standards, those new reasons, are to put an end to the argument and struggle about what is to be done . . . . The pivotal place of the law in the

> [L]aw provides a reason for action for its subjects through being a decree laid down or endorsed by a legitimate authority. Its authoritative nature is itself sufficient to establish that the law is reason for compliance for its subjects, and that independently of and in addition to any sanctions or incentives it may provide.[44]

The idea of an authoritative decree becoming the reason for action becomes clearer through an explanation of Raz's conception of what constitutes legitimate authority.[45] Legitimate authority is achieved when it can be said that if a person follows the directives of the authority, their actions will tend to conform with reason better than they would if they made independent decisions on the best course of action in every situation. In accepting an authority as legitimate, a person acknowledges that heeding the directives of that authority will result in better-reasoned decisions than not heeding those directives. Since adherence to the authority is supposed to maintain better conformity with reason, the directives of that authority can justifiably pre-empt the person's other reasons for acting in a particular way.[46] Accordingly, a person can do something or refrain from doing something *because* (i.e., "for the exclusive reason that") the authority so orders.[47]

Consider, for instance, the student-teacher relationship. When a student accepts the authority of the teacher as legitimate, in Raz's conception, it means that the student will heed the directives of the teacher because they believe that those directives will result in better reasoned action compared to not following the teacher's directives. In that context, where the student has accepted the legitimacy of the teacher's authority, if the teacher directs the student to read a certain book, for example, the student can heed that directive for the exclusive reason

---

organization of society is precisely in its authoritative nature. That is why I can say that for the time being, that is while it is in force, the law resolves the argument and the struggle about how things should be in society.

44 Raz, *Authority and Interpretation*, above note 41 at 108.

45 See generally, Raz, *Authority of Law*, above note 40 at 1–33.

46 Raz, *Authority and Interpretation*, above note 41: "In postulating that authorities are legitimate only if their directives enable their subjects to better conform to reason, we see authority for what it is: not a denial of people's capacity for rational action, but simply one device, one method, through the use of which people can achieve the goal (*telos*) of their capacity for rational action, albeit not through its direct use," at 140.

47 Joseph Raz, "The Problem of Authority: Revising the Service Conception" (2006) 90 *Minnesota Law Review* 1010, reprinted in Raz, *Authority and Interpretation*, above note 41 at 126.

that the teacher has so directed, without assessing for themself whether or not to read the book. In the same way, a citizen who accepts the legitimate authority of the legal system can say, "I do 'X' because 'X' is the law," without resorting to any other reason for doing "X".[48] In Raz's words:

> The authority's directives become our reasons. While the acceptance of the authority is based on belief that its directives are well-founded in reason, they are understood to yield the benefits they are meant to bring only if we do rely on them rather than on our own independent judgment of the merits of each case to which they apply.[49]

For Raz, legal systems, by their nature, claim to have legitimate authority, and claim that the rules and standards endorsed by their legal institutions are legitimately authoritative.[50] While Raz maintains that it is essential to law that it *claims* legitimate authority and be capable in principle of having it, a vital feature of his theory is that actually having legitimate authority is only an aspiration. It is not a necessary factual condition for the existence of law.[51]

In other words, in order to be classified as a legal system, the Canadian political system must claim to have legitimate authority. That

---

48   The critique of Raz's position that I am offering now regards his notion that legal validity is contingent on a *claim* of legitimate authority but not on actual achievement of that legitimate authority. At this stage, contesting or endorsing the particulars of Raz's conception of what makes authority legitimate is not necessary. I will, however, return to Raz's idea of aligning conformity with reason and legitimacy when I turn to substantiating my own conception of legitimate adjudicative fact-finding in chapter 3. Many authors have criticized Raz's perspective on authority from a variety of angles. For a sampling, see Stephen Lukes, "Perspectives on Authority" in Joseph Raz (ed), *Authority* (New York: New York Press, 1990) at 203–17; Ronald Dworkin, "Thirty Years On" (2002) 114 *Harvard Law Review* 1655 at 1671–76; Kenneth Himma, "Just 'Cause You're Smarter Than Me Doesn't Give You a Right to Tell Me What to Do: Legitimate Authority and the Normal Justification Thesis" (2007) 27 *Oxford Journal of Legal Studies* 121.

49   Joseph Raz, *Practical Reason and Norms*, 2d ed (Princeton University Press: Princeton, 1990) at 193.

50   Raz, *Authority and Interpretation*, above note 41 at 104. See also Raz, *Ethics in the Public Domain* (Oxford: Clarendon Press, 1994) at 194–221 [also Raz, *Ethics in the Public Domain*]. In Raz, *Authority of Law*, above note 40 at 33, Raz states, "The law presents itself as a body of authoritative standards and requires all those to whom they apply to acknowledge their authority."

51   *Raz, Authority and Interpretation*, above note 41 at 104, 111. And Raz, *Ethics in the Public Domain*, above note 50 at 215: "Though a legal system may not have legitimate authority, or though its legitimate authority may not be as extensive as it claims, every legal system claims that it possesses legitimate authority."

claim contains an assertion that when people adhere to its directives, their actions will maintain better conformity with reason. Still, the government may end up passing laws that do not, in fact, ensure the best-reasoned action. Take for instance the laws that criminalize all forms of assisted suicide. Some would argue that adherence to those criminal laws would not actually ensure the most reasonable actions. If that were true, then those laws would maintain legal validity, because they emerged from a legal system that claims legitimate authority, but their authority would not be legitimate, *in fact*.

For Raz, many or even all the citizens and officials of the political community may believe that the law has legitimate authority and therefore act according to its directives, but it does not follow that law actually does have the legitimate authority that it asserts. Neither the assertion of legitimacy nor the legal subject's acceptance of the law in fact *justifies* law's authority. Law's authority is only actually justified if it is in fact legitimate, in the sense that it best enables conformity with reason.[52] Accordingly, under Raz's theory, like Hart's, legal validity is not contingent on the justifiability of law. Of course, Raz commits to the descriptive truth that law *is* authoritative on the basis of its legal validity. But like Hart, he maintains that its authoritative quality is not necessarily legitimate by virtue of legal validity.

Much like Hart, Raz is adamant that the question of law's justification must remain distinct from the question of what constitutes a valid law in a particular community. In fact, it is in-built within Raz's theory that law is identifiable without resort to any deliberation over what the law should be. For Raz, the authority of an institution is derived from its *claim* that adhering to its directives will better enable conformity with reason compared with disregarding the directives and attempting to conform to right reason on our own. This requires that the subjects of the authority be able to establish the content of the law. They can discern that content, Raz explains, "by establishing which rules were made or endorsed by the authorities."[53] Subjects must not have to establish the legitimacy of the law's authority, because the very purpose of the institutions of authority is to pre-empt that reasoning.[54] Accordingly, the question of whether or not a rule has the status of

---

52   Raz, *Authority and Interpretation*, above note 41 at 112.

53   *Ibid* at 114.

54   Raz makes this point in *Ethics in the Public Domain*, above note 50 at 219 as follows: People who are subjects to an authority "can benefit by its decisions only if they can establish

law must be independent of considerations of what the law ought to be, which in Raz's conception is that it should enable conformity with reason.[55]

Consider the example of the teacher and the student again. When a student takes the teacher as a legitimate authority, they would not themself consider the legitimacy of each (or any) of the teacher's directives before acting on them. Doing so would defeat the purpose of the teacher's authority, which is to steer the student toward more reasonable actions than the student would take absent the teacher's directives. In the same way, a citizen should not have to evaluate the legitimacy of each law before considering it valid, because that defeats the purpose of law pre-empting that very reasoning. So, Raz's theory contains a clear and strong endorsement of the separation thesis: the validity of law and its legitimacy are separate questions.[56]

Raz opines that opposition to the separation thesis is premised on the assertion of a necessary moral duty to obey the law. The existence of a duty to obey law implies a requisite connection between law and morality, because it would be contradictory to say that there is a moral duty to obey that which is immoral. Therefore, whatever is law must actually have the moral legitimacy that it claims.[57] Raz agrees that only legitimate authority can "vindicate a general obligation to obey the law in any country."[58] Flowing from this assertion, Raz

---

their existence and content in ways which do not depend on raising the very same issues which the authority is there to settle."

55   A similar argument is captured in Richard Friedman, "On the Concept of Authority in Political Philosophy" in R. Flathman (ed), *Concepts in Social and Political Philosophy* (New York: Macmillan, 1973) at 132 as follows, "[I]f there is no way of telling whether an utterance is authoritative, except by evaluating its contents to see whether it deserves to be accepted in its own right, then the distinction between an authoritative utterance and advice or rational persuasion will have collapsed."

56   Raz, *Authority and Interpretation*, above note 41 at 114. Through his assertion that moral criteria can be neither necessary nor sufficient conditions for determining whether a rule has status as law, Raz sides with proponents of "exclusive legal positivism." Contemporary debates around inclusive versus exclusive legal positivism contain elaborate discussions of the claim that law does not have any *necessary* dependency on morality. For more on those discussions, see Kenneth Einar Himma, "Inclusive Legal Positivism" and Andrei Marmor, "Exclusive Legal Positivism," both in Jules Coleman & Scott Shapiro (eds), *The Oxford Handbook of Jurisprudence and Philosophy of Law* (Oxford: Oxford University Press, 2002); Jules Coleman, "Negative and Positive Positivism" (1982) 11 *Journal of Legal Studies* 139.

57   Raz, *Authority and Interpretation*, above note 41 at 114.

58   Joseph Raz, "About the Morality and the Nature of Law," in Joseph Raz, *Authority and Interpretation*, above note 41 at 175.

maintains that since the existence of a legal system and the status as law is not, and cannot be, contingent on the legitimacy of its authority, there also must not be any general obligation to obey law purely on the basis of its status as law.[59] Summing up his position in this respect, Raz states:

> [L]aw is good if it provides prudential reasons for action where and when this is advisable and if it marks out certain standards as socially required where it is appropriate to do so. If the law does so properly, then it reinforces protection of morally valuable possibilities and interests and encourages and supports worthwhile forms of social cooperation. But neither of these legal techniques even when admirably used gives rise to an obligation to obey the law. *It makes sense to judge the law as a useful and important social institution and to judge the legal system good or even perfect while denying that there is an obligation to obey its laws.*[60]

As noted above, Hart similarly acknowledged the possibility of valid laws that are morally reprehensible, and like Raz, reasoned that there is no necessary *moral* obligation to obey law on the basis of its status as law alone.

By revoking any moral obligation of loyalty to the law, Hart and Raz effectively assert that there is in no *moral* dilemma when a person is faced with a valid law that is too morally reprehensible to be obeyed. The moral evaluation of the law is made by reference to considerations that are external to the question of legality.[61] David Dyzenhaus explains this point as follows: "when positivists use the example of a particular immoral law, they seem to assume that there is a legally unproblematic fact of the matter about the law's immoral content, i.e. that it has a determinate

---

59　See generally, Raz, *Authority of Law*, above note 40 at 233–49. Raz opens the chapter at 233 as follows:

> I shall argue that there is no obligation to obey the law. It is generally agreed that there is no absolute or conclusive obligation to obey the law. I shall suggest that there is not even a prima facie obligation to obey it. Such a view may be the outcome of a very pessimistic outlook of the value of law and the possibilities of its reform. My argument will not be based on such pessimistic assumptions. I shall argue that there is no obligation to obey the law even in a good society whose legal system is just.

60　Raz, *Authority of Law*, above note 40 at 249 [emphasis added].

61　David Dyzenhaus, *Hard Cases in Wicked Legal Systems: Pathologies of Law*, 2d ed (Oxford: Oxford University Press) at 167 [Dyzenhaus, *Wicked Legal Systems*].

content that is morally but not legally problematic."[62] Dyzenhaus goes on to explain criticisms of this position, which he attributes to Lon Fuller and Ronald Dworkin,[63] as follows:

> What legal positivism misses in this situation is that for there to be a genuine problem for the citizen, the citizen must find him or her self in a moral dilemma – pulled in different directions by conflicting moral values. That entails that law must exert its own independent moral force in order to create the dilemmas.[64]

The criticism seems to go that positivism improperly disregards the fact that an individual *does* experience a dilemma when faced with an immoral law, which suggests that law *does* have some sort of moral pull. The existence of that moral pull indicates that there must be some necessary moral content in law. This may be persuasive, but my own assertion that legal validity must contain normative legitimacy does not rest on this critique, and is also not contingent on the existence of a moral obligation to obey the law. Rather, my assertion is founded on the descriptive reality that both Hart and Raz point out: having status as law brings authoritative implications — the law is applicable and enforceable on the basis of its legal validity. Without legitimacy, that authority is ungrounded and unjustified.

Consider a citizen, a son, who has an ailing mother who is severely suffering and wishes to end her life. He is faced with the law prohibiting euthanasia or assisted suicide, which they consider an immoral law, given his circumstances. He interprets himself as having a moral obligation to disobey the law, and assist in his mother's death. At the same time, he is confronted with a distinct legal obligation to obey the law. That legal obligation is authoritative in the society — it is a binding and enforceable obligation on the basis of its legal status. Even if there is no moral obligation to obey the law, the son is nonetheless placed in a dilemma in terms of what action he should take, because of the authoritative quality of law, *whether or not that authoritative quality is moral*: if he does not assist in his mother's death, he prolongs her suffering, which he may reasonably consider immoral;

---

62   *Ibid.*

63   Lon Fuller, "Positivism and Fidelity to Law – A Reply to Professor Hart" (1957) 71 *Harvard Law Review* 630 and Ronald Dworkin, "A Reply" in Marshall Cohen (ed), *Ronald Dworkin and Contemporary Jurisprudence* (Totowa, NJ: Roman & Allenheld, 1984).

64   Dyzenhaus, *Wicked Legal Systems*, above note 61 at 167.

if he fulfills his moral duty to relieve his mother, however, he faces legal consequences because of the legal validity of the criminalization of assisted death. In this situation, even if the son does not consider obedience to the law to be a moral duty, the validity of the law causes him a dilemma.

The fact that this dilemma can be imposed on a citizen requires justification. If not, then law, due to its authoritative quality, erodes a person's ability to engage in autonomous moral reasoning and take action purely on the basis of his own moral reasoning, without any justification.[65] The son's moral obligation, at least in his own interpretation, is to relieve his mother, but the legal validity of the laws prohibiting assisted death prevents him from acting purely on the basis of his moral reasoning. For me, this is the most persuasive reason for why status as law requires in-built justification, or legitimacy.[66]

For both Hart and Raz, having legal status brings the definitive implication that the rule is authoritative — both theorists are clear that as soon as a rule has legal validity, that rule will be enforced and applied to members of the community. But since they do not approach legal validity as a normative enterprise, they move to deny any moral implications that may come with having status as law. This denial also leaves them unable to account for the legitimacy of the authoritative

---

65   R.P. Wolff, *In Defense of Anarchism* (Berkeley, CA: University of California Press, 1970) at 9 has offered a defence of anarchism upon a similar conclusion: "If the individual retains his autonomy by reserving to himself in each instance the final decision whether to co-operate, he thereby denies the authority of the state; if, on the other hand, he submits to the state and accepts its claim to authority then . . . he loses his autonomy." See also Neil MacCormick, "The Concept of Law and *The Concept of Law*" in Robert George (ed), *The Autonomy of Law: Essays on Legal Positivism* (Oxford: Clarendon Press, 1996) at 170 for a discussion around the distinction between legal obligations and moral obligations on the basis that "law is heteronomous, binding us from without, while morality is autonomous, binding us by our own reflective judgment and will."

66   A number of theorists have denied an obligation to obey the law, while maintaining that law can still be entitled to have authority. See for example, M.B.E. Smith, "Is There a Prima Facie Obligation to Obey the Law" (1972–1973) 82 *Yale Law Journal* 950; William Edmundson, *Three Anarchical Fallacies* (New York: Cambridge University Press, 1998) and "Legitimate Authority without Political Obligation" (1998) 17(1) *Law and Philosophy* 43; A.J. Simmons, *Moral Principles and Political Obligations* (Princeton, NJ: Princeton University Press, 1979); and for a comprehensive review of the state of the discussion around the existence of a duty to obey the law see Leslie Green, "Law and Obligations" in Jules Coleman & Scott J. Shapiro (eds), *The Oxford Handbook of Jurisprudence and Philosophy of Law* (Oxford: Oxford University Press, 2002).

implications that come with legal validity. This gap is why I consider Hart's and Raz's positivist approaches problematic.[67]

So far, my goal has been to outline the positivist approach to explaining legal validity, and highlighting my contention with the insistence on separating the validity of laws and their legitimacy. I have not yet commented, however, on those positivist notions that I consider agreeable. In the next section, my aim is to reconcile the meritorious aspects of the positivist separation thesis with my resolve that legal validity requires normativity in order to account for the authoritative quality of law, whether that law is substantively good or bad. This, as I explain below, paves the road for my turn to a substantiated procedural model for legal validity as well as its legitimacy.

C. Merging Description with Normativity, Validity with Legitimacy

Hart and Raz, and any proponent of the separation thesis, will hold that conceiving of law and its evaluation as wholly distinct is descriptively accurate, and essential to maintaining the discernibility of law. It enables individuals to know what the law is without having to evaluate it as good or bad, moral or immoral. In modern multi-moral communities where individuals may reasonably disagree on their evaluation of the law, this seems sound and necessary.[68] Moreover, if the question of "what is the law?" depended on subjective deliberation on the merits of that law, then the authoritative rules that govern a society would be ambiguous. Applying and enforcing ambiguous or uncertain rules

---

67   Scholars have pointed to conceptual tensions arising from the idea that law claims legitimate authority without necessarily achieving it, but still maintains *de facto* authority. See for example: Kristen Rundle, *Forms Liberate: Reclaiming the Jurisprudence of Lon Fuller* (Oxford and Portland, Oregon: Hart Publishing, 2012) [Rundle, *Forms Liberate*] at 154–59; W. J. Waluchow, *Inclusive Legal Positivism* (Oxford: Oxford University Press, 1994) at 129–40; Kenneth I. Himma (2001) "The Instantiation Thesis and Raz's Critique of Inclusive Positivism" 20 *Law and Philosophy* at 61–79; Dale Smith, "Must the Law be Capable of Possessing Authority?" (2012) 18 *Legal Theory* 69; and Jules Coleman, "Authority and Reason," above note 38.

68   See Jürgen Habermas, *Between Facts and Norms: Contributions to Discourse Theory of Law and Democracy* (Cambridge, MA: MIT Press, 1996) at 200: "in a pluralistic society in which various belief systems compete with each other, recourse to a prevailing ethos developed through interpretation does not offer a convincing basis for legal discourse. What counts for one person as a historically proven topos is for another ideology or sheer prejudice." [Habermas, *Between Facts and Norms*].

cannot be considered fair.[69] I share, therefore, Hart's and Raz's commitment to the discernibility aspect of the separation thesis — what rules have status as law in a society surely must be discernible by those for whom the law is authoritative. Owing to their commitment to the discernibility element, Hart and Raz hold that having status as law cannot depend on the justifiability of the content of a rule. This seems to be descriptively and logically accurate, as I noted in chapter 1. It does not follow, however, that legal validity can be devoid of any necessary normativity altogether, as Hart and Raz hold.

As outlined above, in both Hart's and Raz's theories, valid law is authoritative for community members, but it is not necessary that valid law deserves its authoritative status. Accordingly, a valid law may lack moral aptness or any kind of legitimate authority.[70] Consequently, there is a gap between the ideal situation where all valid law would have legitimate authority, and the inescapable reality that a valid law may be immoral or does not enable better conformity with reason, in Raz's sense. This means that there is the inevitable potential that a "bad" law gains legal validity, and on that basis, it will be applied and enforced in a society. Hart's and Raz's theories demonstrate this gap, but their projects are not directed toward offering any normative justification for it. In my view, however, status as law must be substantiated in some way in order to legitimize the very fact that law may not live up to its substantive ideal, whatever that ideal may be, yet it can still bear the authoritative implications that are parceled within having status as law.

I am concerned with the justification for this gap, because that justification can indicate from where the legitimacy of the status of law, in its own right, is ultimately derived. That inquiry is analogous to my ultimate inquiry about the legitimacy of adjudicative fact-finding. My goal is to answer why adjudicative outcomes are legitimate when they are dependent on a process of fact-finding that allows for the potential that valid legal facts are factually inaccurate. I am seeking the normative justification for the gap between the obvious ideal of accurate fact-finding all the time, and the reality of factual uncertainty that

---

69 As I note below, clarity is one of Lon Fuller's criteria for legal validity and is therefore an essential characteristic of law.

70 For example, Raz, *Authority and Interpretation*, above note 41 at 112: "the law can fail morally. It may not justify the moral claims it is making. If it were not so then the very idea of criticizing the law, or at least of criticizing it on moral grounds would be incoherent."

causes us to accept that legal facts may not be substantively accurate, but nonetheless, valid.

This gives rise to the question of how the discernibility element of the separation thesis can be reconciled with the fact that status as law requires some justificatory substantiation. The reconciliation is possible by abandoning Hart's and Raz's commitment that the legitimizing virtue of law can only be located within its substantive content, and by shifting the location of the virtue into the process of *becoming* law. Through this shift, the justifying virtue that vindicates law's status, and the gaining of that status occur simultaneously because they are fused together. In other words, resolving the descriptive accuracy of the positivist approach against the problem of its substantive hollowness is possible through a thinly substantiated procedural model that acts as a criterion for legal validity *and* the legitimacy of the authority that comes with legal validity, while simultaneously providing a justificatory reason for legal authority. This criterion will then provide a normative basis for the fact that a law, based on its legal validity, is applicable and enforceable in a community *even if* a community member disagrees with the law in substance.

By ensuring that the process of a rule becoming law is virtuous, the outcomes of that procedure emerge endowed with a form of legitimacy as a consequence of their being a product of a worthy procedure. The virtue located within the legal procedure transfers into the law, thus providing the law with some substantiation to justify its authoritative status. Only such an approach to legal validity can maintain that the question of what *is* law remains discernible without resort to justifying its content, because the law is whatever emerges from acceptable legal procedures. Simultaneously, this approach avoids law being devoid of any normativity. The substantiated procedural approach opens an avenue to responding to the fact that a law's substantive morality may be questionable, its content may be disagreeable, or even unjustified in a community member's reasonable opinion, and on the basis of their autonomous moral reasoning, a community member may decide to act in contravention of it, but the law is nonetheless legitimate and justifiably applicable and enforceable for all community members.

There is one point worth clarifying before proceeding: I do not suggest that a thinly substantiated procedural model invokes a moral obligation to obey the law. That is, even in a system that has a procedurally legitimate legal system, I do not suggest that community members *should* obey the law in a moral sense. My claim is that when a law is legitimate, its authority is normatively grounded, so there is a justificatory reason for treating the law as authoritative even though a person might reasonably think that they have no *moral* obligation to obey that law, or even a moral obligation to disobey it.[71]

Ending up with the claim that only a substantiated proceduralist account can provide an adequate explanation for the legitimacy of law's status as law reveals that my inquiry into the legitimacy of adjudicative outcomes cannot rest on the mere "status as law" of adjudicative procedures. Although primary rules (to borrow Hart's terminology) may be legitimized based on their status as law, my inquiry refers to the propriety of procedural or secondary rules of adjudication. Adoption of a proceduralist theory of the legitimacy of law means that those procedures, which themselves must give rise to valid and legitimate law, must substantively embody the very same virtue that legitimized their own status as law. Being a product of a virtuous procedure can render any law worthy of its status as law, despite its potential substantive moral failing; in the same way, legal facts can be considered worthy of grounding adjudicative decisions through the virtues located in the process of adjudicative fact-finding, despite their potential for substantive inaccuracy.

My next step is to consider what virtue the procedure must reflect in order to support its legitimizing role. Essentially, this step can be described as a substantiation of Hart's foundational idea that laws are valid based on their adherence to secondary rules. I criticized Hart's theory because he does not provide any reason why adherence to the secondary rules legitimately provides laws with their authoritative status. That lack, I suggested, rendered his theory descriptively accurate, but normatively hollow. I turn now to reviewing the contributions of two theorists who have offered a substantiation: Lon Fuller and Jürgen Habermas. Both authors have concluded that legal validity requires in-built normative justification, legitimacy, which serves as the reason that community members can rationally assent to law's authority.

---

71   This is a point of divergence between Lon Fuller's jurisprudence and my understanding, as I explain further below.

PART 2. PROCEDURALIST PARADIGMS: LON FULLER AND JÜRGEN HABERMAS

In this Part, my first goal is to demonstrate how Lon Fuller's and Jürgen Habermas's insights support the assertion that gaining legal validity must simultaneously entail gaining legitimacy. My second aim is to delineate Fuller's and Habermas's conceptions of the source of law's legitimacy. The cornerstone of both accounts, in my interpretation, is that legal subjects must have a rational reason to assent to law's authoritative nature — the fact that it will be enforced and applied in the community. That reason is law's legitimacy, and it is derived from the legal system's respect for its subjects as rationally acting autonomous agents. That commitment is demonstrable within law-making procedures. Not only do Fuller's and Habermas's accounts embolden the claim that law's legitimization occurs in the procedural arena; they also provide the substantive qualities that legal procedures must embody in order to play their role of legitimizing their emergent outcomes.

A. The Legal Theory of Lon Fuller

(1) Why Law Needs Legitimacy

My reactions to Hart's approach parallel Fuller's response to Hart in, "Positivism and Fidelity to Law – A Reply to Professor Hart."[72] Ultimately, Fuller complains of lack of substantiation in Hart's theory, similar to my complaint that the positivist perspective leaves the status as law hollow. The central theme in Fuller's response to Hart in their famous 1958 exchange is that a complete concept of law must contain a reason that law warrants its demand for the fidelity of its subjects. According to Fuller, while Hart maintains that law is presumptively authoritative and requires obedience, his concept of law does not delineate any reason for those qualities, it only asserts them. On that basis, Fuller finds Hart's concept of law inadequate:

> Professor Hart's thesis as it now stands is essentially incomplete and . . .
> before he can attain the goals he seeks he will have to concern himself

---

72   Lon Fuller, "Positivism and Fidelity to Law – A Reply to Professor Hart" (1957) 71 *Harvard Law Review* 630 [Fuller, "Reply to Hart"].

more closely with a definition of law that will make meaningful the obligation of fidelity to law.[73]

And later, "I do not think it is unfair to the positivistic philosophy to say that it never gives any coherent meaning to the moral obligation of fidelity to law."[74]

As the above excerpts indicate, Fuller maintains a presumption that there is a moral obligation of loyalty to the law. That presumption leads him to conclude that there must be some moral quality about law that vindicates the subject's moral obligation of obedience to it. As noted previously, I do not share the presumption that law necessarily invokes a moral obligation of fidelity, and my derivation of the claim that law requires legitimacy does not depend on that presumption. But I share Fuller's notion that law does, by its nature, demand and enforce fidelity, and the positivist conception of law falls short insofar as it refuses to vindicate that demand.

In his "Reply to Hart," Fuller reveals that he anticipated (errone-ously) that Hart would arrive at the conclusion that the legitimizing vir-tue of law is located within the procedures of lawmaking, given Hart's conclusions that "the foundation of a legal system is not coercive power, but certain 'fundamental accepted rules specifying the essential law-making procedures.'"[75] Considering that legal validity hinges on those law-making procedures, Fuller's surprise that Hart leaves the question of the necessary nature of those procedures undefined is understand-able.[76] The result is that Hart's concept of the status as law remains empty, leaving Fuller to wonder, "how are we to define the words 'fun-damental' and 'essential' in Professor Hart's own formulation?"[77] These words require definition if there is to be a comprehensive concept of legal validity. Fuller's central contribution can be seen as providing

---

73   *Ibid* at 634–35.

74   *Ibid* at 656.

75   *Ibid* at 639.

76   The same surprise is shared by Dan Priel in "Reconstructing Fuller's Argument against Legal Positivism" Osgoode Hall Law School Comparative Research in Law and Political Economy Research Paper Series no 16/2013 at 8: "Once Fuller's real position is acknowledged, it is Hart's view that appears surprising, or at least incomplete. It is surprising because it suggests that the considerations relevant for the first step – Hart's secondary rules – are utterly different from the factors relevant for the second step – the principles of legality. While this view is logically possible, it appears odd without further argument, and one that Hart never provides."

77   Fuller, "Reply to Hart," above note 72 at 641.

some definition to these phrases, and thereby arriving at a richer concept of law that has in-built substantiation or legitimacy.

The seeds of this contribution are planted in Fuller's "Reply to Hart" when he discusses "the Morality of Law Itself".[78] Suggesting that Hart's position can be conceived as drawing a distinction between order (law) and good order (good law), Fuller proposes that order itself (whether good or bad) has a morality of its own. Defining the morality of order amounts to giving substance to Hart's "fundamental" and "essential" procedural rules of lawmaking. Even a tyrannical monarch, Fuller explains, would have to follow certain rules of form to achieve order. For instance, they would have to ensure that they reward what they say they will reward, and punish what they say he will punish, whatever it is that warrants reward or punishment under their rule. And whatever their order are in substance, they must be discernible, so the subjects know what is required of them. If such rules are not adhered to, the monarch's decrees would hold no meaning, and order would not be achieved.[79] The formal principles that are necessary to achieve order at all, Fuller calls the implicit morality of order, or the internal morality of law. These formal principles, Fuller suggests, are the rules that make law possible.

In the "Reply to Hart," Fuller introduces his theme that respecting the internal morality of law is essential to both gaining status as law and warranting that status. But he does not suggest that adhering to those principles makes law necessarily good: "The morality of order must be respected," Fuller explains, "if we are to create anything that can be called law, *even bad law*".[80] In his opening, Fuller also alludes to the possibility of bad law in his articulation of the two dimensions that must be explained in order to achieve a meaningful concept of law:

> If laws, *even bad laws*, have a claim to our respect, then law must represent some general direction of human effort that we can understand and describe, and that we can approve in principle even at the moment when it seems to us to miss its mark.[81]

Fuller's insistence that law's demand for loyalty must be defended requires him to argue that in order to properly have status as law, law

---

78   *Ibid* at 644.
79   *Ibid* at 644–45.
80   *Ibid* at 645 [emphasis added].
81   *Ibid* at 632 [emphasis added].

must have some in-built virtuous quality that vindicates its authoritative status. Translated into the terminology that I have adopted here, Fuller's claim is that valid law requires legitimacy. At the same time, evidenced by his clear acceptance of the possibility of "bad" law, Fuller acknowledges that legal validity cannot be contingent on substantive morality. These commitments clearly map onto my view outlined above that there must be some source of legitimacy built into the status as law that can accommodate the potential for valid law that may be reasonably judged as bad. Fuller locates the requisite virtue of law within the formal principles of lawmaking and calls it the internal morality of law:[82]

> What I have called the internal morality of law is in this sense a procedural version of natural law. . . . The term "procedural" is, however, broadly appropriate as indicating that we are concerned, not with the substantive aims of legal rules, but with the ways in which a system of rules for governing human conduct must be constructed and administered if it is to be efficacious and at the same time remain what it purports to be.

The internal morality of law is, for Fuller, the bridge between law requiring substantive morality and law being devoid of justification altogether. Given that Fuller locates the justifiability of law in the formal principles of law-making, my goal of determining the virtue that enables procedural/formal propriety to play its legitimizing role will be furthered by exploring and evaluating his internal morality of law proposal, which becomes his central theme in his book, *The Morality of Law*, which I turn to now.

(2) Locating Legitimacy in Fuller's Account: The Internal Morality of Law

The principles of the internal morality of law that Fuller first introduces in his "Reply to Hart" in 1958 are further developed in his book, *The Morality of Law*. His approach involves analyzing the elements that make law valid, or, the elements of legality. As I demonstrate further below, the overarching implication that he derives from those elements is that the principles that make law possible are all underpinned with a

---

82   Lon Fuller, *The Morality of Law* (New Haven, CT and London: Yale University Press, 1964) at 96–97 [Fuller, *Morality of Law*].

requirement that lawmakers respect their subjects as rationally acting agents. Law is infused with that virtue as a result of being produced through adherence to the formal principles of legality, or the internal morality of law that Fuller delineates. Thereby, Fuller provides a reason that subjects can rationally accept the law just on the basis that it is law, even though they may not appreciate it in substance.

Conceiving of law as the "enterprise of subjecting human conduct to the governance of rules,"[83] Fuller maintains that a system of governance that is incapable of meaningfully enabling citizens to govern their conduct cannot be considered a legal system at all. With this purposive concept of law as his starting point, Fuller discerns eight principles that are inherent to valid law, and that must be respected by lawmakers if a system of rules that is properly a "legal system" is to come about. Taken together, these eight principles of legality reflect the internal morality of law, and overall compliance with each of them is a prerequisite to the existence of law at all.

Fuller unveils the eight principles by relating an anecdote of King Rex, who sets out to become a successful lawmaker. The story unfolds as a dialogue between Rex and his subjects, foreshadowing Fuller's unique commitment that law cannot be conceived as a one-way flow of power but instead, as a two-way interaction where both parties have certain expectations of one another. In the course of his rule, Rex commits eight fatal mistakes, each of which are brought to his attention by his disgruntled subjects, prompting him to make various attempts to respond to them. Each attempt, however, results in an offence against law's internal morality, resulting in a perpetually lawless state. Through the story, Fuller demonstrates that in order for law to guide the conduct of citizens, certain formal principles must be followed. Ensuring compliance with those formal requirements enables the law to be relevant to the subjects' reasoning when they make decisions to conduct their affairs.

First, for a legal system to exist, there must be general rules that govern conduct to begin with. Fuller refers to this principle as the requirement of generality.[84] The generality principle does not imply that every decree that has status as law must be a generalized rule in the sense that it should address general groups rather than specific individuals. If

---

83   *Ibid* at 96.
84   *Ibid* at 46.

substantive generality were a requirement of the existence of law, then judicial decrees that direct an individual to act in a certain way could not have the force of law. Rather, the generality principle for Fuller denotes that "at the very minimum, there must be rules of some kind, however fair or unfair they may be."[85]

Second, the governing rules must be publicly available. If rules are unknown to the subjects, they obviously cannot influence their decision-making. Explaining the principle of promulgation, Fuller advises that the demand is not that every citizen must be made to know the law in order for the law to be valid. Rather, the principle requires that the law be made available to citizens so that they have the opportunity to know what rules govern their conduct.

Protecting a similar requirement that rules must be knowable in order to govern conduct, the third principle of legality is that laws should generally be prospective, not retroactive. In order to bear an impact on a citizen's actions, the rules must *exist* prior to conduct. As Fuller explains, "to speak of governing or directing conduct today by rules that will be enacted tomorrow is to talk in blank prose."[86]

Fourth, a rule that nobody can understand also cannot guide human conduct. For Fuller, the requirement of clarity in laws is "one of the most essential ingredients of legality."[87] It, more obviously than the other principles, flies in the face of the positivist thesis that whatever the legislator (or otherwise appropriate source of law) asserts is law. For Fuller, if the legislator makes laws that are not sufficiently clear to guide human conduct, then it has failed to create law, and the fact that it is a legislative decree does not save its status as law.[88] "Being at the top of the chain of command does not exempt the legislature from its responsibility to respect the demands of the internal morality of law, indeed, it intensifies that responsibility."[89]

Fifth, a system of laws cannot be self-contradictory. If obeying one law would mean breaking another, then it is fairly obvious that law would lose its ability to rationally guide conduct. This rule applies not only to contradictions within one statute, but also to contradictory requirements between statutes as well as laws that are incompatible

---

85   *Ibid* at 47.
86   *Ibid* at 53.
87   *Ibid* at 63.
88   *Ibid*.
89   *Ibid* at 64.

or repugnant to each other: "legislative carelessness about the jibe of statutes with one another can be very hurtful to legality and there is no simple rule by which to undo the damage."[90]

Sixth, the law must be possible for the subjects to comply with. Requiring the impossible is an absurdity when law is taken to have the aim of guiding conduct. Issuing laws that require the impossible would be nothing more than an exercise of brute power.

Seventh, legality requires that laws remain relatively constant in time. Just as it would be impossible to be guided by the laws of a legal system that made regular use of retroactive statutes, it would be impossible to be guided by law in a context of ever-changing rules.[91]

Eighth and finally, Fuller advises that legality requires congruence between administration of the law and the declared law.[92] Preserving this congruence, in most countries, is largely the task allotted to the judiciary. There are many threats to the congruence, Fuller explains, ranging from mistaken interpretation to a striving for personal gain. To his list of potential incongruences, I would add that the plain fact that adjudication occurs in circumstances of factual uncertainty sets the stage for incongruence as well. Although he does not expressly note factual uncertainty, Fuller does advise that the devices that are used to maintain congruence include "most of the elements of due process, such as the right to representation by counsel and the right of cross examining adverse witnesses,"[93] which may be understood as preserving accuracy in terms of both law and fact, in order to protect congruence.

In addition to requiring congruence between the legislated law and judicial application, Fuller also notes that the internal morality principle of congruence applies in the context of judge-made law, as in the arena of torts, where the governing legal principles are, in large part, the product of judicial decree rather than legislation. Incongruence in court-made law is an affront against internal morality in its own right; it also leads to potential overstepping of other principles of the internal morality of law:

> All of the influences that can produce a lack of congruence between
> judicial action and statutory law can, when the court itself makes

---

90   *Ibid* at 69.

91   *Ibid* at 79–80.

92   *Ibid* at 81.

93   *Ibid.*

the law, produce equally damaging departures from other principles of legality: A failure to articulate reasonably clear general rules and an inconstancy in decision manifesting itself in contradictory rulings, frequent changes of direction, and retrospective changes in the law.[94]

In summary, in Fuller's conception, for the existence of a legal system and for the creation of valid laws, human conduct must (1) be governed through general laws that are (2) publicly available, (3) non-retroactive, (4) clear, (5) constant in time, (6) free of contradictions, (7) do not require the impossible, and finally (8) the declared rules and their administration must be congruent. Compliance with these principles ensures that laws are capable of being a rational influence for subjects as they decide how to conduct themselves. This is essential to law, given its purpose of subjecting human conduct to the governance of rules. Since adherence to the principles of legality is necessary for law to be law at all, in Fuller's view, just as the existence of law demands obedience from subjects, it also demands that lawmakers obey the internal morality principles. If not, then like Rex in Fuller's story, the lawmaker fails in his task, and his decrees cannot bear the authoritative implications that come with rules that are properly called laws.

(3) Addressing Critiques of the Internal Morality Principles

Fuller has faced the critique that the principles he enumerates are more properly characterized as morally neutral principles of efficacy, and as such, they do not confer legitimacy to law.[95] It is through his "Reply to Critics" that some of Fuller's more foundational insights into the values underpinning the legitimacy of legality emerge most clearly. In Hart's review of *The Morality of Law*, he maintains that since Fuller derives the internal morality of law principles "solely through a realistic consideration of what is necessary for the efficient execution of the purpose of guiding human conduct by rules,"[96] his

---

94   *Ibid* at 82.

95   Such critics include: H.L.A. Hart, *Book Review of Morality of Law* by Lon Fuller, (1964–1965) 78 *Harvard Law Review* 1281 [Hart, *Review of Morality of Law*] (note: in the revised edition of *The Morality of Law* (published in 1969), Lon L. Fuller added a fifth and final chapter titled "A Reply to Critics"; Ronald Dworkin, "Philosophy, Morality and Law – Observations Prompted by Professor Fuller's Novel Claim" (1965) 113 *University of Pennsylvania Law Review* 668; Marshall Cohen, "Law, Morality and Purpose" (1965) 10(4) *Villanova Law Review* 640; Robert Summers, "Professor Fuller on Morality and Law" (1966) 18 *Journal of Legal Education* 1.

96   Hart, *Review of Morality of Law*, above note 95 at 1284.

classification of these principles as ones of "morality" rather than the principles required to bring about a purpose is improper and confusing:

> The crucial objection to the designation of these principles of good legal craftsmanship as morality, in spite of the qualification of "inner," is that it perpetrates a confusion between two notions that it is vital to hold apart: the notions of purposive activity and morality.[97]

Hart explains the impropriety of equating elements that are necessary for a purposive activity and morality by relating the famous analogy of the "inner morality of poisoning." Poisoning has a definite purpose, and the fulfillment of that purpose can be brought about through adherence to certain principles of successful poisoning. But calling those principles "the morality of poisoning," would be to confuse the principles of fulfilling a purpose with morality. Fuller's eight principles are aimed at fulfilling law's purpose of guiding human conduct, but they are independent of any substantive aims of law, just like the principles of poisoning bring about its purpose but are neutral as to the immoral aim of poisoning someone. Therefore, adherence to Fuller's eight principles of legality, Hart suggests, does not ensure that law is aimed toward any moral purpose. On the contrary, he holds that adherence to them could be "compatible with very great iniquity."[98]

In *The Rule of Law and its Virtue*, Raz has advanced a more nuanced but essentially similar argument that Fuller's principles relate to efficacy of law but do not constitute law's necessary virtue. In that essay, Raz argues that the underlying principle of the rule of law is that the "law must be capable of guiding the behaviour of its subjects."[99] He goes on to list some principles that can be derived from this view of the rule of law. Given the common starting point of law's ability to guide behaviour, the list of principles that Raz articulates is very similar to Fuller's principles of legality.[100]

---

97   *Ibid* at 1286.

98   Hart, *Concept of Law*, above note 2 at 207.

99   Raz, "The Rule of Law and its Virtue" in Raz, *Authority of Law*, above note 40 at 214 [Raz, "The Rule of Law and its Virtue"].

100   Raz's list includes prospectively, clarity, stability, general rules that provide a framework for particular rules, independence of the judiciary, observance of the rules of natural justice, review power for the courts, accessibility to the courts, and limiting the discretion of police and prosecuting authorities.

Since the rule of law is a formal concept, Raz maintains that adherence to it can provide law with some formal virtues, but those do not translate as substantive assurances. Raz argues that while adherence to the rule of law can decrease the possibilities of arbitrary laws and judicial decisions (procedurally), he points out that the rule of law does not guarantee non-arbitrary laws (substantively). He explains that the rule of law can help to secure individual freedom by providing predictability (a procedural/form concept), but he notes that the laws that might be made may not guarantee personal freedom (substantively). Similarly, he maintains that the rule of law is necessary if the law is to respect human dignity, but notes that even if the rule of law is observed, a law can still violate human dignity, substantively. "The law may, for example, institute slavery without violating the rule of law."[101] Raz argues, therefore, that since the rule of law is compatible with substantive aims that could violate the same virtues that adherence to it promotes, it would be incorrect to point to the virtues protected by the rule of law through its formal guarantees as the necessary virtue of law.

Being neutral to the substantive aims of law, critics complain, Fuller's principles are value-neutral, so they do not further his aim of showing that law has an inherent virtue that vindicates its authoritative status. However, by extracting the underpinnings of the principles of legality, Fuller maintains an entirely different jurisprudential orientation than his critics — one that meaningfully accounts for the law's inherent authoritative quality, *even though* it may be substantively unfavourable. And as such, his viewpoint aligns with my aim of accounting for the authority of judicial outcomes that may be substantively inaccurate.

Fuller's analysis aims to explain *why* adherence to the principles of legality constitutes a "morality," or a normative concept of legitimacy. That becomes Fuller's explanation for why valid law emerges endowed with legitimacy, and therefore warranting its authoritative status. That analysis into legality, according to Fuller, is what his contemporary jurisprudence scholars had left undone:

> With writers of all philosophic persuasions it is, I believe, true to say that when they deal with problems of legal morality it is generally in a casual and incidental way. The reason for this is not far to seek. Men do not generally see any need to explain or justify the obvious. . . .

---

101   Raz, "The Rule of Law and its Virtue," above note 99 at 221.

> From one point of view, it is unfortunate that the demands of legal morality should generally seem so obvious. This appearance has obscured subtleties and has misled men into the belief that no pains-taking analysis of the subject is necessary or even possible.[102]

In his Reply to Critics, Fuller echoes the same lamentation contained in the excerpt above, as he diagnoses the divergence between his views and those of his positivist critics by showing the difference in their jurisprudential interests. In the Reply to Critics, he points out that all of his critics agree that some adherence to the principles of legality is necessary in order for law to come about.[103] "On this general issue, then," Fuller writes, "the agreement between my critics and me seems, in words at least, complete."[104] But contrary to the positivists, Fuller orients himself toward the question of *"to what end* is law being so defined that it cannot "exist" without some minimum respect for the principles of legality?"[105] In other words, Fuller's very concept of law is shaped by discerning the implications that can be drawn from the fact that compliance with the principles of legality is necessary for the existence of a legal system and law.[106]

The foundational implication that Fuller discerns is that law is properly conceived as a reciprocal relationship between lawmaker and legal subjects, where the lawmaker must respect the agency of the legal subject in order to expect any acceptance of its decrees.[107] Affirming Simmel's comments, Fuller notes, "there is a kind of reciprocity between government and the citizens with respect to the observance of rules. . . . When this bond of reciprocity is finally and completely ruptured by

---

102 Fuller, *Morality of Law*, above note 82 at 98.

103 Fuller, "Reply to Critics" in *Morality of Law*, above note 96 at 197–98.

104 *Ibid* at 198.

105 *Ibid* [emphasis in the original].

106 As Jeremy Waldron has observed in "Positivism and Legality: Hart's Equivocal Response to Fuller" (2008) 83 *New York University Law Review* 1135 at 1137:

> Fuller's reflections on [the Nazi adherence to the principles of legality] suggest a two-fold agenda for jurisprudence. It might be worth asking, first: what exactly is the relation between the principles of legality and categories of law and legal system which we use to characterize systems of rule? And it might be worth asking, secondly: what exactly is the relation between the principles of legality and the norms like justice, rights, and the common good which we use to evaluate systems of rule?

107 For an in-depth exposition of the relevance and implications of reciprocity and respect for human agency in Fuller's jurisprudence, uniquely defended through references to Fuller's personal correspondence and working notes, see Rundle, *Forms Liberate*, above note 67].

government, nothing is left on which to ground the citizen's duty to observe the rules."[108] This reciprocity is implicit in the fact that the principles of legality are required for there to be law, because those principles translate as positive obligations on the part of lawmakers. Only when those obligations are met can law, with all its authoritative implications, even come about. And since all the lawmaker's obligations are directed toward ensuring that the law has the requisite characteristics to guide subjects in their own rational decision-making, they all contain the underpinning *value-laden* sentiment that a lawmaker must conceive of their subjects as free-acting agents. As Fuller explains:

> Every departure from the principles of law's inner morality is an affront to man's dignity as a responsible agent. To judge his actions by unpublished or retrospective laws, or to order him to do an act that is impossible, is to convey to him your indifference to his powers of self-determination.[109]

Accordingly, the principles of legality represent law's internal *morality*, in the sense that they contain an underlying value: law must respect the agency of its subjects. If the lawmakers fail to adhere to that principle by breaching any element of legality, then law is not created at all, so none of the implications that come with law can attach. By asserting that an attitude of respect for agency is implicit in the requirements of legality, Fuller provides a reason for why citizens can reasonably assent to the authoritative demands of law. As Colleen Murphy notes, "Fuller's account helps to explain why it is rational for citizens to participate in the system of cooperation which the legal system establishes."[110]

That constitutes Fuller's persuasive response to the critique that his internal morality of law is misnamed, and provides only morally neutral requirements of legality.[111] Still, adopting a jurisprudential orientation

---

108   Fuller, *Morality of Law*, above note 82 at 40.

109   *Ibid* at 162.

110   Colleen Murphy, in "Lon Fuller and the Moral Value of the Rule of Law" (2005) 24 *Law and Philosophy* 239 at 243 [Murphy, "Fuller and the Rule of Law"].

111   A number of scholars, including Kristen Rundle in *Forms Liberate*, noted above note 67, have offered interpretations of Fuller that are sympathetic to his position that the principles of legality are not properly characterized as ones of mere efficacy, and that they are, rather, value-underpinned. For instance, David Dyzenhaus, "Process and Substance as Aspects of the Public Law Form" (2015) 74(2) *Cambridge Law Journal* 284 at 294 holds that Fuller argues "that compliance with the principles [of the internal morality of law] makes a positive moral and substantive difference to all legal systems"; Colleen Murphy, "Fuller and the Rule of

that places the moral virtue in process rather than substance faces the critique that substantively immoral laws could pass the test of "procedural morality." That leads to the situation where the authority of a substantively immoral law could be considered morally justified. Fuller has offered a simple and persuasive response that I find convincing: though it may be possible in the abstract, it is difficult to imagine a society where virtuous law-making procedures are genuinely adhered to, but the laws are substantively evil. Responding to the critique that history provides many examples of iniquitous laws that were procedurally proper, Fuller retorts:

> Since my book has been out I have discussed this question with a good many people, and I have yet to encounter a single case to prove this point. South Africa is probably as close as any. But as I tried to show in my final chapter, to the extent that an attempt has been made there to write racial prejudice into law, some impairment of legal morality has taken place.[112]

In fact, even in earlier writing, Fuller had noted that the Nazi regime quite clearly failed to observe the inner morality of law.[113] Nazi rule routinely made use of retroactive and secret laws; Nazis were able to disregard legal forms altogether and rule by terror; Nazi courts could decide cases disregarding even Nazi made laws. These realities suggest

---

Law," above note 110 at 250 holds that Fuller presents the rule of law as "inherently respectful of people's autonomy;" David Luban, "Rule of Law and Human Dignity: Re-examining Fuller's Canons" (2010) 2(1) *Hague Journal on the Rule of Law* 29, claims that Fuller's principles are in fact substantive and make important contributions to protecting human dignity. Evan Fox-Decent, "Is the Rule of Law Really Indifferent to Human Rights?" (2008) 27 *Law and Philosophy* 533, offers an argument about the inherent value of the rule of law as a protection of human rights, inspired by Fuller's theoretical underpinnings that "human agency underlies internal morality" at 538; and Jeremy Waldron, one of the pioneers in the efforts to reclaim Fuller's jurisprudence from the efficacy critique, in "Why Law: Efficacy, Freedom or Fidelity" (1994) 13 *Law and Philosophy* 259 at 276, argues that Fuller's jurisprudence should be considered the starting point for the important and difficult question of what it is about law that warrants its demand for fidelity; and see also Jeremy Waldron, "The Rule of Law and the Importance of Procedure" (2011) 50 *Nomos* 3.

112 Correspondence from Fuller to Walter Berns, quoted in Rundle, *Forms Liberate*, above note 67 at 111. This retort was endorsed by John E. Murray, "Observations on the Morality of Law" (1965) 10(1) *Villanova Law Review* 667 at 668 after hearing Fuller make the same point in an oral presentation discussing his book, *The Morality of Law*, and the critiques proffered by Ronald Dworkin and Marshal Cohen.

113 Fuller, *Reply to Hart*, above note 72 at 650.

that the Nazi regime was not oriented toward order at all and disregarded the internal morality of law. Accordingly, the Nazi regime and its decrees could be justifiably stripped of the title "law:"

> When a system calling itself law is predicated upon a general disregard by judges of the terms of the laws they purport to enforce, when this system habitually cures its legal irregularities, even the grossest, by retroactive statutes, when it has only to resort to forays of terror in the streets, which no one dares challenge, in order to escape even those scant restraints imposed by the pretense of legality – when all of these things have become true of a dictatorship, it is not hard for me, at least, to deny to it the name of law.[114]

Making a similar point, Jeremy Waldron has noted that:

> The outward appearance of the rule of law may be important for the external reputation of a regime. But those who reflect seriously on humanity's experience with tyranny know that, in the real world, this problem of the scrupulously legalistic Nazi is at best a question about the efficacy of cosmetics.[115]

The difficulty in providing an example of substantively evil laws that nonetheless adhere to virtuous legal procedures may be because the requisite procedures are themselves value-laden, and adherence to those procedures demonstrates a governmental commitment to those values. If the government is genuinely committed to the values that must be manifest in the law-making procedures, then it is unlikely that it will contradict those values in the substantive laws that it creates.[116]

---

114 *Ibid* at 660.

115 Jeremy Waldron, "Why Law – Efficacy, Freedom, or Fidelity?" (1994) 13 *Law and Philosophy* 259 at 264. Colleen Murphy, in "Fuller and the Rule of Law," above note 110 makes the same point, endorsing Waldron's above comments at 252.

116 In Rundle, *Forms Liberate*, above note 67, Kristen Rundle suggests that Fuller hinted at, but never elaborated, the point that the same values that underpin the form of law also constrain its ability to pursue iniquitous substantive goals, at least to some extent. According to Rundle, Fuller did so when he denied that laws instituting slavery were compliant with the internal morality of law. For Fuller, as I explain in the upcoming section, the form of law must manifest respect for human agency. A law that reduces a legal subject to a status akin to property is contrary to that virtue, and therefore constitutes an affront to a

Moreover, the problem of potentially immoral laws that, none-theless, bear the title law and have the associated implication of authority is precisely the place where procedural legitimacy does its normative work. As I have noted in chapter 1, modern pluralistic societies can, must, and do accommodate multiple moralities, so law's authority cannot depend on its adherence to particular moral principles. Even so, to be effective, law must be authoritative. Fuller's theory provides a reason to accept the law even if it seems substantively questionable to some people, and that reason is derived from the virtues that are implicit in the formal principles of legality. The analogy to my question regarding the acceptance of legal fact-finding is clear. As noted, my goal is to ascertain what virtues the process of fact-finding must display in order for adjudicative decisions based on legal facts to be acceptable to litigants, despite the potential for substantive inaccuracy. Applying Fuller's concept, just as subjects can accept laws that are substantively disagreeable to them if the process of creating those laws demonstrated respect for their agency, litigants can accept adjudicative facts that are potentially inaccurate if the process of arriving at those facts ensured respect for the agency of those affected.

A number of the themes that emerge in Fuller's writing are present, and more expressly developed, in Jürgen Habermas's contributions. For one, the necessity for maintaining certain, authoritative law in pluralistic societies is more expressly prominent in Habermas's thinking. In addition, both authors understand law as a dialogical process. This is evident in Fuller's foundational idea of reciprocity, which unfolds as a dialogue between King Rex and his disgruntled subjects. Habermas's concept of law as a dialogue unfolds within the democratic context, making its applicability in modern western con-texts more tangible. Finally, Fuller's approach into law as a guide for rational human conduct finds a parallel, and further development, in Habermas's insights into law as a rationally acceptable tool for the social integration of a diverse community. Below, I explain how these concepts unfold in Habermas's writing, and their relevance for my project.

---

substantiated concept of procedural propriety. For Rundle's argument, see, *Forms Liberate*, above note 67 at 111–14.

B. The Legal Theory of Jürgen Habermas

(1) Why Law Needs Legitimacy

The starting point of Habermas's paradigm is his observation that the modern world is largely made up of "post-traditional" societies. These societies are not integrated through a singular, shared morality. Law, Habermas explains, substitutes as an integrative, stabilizing agent.[117] His concept of law and its necessary characteristics is premised on this notion of law as a tool of social integration. That role requires that community members comply with the law, because law clearly cannot be socially integrative if nobody complies with it. That compliance is prompted through two necessary features of law: certainty and legitimacy.[118]

Certainty, for Habermas, means something close to predictable in that the law must be ascertainable, and whatever is law will also be enforceable. In that sense, law contains what Habermas refers to as a "facticity" component. He explains, though, that while compliance can be achieved through enforcement measures, if law is to be truly socially integrative and stabilizing for society, then citizens must have some reason to obey the law out of respect for it, not only out of fear of enforcement.[119] Thus rejecting the positivist approach, which conceives of law as a value-free fact without delineating its necessary normativity,[120] Habermas offers a concept of law that recognizes that valid law must be discernible and enforceable, while simultaneously embodying some normative quality that justifies its demand for compliance.[121] In his own words:

---

117   See for example: Habermas, *Between Facts and Norms: Contributions to Discourse Theory of Law and Democracy* (Cambridge, MA: MIT Press, 1996) at 83: "law must do more than simply meet the functional requirements of a complex society; it must also satisfy the precarious conditions of a social integration." And elsewhere at 1544: "Law is the only medium through which a 'solidarity with strangers' can be secured in complex societies." [Habermas, *Between Facts and Norms*]. For Habermas's discussion of law as a stabilizing tool of social integration, see generally Habermas, *Between Facts and Norms*, chapter 1.

118   *Ibid* at 198.

119   *Ibid.*

120   For Habermas's brief critique of legal positivism, see *ibid* at 201–3.

121   Habermas, "Between Facts and Norms: An Author's Reflections" (1999) 76 *Denver University Law Review* 937 at 937 [Habermas, "Author's Reflections"]:

> Law stands as a substitute for the failures of other integrative mechanisms . . . . This integrative capacity can be explained by the fact that legal norms are particularly functional in virtue of an interesting combination of formal properties: Modern law is cashed out in terms of subjective rights; it is enacted or positive as well as enforced or

We have already seen how the tension between facticity and validity is inherent in the category of law itself and appears in the two dimensions of legal validity. On the one hand, established law guarantees the enforcement of legally expected behaviour and therewith the certainty of law. On the other hand, rational procedures for making and applying law promise to legitimate the expectations that are stabilized in this way; the norms *deserve* legal obedience.[122]

The foundation of Habermas's paradigm is that valid law requires legitimacy, and accordingly, law cannot be conceived as either only fact, or only norm, but it requires both.[123] He writes:

> I take as my starting point the rights citizens must accord one another if they want to legitimately regulate their common life by means of positive law. This formulation already indicates that the system of rights as a whole is shot through with that internal tension between facticity and validity manifest in the ambivalent mode of legal validity.[124]

Recognizing both positivity and legitimacy as necessary characteristics of law, Habermas offers a paradigm for conceiving of law that bridges facticity and normativity of law in the realm of process. For Habermas, "the law receives its full normative sense neither through its legal form per se, nor through an a priori moral content, but through a procedure of lawmaking that begets legitimacy."[125] He explains the requisite procedure of law-making by applying the principles of discourse theory to law.

---

coercive law; and though modern law requires from its addressees nothing more than norm-confirmative behavior, it must nevertheless meet the expectation of legitimacy so that it is at least open to the people to follow norms, if they like, out of respect for the law.

For more on Habermas's discussion of facticity and validity, see Habermas, *Between Facts and Norms*, above note 117, chapter 1: "Law as a Category of Social Mediation between Facts and Norms."

122 Habermas, *Between Facts and Norms*, above note 117 at 198 [emphasis added].

123 James Gordon Finlayson, *Habermas: A Very Short Introduction* (Oxford: Oxford University Press, 2005) at 114: "A valid legal norm or law, Habermas argues, has both a normative and a factual side: on the one hand it is legitimate, and on the other it is positive. Hence the title of his book Between Facts and Norms, which literally translated would be 'Facticity and Validity.'"

124 Habermas, *Between Facts and Norms*, above note 117 at 82.

125 *Ibid* at 135.

(2) Locating Legitimacy in Habermas's Account: The Discourse Principle

Discourse constitutes a deliberative process. Its foundation is that "just those action norms are valid to which all possibly affected persons could agree as participants in rational discourse."[126] Habermas conceives of laws as the product of a discursive process, which makes the discourse theory of rational acceptability transferable to law. Laws have the requisite normative legitimacy, for Habermas, when they are amenable to the consent of community members who are participants in a rational discourse. That is, a law is legitimate when all the members of the community, despite their different values and belief systems, *can* (not necessarily will) rationally assent to it, and that is possible when the law is a product of a sincere rational discourse.

It is the rationality of the discourse process that makes the law acceptable even if a community member finds it substantively disagreeable. For instance, a law preventing hunting may not be agreeable to some community members, but its authority is still justifiable, because the nature of the *process of arriving* at the law (which I elaborate further below) is fair and orientated toward making a rational decision; the law's legitimacy is not dependent on the actual acceptability of the law to every community member, which is obviously impossible to guarantee, but on the acceptability of the process. Accordingly, Habermas's proposed application of the rational discourse principle to law furthers my aim of uncovering requisite features of an acceptable process of arriving at legally valid and rationally acceptable fact-finding outcomes, even if participants cannot agree with the substantive outcomes.

What, then, makes a discourse process rational such that its outcome warrants a community member's rational assent? Understanding Habermas's answer to this question requires looking into his notions about assessing the validity of any action norms through rational discourse. Validity, for Habermas, expresses normative validity, and is akin to what I refer to as legitimacy.[127]

Rational discourses testing normative validity of claims, in Habermas's conception, occur often in everyday life, and they are easiest

---

126 *Ibid* at 107.

127 *Ibid* at 107: "The predicate 'valid' (gultig) pertains to action norms and all the general normative propositions that express the meaning of such norms."

to explain and understand in such routine contexts.[128] Consider, for instance, that a man asks his partner to refrain from drinking alcohol while his parents visit them. The partner may refuse, asserting that her ability to do as she pleases should not be influenced by his parents' presence and preferences. She asks for the reasons behind his request, at which point the validity of his claim begins to get tested through a discourse. He explains that his father is a recovering alcoholic, and he does not want to prompt any temptation. Upon that explanation, the partner may agree to the validity of his request. If so, then the couple has reached a rational consensus through a discourse. The partner may also retort that the father will have to face alcohol temptation at some point. It may be beneficial for the couple to drink alcohol, as they normally would during the parents' visit so that the father can start to become accustomed to refraining from alcohol despite the actions of others. The man may accept this reasoning, and the couple will arrive at the rationally acceptable conclusion that they will not refrain from drinking during the parents' visit. The couple may decide to drink alcohol or to refrain from doing so, and both decisions can be rationally acceptable and valid outcomes. What, then, makes an outcome unacceptable? Suppose the man refuses to consider his partner's point of view and simply asserts that the couple will not drink during the parents' visit. That decision not to drink is not the product of a rational discourse, so the couple cannot be said to have arrived at a rationally acceptable outcome. The validity of their actions is rationally acceptable to all parties as a result of the rational discourse process, irrespective of any external judgment on the moral "rightness" of the outcome. David Dyzenhaus explains Habermas's point as follows:[129]

> What drives this process is what makes communication more than just an implicit threat to open hostilities in the face of disagreement. This is the assumption that there is something to the rightness beyond what we happen to think here and now. In the age of secularism, where

128 *Ibid* at 107–8: "'Rational discourse' should include any attempt to reach an understanding over problematic validity claims insofar as this takes place under conditions of communication that enable free processing of topics and contributions, information and reasons in the public space constituted by illocutionary obligations."

129 David Dyzenhaus, "The Legality of Legitimacy" (1996) 46 *University of Toronto Law Journal* 129 [Dyzenhaus, "Legality of Legitimacy."]

things are not made right by tradition, the only candidate we have for rightness is the beliefs we have in the light of our deliberations about our experience.

A similar process occurs, Habermas explains, when assessing the validity of a truth claim. What is claimed to be true can also be amenable to rational consent, just like the validity of the husband's request above. The validity of a truth claim cannot, in Habermas's conception, depend on substantive accuracy because "there is no 'natural' end to the chain of possible substantial reasons; one cannot exclude the possibility that new information and better reasons will be brought forward."[130] Rather, the criterion of the validity of truth claims is indistinguishable from the criterion for the propriety of the process of settling a claim to truth. Where the argumentative process embodies the ideal conditions of rational discourse, the settled claim can be taken as true, and the assent of the parties to the argument is valid. This should not be taken to mean that there is no such thing as "truth" that is independent of the outcome of a good procedure. Rather, it means that we can rationally accept the outcome of a claim of truth on the basis of the procedure that gave rise to that claim. This aspect of Habermas's thinking lends support to my orientation, given my starting point that the truth of a factual finding cannot be guaranteed, yet litigants are expected to assent to judicial factual determinations.

Habermas uses discourse theory's criteria for rational assessment of the validity of claims as the criteria for determining the rational acceptability of law. Analogous to his approach to testing validity claims, for Habermas, the acceptability of a law or adjudicative outcome does not depend on substantive correctness or accuracy (just as the validity of the husband's claim did not depend on its "rightness" and the validity of a truth claim does not depend on its actual accuracy) but on whether the process of arriving at the outcome reflects, as closely as possible, the conditions of rational discourse.[131]

What are, then, the conditions that can give rise to rationally motivated discourse, and rationally acceptable outcomes? The first and foundational feature of achieving rationally motivated assent is that the

---

130 Habermas, *Between Facts and Norms*, above note 117 at 226–27.
131 Lawrence Solum, "Procedural Justice" (2004) 78 *Southern California Law Review* 181 at 267–68 [Solum, "Procedural Justice"].

parties agreed with the claim of validity on the basis of reason alone, and not on the basis of coercion or other extraneous considerations.[132] In the example above, the partner agreed with the husband's request because of his reason, not because of any coercive influence that he asserted over her. Accordingly, a discourse process must be "immunized against repression and inequality."[133] It must ensure "equal communication rights for participants, it requires sincerity and, it must diffuse any kind of force other than the forceless force of the better arguments."[134]

Lawrence Solum has helpfully defined the necessary conditions of rational discourse in a formulation that was originally suggested by Robert Alexy, and then adopted by Habermas. Solum's presentation of the conditions of rational discourse is as follows:

1. Rule of Participation: Each person who is capable of engaging in communication and action is allowed to participate.

2. Rule of Equality of Communicative Opportunity: Each participant is given equal opportunity to communicate with respect to the following:

    a. Each participant is allowed to call into question any proposal;

    b. Each participant is allowed to introduce any proposal into the discourse; and

    c. Each participant is allowed to express attitudes, sincere beliefs, wishes, and needs.

3. Rule against Compulsion: No participant may be hindered by compulsion – whether arising from inside the discourse or outside of it – from making use of the rules secured under (1) and (2).[135]

Habermas explains that these rules of rational discourse are, on the one hand, necessary presuppositions — they simply cannot be avoided if a truly rational discourse is to take place.[136] It would, for instance,

---

132 Habermas, *Facts and Norms*, above note 117 at 227.

133 *Ibid* at 228.

134 Habermas, "Author's Reflections," above note 121 at 940.

135 Solum, "Procedural Justice," above note 131 at 270.

136 As Thomas McCarthy explains:

> The very act of participating in a discourse involves the supposition that genuine consensus is possible and that it can be distinguished from false consensus. If we did

be internally contradictory to say that a rationally motivated consensus was reached by lying, or by torturing all dissenting parties, or by disallowing certain parties from participating. At the same time, the conditions of rational discourse also represent an ideal.[137]

Democratic principles, for Habermas, most closely approximate the ideal conditions of rational discourse, and thereby provide the requisite legitimacy component to emergent laws.[138] "Specifically," Habermas writes, "the democratic principle states that only those statutes may claim legitimacy that can meet with the assent of all citizens in a discursive process of legislation that in turn has been legally constituted."[139] The guarantee that laws are a product of a rational discourse process provides legal subjects with a reason, independent of fear of coercion, to assent to the law. That reason is the law's legitimacy, which it derives as a result of emerging from a process that, as closely as possible, reflects the principle of rational discourse. Habermas explains:

> Valid legal norms are . . . legitimate in the sense that they additionally express an authentic self-understanding of the legal community, the fair consideration of the values and interests distributed in it, and the purposive-rational choice of strategies and means in the pursuit of policies.[140]

The virtue of the democratic principle, and of the rational discourse process generally, is that it ensures that all people who will be affected by the outcome had equal and free opportunity to engage in a sincere process of rational discussion leading to rational decision-making.[141]

---

not suppose this, then the very meaning of discourse would be called into question. In attempting to come to a rational decision about truth claim, we must suppose that the outcome of our discussion will be (or at least can be) the result simply of the force of the better argument and not of accidental or systematic constraints on communication.

Thomas, McCarthy, *The Critical Theory of Jürgen Habermas* (Cambridge, MA: MIT Press, 1978) at 306. Compare with David Dyzenhaus, "The Legality of Legitimacy," above note 129, pointing out the problems associated with the idealization that inheres in the supposition of a genuine consensus being achievable.

137 Stephen White, *Cambridge Companion to Habermas* (Cambridge: Cambridge University Press, 1995) at 44.

138 Habermas, *Between Facts and Norms*, above note 117 at 110.

139 *Ibid.*

140 *Ibid* at 156.

141 I note that the concept of a rational discourse procedure is, of course, an idealization. Canadian civil litigation systems do not emulate these theoretical ideals in practical terms.

Without these basic guarantees, a rational discourse process is not possible. But through them, all members affected by the outcome, treated as equal, free, rationally acting agents, have a reason to assent to the law's authority beyond fear of enforcement. That, Habermas suggests, makes for a stable society.

David Dyzenhaus has highlighted an important point of vulnerability in Habermas's theory. He suggests that there are potentially dangerous impracticalities/idealizations in Habermas's application of the concept of rational discourse to a theory of legal legitimacy. Dyzenhaus reiterates that the principle underpinning Habermas's theory, based on the concept of ideal speech conditions as explained above, is that in order to determine right action, individuals must engage in a noncoercive argumentative process, which entails that they commit to understanding the others' viewpoints and having their own challenged, all with a view to coming to a final agreement that will bind the participants.[142] This deliberative process results in a valid outcome. The problem, Dyzenhaus suggests, occurs when applying this ideal concept of rational discourse in the legal context.

Habermas's notion of true communicative action implies that all participants accept the ideal speech conditions and ultimately come to a consensus that is grounded in reason. As such, the outcome does not require coercion to ensure compliance. But such universal acceptance is impractical in a legal arena, and it can be dangerous to underemphasize the potential for disagreement about legal outcomes.[143] Dyzenhaus explains:[144]

> Given the fact of pluralism, it either seems utterly impractical or, if one attempts to bring it down to earth, it seems dangerous. It is dangerous just because a claim that any institutional order realizes this ideal seems to entail that those who disagree are simply wrong to do so. The dissenters exclude themselves from the community of participants

---

One needs only to turn to the access to justice discourses in Canadian legal scholarship to learn that inability to participate due to inaccessibility to legal systems pose significant challenges to maintaining the justifiability of Canadian legal systems. My purpose in this project is not to assess the civil litigation processes from a pragmatic perspective. My aim is to outline what principles should guide the Canadian civil litigation system, and how they should manifest when it comes to judicial fact-finding.

142 Dyzenhaus, "The Legitimacy of Legality," above note 12 at 167.

143 *Ibid* at 167–68.

144 *Ibid* at 167.

by their disagreement, and hence it can be claimed that there is no coercion within the community. Those who disagree find themselves relegated to being at best marginal disruptions to the community of reasoners.

Dyzenhaus suggests, in my reading, that applying discourse theory as a concept that can legitimize legality can be problematic if it is understood as resulting in universal acceptability of legal outcomes, because that has the effect of disengaging with the inevitability of dissent *after* a law is rendered. The way around this problem, Dyzenhaus suggests, is to abandon the ideal of universalizability, because it is an impractical aspiration in a context of secularism along with plurality: "Secularism precludes appeal to religion or tradition, while pluralism requires recognition of the fact that not all will agree to any solution, no matter how reasonable."[145] Rather than striving to be universal, Dyzenhaus suggests, law should meet a threshold of "general interpretability," which requires that the law be public and understandable[146] so that it can be subjected to continued dialogue even after it is rendered:[147]

> In meeting that threshold, it does not attract the assent of everyone, since even the most reasonable citizens will disagree on what should be done. But what they can agree on, if they wish to conduct their affairs rationally, is that decisions should be taken as a result of deliberation and then made subject to further deliberation in light of experience.

Dyzenhaus uses the concept of deliberation itself to manoeuvre around the above noted problem. In making this turn, he seems to combine Habermas's approach with some of Fuller's deepest insights.[148] Generality, publicity, and intelligibility (all of which are required in order for law to be continually deliberated on) are key features of Fuller's

---

145   *Ibid* at 171.

146   *Ibid* at 173: "In short, publicizability, or meeting a threshold of general interpretability, is a precondition of a communication being properly public. Not only does it have to have the marks of publicity that make it recognizable as law – positivism's exclusive focus – but its content must be understandable or interpretable by the public to which it is addressed."

147   *Ibid* at 176.

148   Dyzenhaus notes his turn to Fuller throughout, and specifically points out that Habermas "can take a more direct route from the idea of deliberation to the idea of legitimacy of legality ... [a route that has] already been elaborated independently by two legal philosophers, Lon Fuller and the Weimar public lawyer Hermann Heller." *Ibid* at 169.

internal morality of law principles. As noted above, Fuller's principles implicitly recognize legal subjects as active, rational participants in legal discourse, much like Dyzenhaus does when he calls for continued public deliberation about the law.

Dyzenhaus's worthwhile contributions highlight, again, the impracticality of achieving perfection (defined here as universal acceptance) in the legal order. This is a helpful and relevant reminder, given that my project is premised on the impossibility of guaranteeing factual accuracy (and therefore universal acceptance, presumably) of judicial fact-finding decisions. Dyzenhaus explains that we do not need to expect universal acceptance in order to achieve legitimacy. This reminder is important, as is Dyzenhaus's insight as to the way forward. The idea that laws should be continually subjected to public debates and deliberation serves as an important recognition of law's fallibility, and accounts for the potential for dissent in a manner that is at least more clear and express that Habermas provided.

Ultimately, Dyzenhaus's proposal provides a necessary pragmatism to Habermas's sometimes extremely theoretical commitments. For now, most importantly, Dyzenhaus arrives at the same key principles that underpin both Fuller's and Habermas's commitments. "As both Fuller and Heller saw, nothing more is needed," he states, "to found this project than a commitment to institutionalizing the recognition by all citizens of each other as free and equal."[149]

C. Summing up Fuller and Habermas and Their Relation to Hart and Raz

Fuller and Habermas offer ideas of law that align with my ultimate goal of explaining why we, as members of a political community, should accept the validity of adjudicative fact-finding. The positivist positions of Hart and Raz, while undoubtedly insightful, do not further my aim, because of their resistance to incorporating a normative concept into legal validity. Fuller and Habermas, on the other hand, offer a concept of law that accommodates the necessary aspects of positivism — the inability to make legal validity contingent on the substantive morality of the content of each law — but they pick up where Hart and Raz's positivist theories fall short.

---

149   *Ibid* at 177.

Fuller's "completion" of Hart's theory is fairly express. He complains that Hart fails to give any substance or definition to the secondary rules of law-making, despite their being the foundation of legal validity. He sets out, then, to offer that substantiation through the internal morality of law principles, through which he offers a reason for why the law warrants the authoritative demands it makes, an answer that positivist jurisprudence does not turn toward. I interpret Habermas's theory as providing a similar "completion" to Raz's version of positivism.

Recall that for Raz, a law is a directive that is endorsed by an authoritative institution that makes a claim to having legitimate authority. But although law makes a claim to legitimate authority, it is not necessary that law achieve that legitimacy. Since status as law is dependent on a claim to legitimate authority, Raz's theory could provide a plausible answer for why the law's authority is justifiable if he provided some grounding for its claim of legitimacy. The first step at grounding the claim to legitimate authority is to draw a distinction between determining whether the authority is *in fact* legitimate versus whether *the claim* of legitimate authority is itself legitimate. In order to substantiate the claim to legitimate authority, without resorting to determining whether the claim is correct (i.e., without determining if there actually is legitimate authority), amounts to an assessment of whether the claim to legitimate authority is actually genuine.

To test the genuineness of the claim (without testing the truth of the claim itself), the inquiry must shift from a substantive determination of whether the law is *in fact* the most rational outcome, to whether the legal institution is sincerely *aimed toward* arriving at the most rational outcome. In other words, the relevant question in order to substantiate the claim to legitimate authority, is *how* the institution purports to discharge that claim, not whether the institution actually discharges it. If the procedures that an institution follows orient the institution toward the aspiration of providing directives that enable conformity with reason, which constitutes legitimate authority in Raz's conception, then the *claim* to legitimate authority may be vindicated.

Even though the claim to legitimate authority is the necessary characteristic of a valid legal system in his theory, Raz does not explain how a legal system's claim to legitimate authority is grounded or how it can be tested.[150] Habermas's theory does. The discourse principle provides the procedural characteristics that delineate a genuine rational discourse, where parties are sincerely motivated to arrive at rational and reasoned outcomes. When the elements of a rational discourse are present, the parties to the communication can defensibly claim that they aspire to arrive at an outcome that best conforms with reason. In the same way, testing a legal system's claim to legitimate authority can be accomplished by considering whether the elements of rational discourse are present, to the most feasible extent, in its decision-making processes. If so, then the claim to legitimate authority can be vindicated.

CONCLUSION

My conclusion in chapter 1 was that the legitimacy of factual judicial outcomes is contingent on consistent adherence to the legal procedures of fact-finding. This conclusion invoked the question of whether there must be some features that are present in legal procedures that enable their legitimizing role. The aim of this chapter was to find an answer to that question and, thereby, substantiate the claim of procedural legitimacy.

In my discussion of positivist approaches, I intended to uncover the shortcomings of an approach to legal validity that does not simultaneously account for legitimacy. Through that commentary, I have reaffirmed the conclusion that legitimacy must be a procedural phenomenon. This claim is supported in Lon Fuller's and Jürgen Habermas's accounts of law. Their viewpoints have provided grounding for my upcoming discussions about the necessary features of legitimate procedures for adjudicative fact-finding.

For both Fuller and Habermas, law, being an integrative guide for human conduct, requires a vindicating virtue. For both, that virtue is not contingent on adherence to any standard of morality or substantive correctness, but is a procedural concept. The process of law-making, in

---

150　Of course, Raz does maintain that since it is the nature of law that it claims legitimate authority, a source of law in a given legal system must also be *capable* of possessing legitimate authority: Joseph Raz, "Authority, Law and Morality," in Raz, *Authority of Law*, above note 40 at 215: a legal system "must be a system of a kind which is capable in principle of possessing the requisite moral properties of authority." My point here is to note that Raz does not elaborate on how to test whether an institution's capacity for legitimate authority is being genuinely exercised.

both accounts, must manifest respect for legal subjects as free-acting rational agents. If so, then legal validity has legitimacy, and legal subjects would have a reason to accept the authority of a law on the basis of its legal validity.

As Fuller and Habermas maintain, just as the rational assent of subjects depends on the procedural qualities of law rather than its substantive moral qualities, similarly, litigants can rationally accept adjudicative facts that are potentially substantively inaccurate if the process of arriving at those facts genuinely respects their status as free-acting agents. In the next chapter, I open with a discussion of Fuller's and Habermas's relatively brief explanations for how their concepts of law generally translate in the adjudicative sphere. With that guidance as my starting point, I will consider how those concepts can be transferred into the specific context of adjudicative fact-finding procedures. That will culminate in a notion that consistent adherence to particular fact-finding procedures infuses judicial fact-finding decisions with legitimacy, such that their authority is warranted. So, what comes next is a transition from general legal theory to applied jurisprudence in the specific arena of fact-finding.

CHAPTER THREE

Procedural Legitimacy in Adjudicative Fact-Finding

INTRODUCTION

This chapter brings us to the central aim of this book: delineating the key characteristics of a legitimate fact-finding process. It comprises an application of the jurisprudential analysis of law and its legitimacy in the previous chapters to the question of how and on what basis adjudicative fact-finding procedures can be considered legitimate.

In chapter 2, I concluded that law must have an in-built source of legitimacy that forms the basis upon which legal subjects can rationally accept the law and its authoritative implications. In arriving at that conclusion, I adopted the jurisprudential insights of Lon Fuller and Jürgen Habermas. Fuller and Habermas both maintain that the legitimacy of law depends on the process of becoming law, and not an assessment of its substantive content. If that process embodies a genuine respect for citizens as autonomous agents, then the law is capable of eliciting the rational assent of its subjects. On that basis, its authoritative nature is grounded, even if the law appears substantively disagreeable. Along those lines, I maintain that the legitimacy of judicial fact-finding is also sourced in the process of making factual determinations. Litigants can rationally accept adjudicative fact-finding on the basis of an application of a fact-finding process that genuinely

---

I first explored and presented the themes presented in this chapter (particularly in relation to how Habermas's theory applies to fact-finding processes) in Nayha Acharya, "Deciding, 'What Happened?' When We Don't Really Know: Finding Theoretical Grounding for Legitimate Judicial Fact-Finding" (2020) 33 *Canadian JL & Jurisprudence* 1.

respects them as free-acting agents. And just as the substance of a law is not itself determinative of the law's legitimacy, the substantive accuracy of adjudicative fact-finding does not determine the legitimacy of that factual finding.

The goal of this chapter is to uncover how maintaining respect for litigants as autonomous agents can be reflected in judicial fact-finding. This provides the answer for the central question of why and on what basis community members can rationally accept judicial outcomes despite the inescapable reality of risk of factual inaccuracy.

Given my alignment with Fuller's and Habermas's jurisprudential thinking, in Part 1, I consider how they transfer their concepts of legal legitimacy into the adjudicative sphere. Using their foundational insights as a springboard, in Part 2, I delineate the necessary features of legitimate adjudicative fact-finding.

I conclude that demonstrable respect for human agency in fact-finding procedures has two categories of necessary features: factual reliability and participation rights. Judicial fact-finding should be factually reliable in the sense that the fact-finding process embodies a genuine effort toward achieving accurate factual determinations. Below, I expand further on what that entails and suggest how to assess the justifiability of compromises to the likelihood of factual accuracy and manage the risk of inaccuracy while maintaining a genuine commitment to getting the outcomes factually right. Along with maintaining factual reliability, in order to give full expression to respecting human agency, fact-finding procedures must include meaningful participation rights for affected parties.

This chapter concludes with the assertion that when fact-finding procedures that reflect respect for litigants as rational agents are applied consistently, the fact-finding system is legitimate, and the authority of a judicial factual determination can be rationally accepted despite the risk of inaccuracy.

PART 1. FULLER AND HABERMAS ON ADJUDICATION

A. Lon Fuller on Adjudication: Participation, Rationality, and Agency

Lon Fuller's most comprehensive discussion on adjudication is found in his article, "The Forms and Limits of Adjudication," where he offers his study of the adjudicative process, its aims, and its necessary elements.[1] Fuller's analysis of adjudication takes a similar form to his analysis of legality. In his discussion of the nature of law, Fuller starts with the premise that law's purpose is to guide human conduct, and then describes the distinguishing elements of law that enable it to discharge that purpose. From there, he infers the implicit normative values contained within those elements. That leads to his presentation of the eight principles of legality as the "internal morality of law."[2] In a similar form, Fuller premises his analysis of adjudication on his conception of the purpose of adjudication, then discerns the features of adjudication that are conducive to that purpose. Then, he infers the implicit normative commitments contained within those features.

For Fuller, adjudication is both a mechanism of authoritative resolution of legal disputes and a method of "social ordering."[3] Just like law generally, judicial decisions guide human conduct — parties will tend to govern themselves upon consideration of either actual judicial reasons or upon some estimation of a likely judicial response.[4]

The distinguishing feature of adjudication as a method of social ordering is that parties participate through their "presentation of proofs and reasoned arguments."[5] It is that distinctive form of participation that, for Fuller, holds the key to determining the optimal form of adjudication and its normative value:

> This whole analysis will derive from one simple proposition, namely, that the distinguishing characteristic of adjudication lies in the fact

---

1   Lon Fuller & Kenneth Winston, "The Forms and Limits of Adjudication" (1978) 92(2) *Harvard Law Review* 353 at 354 [Fuller, "Forms and Limits"]: "By the forms of adjudication I refer to the ways in which adjudication may be organized and conducted . . . . In general, the questions posed for consideration are: What are the permissible variations in the forms of adjudication? When has its nature been so altered that we are compelled to speak of an 'abuse' or a 'perversion' of the adjudicative process?"

2   Lon Fuller, *The Morality of Law* (New Haven, CT and London: Yale University Press, 1964), c 3 [Fuller, *Morality of Law*]. I have summarized Fuller's concept of the internal morality of law in chapter 2, part 2A.

3   Fuller explains, "It is customary to think of adjudication as a means of settling disputes or controversies. . . . More fundamentally, however, adjudication should be viewed as a form of social ordering, as a way in which the relations of men to one another are governed and regulated." Fuller, "Forms and Limits," above note 1 at 357. See also Robert Bone, "Lon Fuller's Theory of Adjudication and The False Dichotomy Between Dispute Resolution and Public Law Models of Litigation" (1995) 75 *Boston University Law Review* 1273 for his argument that Fuller's theory of adjudication has sometimes been mischaracterized as being fundamentally a dispute resolution model [Bone, "Fuller's Theory of Adjudication"]. That characterization, Bone argues, has resulted in a misunderstanding of Fuller's normative commitments.

4   Fuller, "Forms and Limits," above note 1.

5   *Ibid* at 363.

that it confers on the affected party a peculiar form of participation in the decision, that of presenting proofs and reasoned arguments for a decision in his favour. Whatever heightens the significance of this participation lifts adjudication toward its optimum expression. Whatever destroys the meaning of that participation destroys the integrity of adjudication itself. . . . The purpose of this paper is to trace out the . . . implications of the proposition that the distinguishing feature of adjudication lies in the mode of participation which is afforded to the party affected by the decision.[6]

What, then, is so significant about the nature of adjudicative participation? For Fuller, enabling parties to present their own evidence and argument for the purpose of adjudicating their claims implies an underpinning commitment to the rationality of a judicial outcome. He argues that if arriving at a reasoned, rational outcome were not a foundational feature of adjudication, then opportunities to present evidence and arguments to an impartial decision-maker would be superfluous and insincere.[7] In other words, the fact that presentation of evidence and reasons is allowed means that the decision-maker will *rely on* evidence and reasons. When a decision-maker commits to relying on evidence and argument to arrive at a conclusion, the implication is that they are committed to making a rational decision. Expressing this insight, Fuller describes adjudication as, "a device which gives formal and institutional expression to the influence of reasoned argument in human affairs. . . . A decision which is the product of reasoned argument must be prepared itself to meet the test of reason."[8]

Fuller's portrayal of adjudication as a method of arriving at a rational outcome challenged the view that grew from Hume's philosophy (which, Fuller notes, seems to have been gaining more widespread acceptance at the time), which claimed that empirical/scientific inquiry and logical inference were the only arenas where human reason could find meaningful expression.[9] Fuller, however, finds this view improperly restrictive, because it excludes "rational discourse," which for Fuller, also embraces the capacity for human rationality and constitutes a valid

---

6   *Ibid* at 364.

7   *Ibid* at 365–72. A specific example appears at 367: "If, as in adjudication, the only mode of participation consists in the opportunity to present proofs and arguments, the purpose of this participation is frustrated, and the whole proceeding becomes a farce, should the decision that emerges make no pretense whatever to rationality."

8   *Ibid* at 366–67.

9   *Ibid* at 379–80.

method of arriving at a reasoned outcome.[10] It is that process of rational discourse that constitutes the framework for the essential conditions of adjudication.[11]

There is not, unfortunately, much elaboration on the notion of "rational discourse" and its necessary features in Fuller's writing, but his message is clear that rational discourse occurs in the adjudicative context by providing a space for full participation of partisan parties.[12] Accordingly, various procedural elements of adjudicative decision-making can be tested on the basis of whether they "affec[t] adversely the meaning of the affected party's participation in the decision by proofs and reasoned arguments?"[13] For instance, an adjudicator that had already made up their mind before hearing the parties' evidence and argument, or an adjudicator who had some interest in a particular outcome, would be unacceptable because those conditions would diminish the meaningfulness of the litigants' participation rights. If so, then the strong commitment to rationality in adjudication is diminished as a result of the compromise to the optimal process of adjudication.[14]

Fuller's critical insight is that adjudication is committed to rationality, evidenced by the form of participation that adjudication enables — presentation of evidence and argument by affected parties forms the basis of the adjudicative decision. This insight can be understood more holistically if Fuller's discussion of adjudication is read in light of jurisprudential thinking on legality generally. In chapter 2, I endorsed the reading of Fuller's jurisprudence that understands his central theme to be that law-making procedures that embody respect for legal subjects as autonomous agents ground both the law's authoritative demands and

---

10　*Ibid* at 381.

11　*Ibid*: "However we may define this third area [i.e., rational discourse], a rigid adherence to the Humean view is, I believe, destructive of any understanding of the problems of adjudication. It not only falsifies the conditions essential for the effective operation of adjudication but distorts the meaning of any adjudicative process that is functioning successfully."

12　This is consistent with Robert Bone's assessment of Fuller's views on adjudication. As he states, for Fuller, adjudication enables people to "motivate reason by purposive interaction and to provide a sufficiently broad field for the free play of ideas. With lively competition, the ideas that prevailed would be those that appealed to the sense of rightness and reasonableness that all people shared as part of their capacity for reason." Robert Bone, "Fuller's Theory of Adjudication," above note 3 at 1289.

13　Fuller, "Forms and Limits," above note 1 at 382.

14　Fuller notes this problem within his discussion of why an arbitrator should not "act on his own motion in initiating [a] case," in "Forms and Limits," above note 1 at 385.

elicit the subjects' acceptance of them.[15] In other words, that respect for human agency, implicit in the necessarily formal principles of legality, provides law with legitimacy. Although Fuller does not expressly discuss this in "Forms and Limits," in my reading, that same respect for human agency can be defensibly read in as his implicit commitment in the adjudicative sphere as well.

First, Fuller notes that participation through proof and argument is inherent to adjudication.[16] That implicitly characterizes litigants as free-acting, rational agents that are *capable of* presenting their own cases on their own terms. Optimal adjudication, Fuller advises, preserves their right to do just that.[17] Second, the value that Fuller places on the commitment to rational adjudicative outcomes implies, I suggest, that affected parties *deserve* and are entitled to rational outcomes. That implication embraces respect for human agency. Just as Fuller's account of legality stipulates that subjects cannot be subjected to irrational laws (like those that simply cannot be obeyed, or those that are retrospective) due to the associated affront to human agency, his analysis of adjudication similarly stipulates that litigants should not be subject to irrational adjudicative decisions. That would amount to an affront to their position as free, rationally-acting individuals who can only be justifiably guided in their actions if that guidance is itself rational.

This reading of Fuller on adjudication finds some express support in his comments in *The Law in Quest of Itself* where he refers to adjudicative law as a system of "autonomous order" and comments that:[18]

> The common law imperceptibly becomes part of men's common beliefs, and exercises frictionless control over their activities which derives its sanction not from its source but from a conviction of its essential rightness.

This comment, taken together with Fuller's discussion of adjudication as a mechanism of achieving a rational outcome, suggests a number of normative commitments. First, for Fuller, adjudication needs a normative sanction. That is, community members should be able to accept the adjudicative system and its outcomes for a reason beyond the bare reason that it is an authoritative pronouncement of a judge.

---

15   See chapter 1, Part 2A.

16   Fuller, "Forms and Limits," above note 1 at 365–72.

17   *Ibid.*

18   Lon Fuller, *The Law in Quest of Itself* (Boston: Beacon Press, 1940) at 134.

The adjudicative decision can be sanctioned on the basis of it being right. And second, for Fuller, "essential rightness" is synonymous with a rational decision based on the evidence and argument presented by affected parties. Taken together, this supports the interpretation that Fuller's position is that adjudicative decision-making should demonstrably respect the litigants as autonomous agents whose sanction matters.[19]

Fuller's ideas set the stage for an argument that the right process for adjudicative fact-finding must (among other things) maintain the effectiveness of a party's right to present their own evidence and argument. But his themes of participation, its connection to rationality, along with the implicit commitment to respect for human agency are underdeveloped and somewhat ambiguous. For instance, Fuller is clear that meaningful participation rights are indicative of a commitment to a rational outcome, but if it is the rationality of the outcome that is the key normative feature of adjudication, is it possible to endorse a system of decision-making that provides rational results without promising participation rights? Moreover, although Fuller is clearly committed to the idea that adjudication should generate reasoned or rational decisions, he does not provide much by way of defining what exactly he means by "reasoned" and "rational."

Habermas's application of discourse theory to law contains strikingly similar themes of participation and rationality as Fuller's account.[20] But these core concepts are developed with more precision, more substantive content, and more express normative heft in Habermas's discussion. Accordingly, some of the concepts introduced earlier by Fuller gain a more complete expression through reference to Habermas's demonstration of how rational discourse finds expression in adjudication and yields legitimate judicial outcomes.

---

19   Explaining Fuller's principles of law in relation to adjudicative process, Jeremy Waldron explains that they "capture a deep and important sense associated foundationally with the idea of a legal system, that law is a mode of governing people that treats them with respect, as though they had a view or perspective of their own to present on the application of the norm to their conduct and situation." See Jeremy Waldron, "The Rule of Law and the Importance of Procedure" (2011) 50 *Nomos* 3 at 13–14.

20   Despite which Habermas offers Fuller only a passing reference as an example of an (unnamed) theorist who has analyzed the "rational implications" of the "classical concept of legal certainty," in Jürgen Habermas, *Between Facts and Norms: Contributions to Discourse Theory of Law and Democracy* (Cambridge, MA: MIT Press, 1996) at 220 [Habermas, *Between Facts and Norms*].

B. Habermas on Adjudication: Rational Discourse

Like Fuller, Habermas's conception of adjudication develops in a parallel course to his jurisprudential presentation of law, its purpose, and its necessary features in light of that purpose. As I have illustrated in chapter 2, for Habermas, law plays an integrative and stabilizing role in society and, in order to discharge this role, law must have two elements: certainty or facticity, and legitimacy.[21] Law must be certain in the sense that subjects should know (or be able to know) what the enforceable rules in the society are, and to know that those rules will indeed be enforced. Second, laws must also have a normative quality that grounds the legal subject's rational acceptance of them.[22] Without that normative quality, law may be coercive, but would not function as a socially integrative agent.[23]

In Habermas's theory, a law is rationally acceptable when it is a product of a rational discourse process. When a law-making process embodies, as far as possible, an equal and free exchange of information and reasons, and participants are sincerely committed to arriving at an outcome motivated by the force of reason alone, the emergent law can be said to be rationally acceptable, irrespective of its ultimate substantive content. Accordingly, the legitimacy of the outcome depends on a process where legal subjects are treated as free acting agents whose voices matter equally.

A parallel line of reasoning gives rise to Habermas's application of discourse theory to adjudication.[24] First, adjudicative law plays a socially integrative function, just like legislative law.[25] Legislative law establishes a system of rights and adjudication interprets and gives content to that system of rights.[26] Consequently, just as the two aspects of

---

21   See my discussion in chapter 2, Part 2, and Habermas, *Between Facts and Norms, ibid* at 197–203.

22   *Ibid* at 198. Habermas refers to the normative element of law sometimes as "validity" and sometimes as "legitimacy." The normative element is in line with what I have defined as the concept of "legitimacy," so for the sake of clarity and consistency, I use "legitimacy" in my discussion of Habermas's account.

23   *Ibid.*

24   I note that Habermas's grounding is in the German civil law tradition. In my view, this does not affect the applicability of his insights to the context of legal fact-finding.

25   *Ibid.*

26   This is consistent with Klaus Gunther's explanation of Habermas's theory: "Rational discourse is the internal procedural structure of legislation as interpreting and shaping the system of rights as it is laid down in the constitution. According to Habermas, legal

facticity/certainty and legitimacy must be manifest in legislative law, they must also be present in adjudicative law:

> Both guarantees, certainty and legitimacy, must be simultaneously redeemed at the level of judicial decision making. . . . In order to fulfill the socially integrative function of the legal order and the legitimacy claim of law, court rulings must satisfy simultaneously the conditions of *consistent decision-making* and *rational acceptability*.[27]

As the excerpt above indicates, Habermas advises that consistent decision-making ensures the certainty of law, at least in part, by maintaining a predictable and equally applicable application of law. But that basic value of formal justice through treating like cases alike is not itself sufficient to establish adjudicative legitimacy. Along with maintaining the minimal respect for equal treatment through bare formalism, judicial decisions must also be "right" in the sense of being rationally acceptable.[28] If not, the socially integrative function that is as much relevant to adjudicative law as it is to legislative law could not be discharged.

The task of his theory of adjudication, Habermas explains, is to harmonize the two elements of certainty and legitimacy, but as he notes, that harmonization is not always easy.[29] The difficulty is clearly discernible where legal principles are developed through common law. In the arena of tortious injury, courts have, for instance, introduced new tests for causation into Canadian law to complement the "but for" test,[30] or have extended tort liability to include psychiatric injury when it was

---

adjudication also 'interprets and shapes' the system of rights within another form of communication, the legal discourse of application." Klaus Gunther, "Legal Adjudication and Democracy: Some Remarks on Dworkin and Habermas" (1995) 3(4) *European Journal of Legal Philosophy* 36 at 47. This also bears a similarity to Fuller's notion that adjudicative outcomes guide human conduct in a way comparative to legislative law.

27 Habermas, *Between Facts and Norms*, above note 20 at 198 (emphasis in the original). For Habermas, certainty is a derivative of the facticity of law, and legitimacy is derivative of rational acceptability: "On the one hand, established law guarantees the enforcement of legally expected behavior and therewith the certainty of law. On the other hand, rational procedures for making and applying law promise to legitimate the expectations that are stabilized in this way; the norms *deserve* legal obedience."

28 This bears a notable similarity to Fuller's perception of what constitutes a "right" decision, as discussed above.

29 Habermas, *Between Facts and Norms*, above note 20 at 198.

30 See for instance *Athey v Leonati* [1996] 3 SCR 458, *Resurfice v Hanke* 2007 SCC 7, *Clements v Clements* 2012 SCC 32, and *Henry v British Columbia (Attorney General)* 2015 SCC 24.

once limited to physical injury.[31] The implication is that such new principles are "right," yet where there are shifts in what constitutes "right" law in Canada, legal certainty becomes compromised.

Habermas explains the tension between certainty and rightness as a problem of legal indeterminacy. Legislated law is necessarily general in character, so its content in terms of how it would apply in specific situations is not always clearly ascertainable. In that sense, the content of a legislated law is not fully defined, and judges are tasked with providing it with further definition through application.[32]

For Habermas, given that law and its application can be indeterminate, it is not possible to guarantee a consistent and predictable "right" interpretation of exactly the nature of the rights protected by general laws especially in novel situations. This is because the rights guaranteed by laws are not empirical facts and are not discernible through some type of determinative empirical test.[33] Rather, the correct expression of a particular right is subject to argument and competing reasons in favour of one interpretation over another. As Habermas explains, "there is no "natural" end to the chain of possible substantial reasons; one cannot exclude the possibility that new information and better reasons will be brought forward."[34] Accordingly, a singular right answer does not necessarily exist.[35] This gives rise to what Habermas calls "the rationality problem": "how can the application of a contingently emergent law be carried out with both internal consistency and rational external justification, so as to guarantee simultaneously *the certainty of law* and its *rightness?*"[36]

This question that Habermas poses in light of legal indeterminacy parallels my purpose of reconciling the analogous tension that arises in adjudication due to *factual* indeterminacy. Just as judges are tasked with making authoritative conclusions with respect to the sometimes uncertain question, "what is the law?," they are also tasked with authoritatively resolving the often uncertain question, "what happened?" Even in

---

31   See for instance, *Mustapha v Culligan of Canada Ltd* [2008] 2 SCR 114.

32   Habermas, *Between Facts and Norms*, above note 20 at 198–99.

33   *Ibid* at 226.

34   *Ibid* at 227.

35   Habermas's notion of no right answer can be contrasted with Ronald Dworkin's position, which maintains the necessity and possibility of a right, or at least, best answer. See chapter 1 for my discussion of Dworkin's approach. For Habermas's discussion of Dworkin's theory, see Habermas, *Between Facts and Norms*, above note 20 at 203–22.

36   *Ibid* at 199 [emphasis in original].

cases where the applicable legal principles are generally agreed upon, as in my arena of liability for tortious injury, resolving the relevant factual questions is often arduous. For instance, while the general framework of tort law may not be at issue, determining the cause of an injury can involve consideration of contradicting medical expert opinions; determining financial losses can similarly involve making sense of challenging and potentially conflicting actuarial evidence. Given the inevitability of factual uncertainty and indeterminacy, accurate resolution to these factual questions cannot be guaranteed. How, then, can the adjudicative system reconcile the need for a final and certain legal outcome along with the need for a "correct" resolution of the dispute?

Habermas reconciles the certainty and legitimacy issue by turning to the discursive principle that he applies to law generally. My goal is to use those insights as the starting point for understanding how to reconcile the comparable tension that arises in adjudication due to indeterminate or uncertain factual questions.

Habermas's move is to transfer both elements, certainty and rightness (i.e., legitimacy), from outcome to process. Rather than insisting on the existence of a particular substantively right answer, Habermas's theory places the rightness of the outcome within the process of arriving at that outcome: "Procedural rights," he explains, "guarantee each legal person the claim to a fair procedure that in turn guarantees not certainty of outcome but a discursive clarification of the pertinent facts and legal questions."[37] In other words, the certainty component does not guarantee any certain outcome, but it does guarantee that the outcome will be the product of a certain *procedure*.

Of course, satisfaction of the certainty element in this way is essentially an expression of formal justice, and does not account fully for the "rightness" guarantee, which requires a stronger normative commitment. That normative commitment is also located in the realm of process — legitimacy is imported into the judicial outcome via the virtues of the process of arriving at the outcome. As Habermas puts it, "procedural principles that secure the validity of the outcome of a procedurally fair decision-making practice require internal justification."[38] That is, given that process is the source of the rightness of a legal outcome, that process itself needs to be a justifiable

---

37   *Ibid* at 220.
38   *Ibid* at 225.

one. The internal justification of the procedural principles constitutes the "rightness" or legitimacy guarantee. When an internally justified procedure is consistently employed for the purpose of adjudicative decision-making, the outcome contains not only the certainty guarantee, but also the legitimacy guarantee on which legal outcomes are contingent.

That internal justification, Habermas explains, comes from the principles of discourse theory. Just as the approximation of the discourse principles within democratic process gives rise to the rational acceptability of law in general, adjudicative procedures that approximate discourse principles give rise to the rational acceptability of judicial outcomes.[39] Accordingly, Habermas's theory postulates that "'rightness' means rational acceptability supported by good reasons,"[40] which is attainable through an approximation of discourse principles. And certainty is achieved through a guaranteed, consistent adherence to these procedures in the resolution of legal disputes.

How, then, can the discourse principles be reflected in the adjudicative process? In its ideal manifestation, a rational discourse will contain a number of presumptive preconditions. The process will:[41]

1. Prevent a rationally unmotivated termination of argumentation;[42]

2. Secure both freedom in the choice of topics and inclusion of the best information and reasons through universal and equal access to, as well as equal and symmetrical participation in argumentation;

3. Exclude every kind of coercion — whether originating outside the process of reaching understanding or within it — other than

---

39 *Ibid* at 226: As Habermas puts it, "A discourse theory of law … relies on a strong concept of procedural rationality that locates the properties constitutive of a decision's validity not only in the logicosemantic dimension of constructing arguments and connecting statements but also in the pragmatic dimension of the justification process itself."

40 *Ibid*. (Habermas's statement here is somewhat obtuse because it seems redundant to express that rational acceptability must be supported by good reasons, as good reasons are inherent to rational acceptability.)

41 *Ibid* at 230, citing Robert Alexy, *A Theory of Legal Argumentation: The Theory of Rational Discourse as Theory of Legal Justification*, translated by Ruth Adler and Neil MacCormick (Oxford: Oxford University Press, 1989).

42 I take this statement to mean that if a discourse is terminated for any reason other than rational assent of parties (for instance, termination due to frustration, hurt, or fatigue), it cannot be considered a true rational discourse.

that of the better argument, so that all motives except that of the cooperative search for truth are neutralized.

Naturally these principles cannot be reflected in adjudication absolutely given the practical restrictions of timely and economically feasible dispute resolution.[43] Rather, those ideal conditions provide guidance to the effect that justifiable procedural conditions should "ensure that all the relevant reasons and information available for a given issue at a particular time are in no way suppressed, that is, they can develop their inherent force for rational motivation."[44] Just as the ideal discourse conditions protect against unequal ability to participate, the requisite features of adjudicative decision-making calls for free and equal ability for affected members to put forth arguments and reasons, bearing in mind the practical realities involved in maintaining adjudicative efficacy. As Habermas puts it:

> Procedural law does not regulate normative-legal discourse as such but secures, in the temporal, social, and substantive dimensions, the institutional framework that *clears the way* for processes of communication governed by the logic of application discourses.[45]

Put another way, adjudicative procedural rules are a mechanism for ensuring a place where the essence of rational discourse can be maintained, limited by the pragmatics of legal adjudication. They "institutionally carve out an internal space for the free exchange of arguments in an application discourse."[46] In doing so, they maintain that the judicial outcome will be rationally motivated by the evidence and argument presented by affected parties, and the outcomes, therefore, have a basis for acceptance. Accordingly, the adjudicative procedures are internally justified when they treat parties as equal and free autonomous agents who are entitled to present their cases, and who are entitled to rational decisions respecting their legal entitlements and obligations.

---

43   Habermas, *Between Facts and Norms*, above note 20 at 235. "Practical realities" may also involve indiscretions including adversarial attempts at thwarting fact-finding. I discuss this briefly in chapter 4 in the context of the role of lawyers and experts when fact-finding depends on technical or scientific evidence.

44   *Ibid* at 227.

45   *Ibid* at 235 [emphasis in the original].

46   *Ibid.*

C. Summing up Fuller and Habermas on Adjudication

Adopting the insights of Fuller and Habermas, adjudicative legitimacy lies in the *rationality* of the judicial outcome. In keeping with their normative commitments regarding law generally, as presented in chapter 2, rationality of outcome is expressed through an adjudicative process that demonstrably recognizes legal subjects as autonomous agents by preserving their right to present evidence and arguments in advancement of their own claims. The assurance of a sincerely rationally motivated outcome, as evidenced through a process that relies on the evidence and argument freely presented by affected parties, provides a normative grounding — legitimacy — for the authority of judicial decisions.

Fuller's and Habermas's commentaries on adjudication provide the grounding for my ultimate question of locating the source of legitimacy of judicial resolution of factual indeterminacy. Although Fuller and Habermas, like most jurisprudential discussions of adjudication, focus on legal indeterminacy, and do not consider factual indeterminacy directly, their insights are applicable by analogy. As explained above, just as legal indeterminacy causes uncertainty in adjudication, so does factual indeterminacy, and litigants are entitled to legitimate resolution of factual questions, considering that the resolution of those questions underpins the subsequent application of legal principles leading to resolution of disputes.

Just as legal subjects have a reason to respect judicial resolution of legal indeterminacy by virtue of a rational decision-making process, they can similarly respect judicial resolution of factual indeterminacy so long as the fact-finding processes embody a genuine commitment to a rational determination of the relevant facts. As Fuller and Habermas suggest, this requires that parties are enabled to present evidence and argument in favour of a particular factual determination, and are assured that the ultimate outcome will be sincerely rationally motivated. In this way, the process of fact-finding maintains a discernible respect for litigants as equal, autonomous agents, which provides the normative justification for an authoritative determination of the uncertain question, "what happened?" The remainder of this chapter is dedicated to a more specific delineation of how these virtues can be reflected in the basic features of adjudicative fact-finding in the civil litigation context.

PART 2. DELINEATING LEGITIMATE ADJUDICATIVE FACT-FINDING

In this Part, I consider the necessary features of an adjudicative fact-finding process that demonstrably respects legal subjects as autonomous agents, deserving of rational decision-making. I conclude that a legitimate adjudicative process of fact-finding has two independent, yet related, features. First, as both Fuller and Habermas set out, the adjudicative process should assure meaningful participation rights that enable affected parties to present relevant evidence in furtherance of their positions. An adjudicative process that does not enable decision-making on the basis of parties' evidence and reasons (within the confines of legal principles that justifiably restrict admissible evidence or arguments) cannot be considered either committed to rational outcomes or respectful of the agency of legal subjects.

Second, while fact-finding procedures cannot guarantee accuracy, the process must assure factual reliability. That is achieved, I suggest below, when the adjudication process is genuinely oriented toward achieving factually accurate outcomes. A fact-finding process that is not committed to making a best effort to finding true facts is inherently irrational and disrespectful of legal subjects. Of course, compromises to accuracy are inevitable. Those compromises should be justifiable in light of the principles of legitimate fact-finding, which I outline below.

I note that the framework for legitimate fact-finding I offer below does not solely rest on the value of striving for outcome accuracy. Rather, what is paramount in the framework provided is the expression of the two values noted above — equality and autonomy. Ensuring a reliable fact-finding process is part of manifesting those values, but, as I hope is made clear below, it is not enough on its own. After all, a process may be factually reliable, but may compromise the values of autonomy or equality. Consider, for instance, a process that allows men to present their own evidence but demands that all women's evidence is presented by an able representative. This may have no necessary impact on the factual reliability of the process, but the values of equality and autonomy are nonetheless compromised. Such a process is clearly repugnant, and cannot yield legitimate legal outcomes, even if those outcomes are factually reliable. As such, where applicable, this discussion contains references to maintaining meaningful participation rights, but I provide a more express discussion of the necessity and form of participation rights at the end of the chapter.

A. Factual Reliability

(1) Accuracy Matters: The Importance of Accuracy Expressed as Reliability

An argument for procedural legitimacy can be critiqued on the basis that it is improperly forgiving of the injustice caused by factual inaccuracy.[47] That criticism does not hold, however, in the context of the case for procedural legitimacy that I endorse here. As I introduced in chapter 1, although the procedural legitimacy notion refrains from the impractical ideal of pinning legitimacy to factual accuracy of each outcome, it does not follow that a process that is altogether unconcerned with outcome-accuracy is acceptable under a procedural legitimacy framework.[48] The goal of outcome-accuracy is, however, expressed as a genu-

---

47   See for instance Hock Lai Ho, *Philosophy of Evidence Law: Justice in the Search for Truth* (Oxford, New York: Oxford University Press, 2008) at 65 [Ho, *Philosophy of Evidence Law*], where he rejects the notion of pure procedural justice on the basis that: "A party is unjustly treated if and when the court withholds from her substantive entitlements under the law, however unintentional the error." Similarly, in the criminal context, David Paciocco, "Balancing the Rights of the Individual and Society in Matters of Truth and Proof: Part II – Evidence about Innocence" (2008) 81 *Canadian Bar Review* 39 at 44: "When we recognize a wrongful conviction we, quite rightly, consider it to be an inexcusable tragedy. It is no answer to the factually innocent to say, 'Well. Even though you are factually innocent it is fair to leave you convicted because the law was applied with perfection during your trial.'" See also William Twining, *Rethinking Evidence: Exploratory Essays*, 2d ed (Cambridge University Press, 2006) for an interpretation of evidence law that places fact-finding in a broader social and legal context, highlighting the limits on purely truth-oriented models.

48   David Estlund is well-known for advancing a theory known as "epistemic proceduralism" in the context of democratic legitimacy. He argues that democratic procedures produce legitimate results because they emerge from a process that *tends to* arrive at correct outcomes; importantly, the legitimacy of the outcome does not depend on its correctness — incorrect outcomes can also be legitimate on the basis of the democratic process from which they emerged. See David Estlund, *Democratic Authority: A Philosophical Framework* (Princeton, NJ: Princeton University Press, 2008), particularly chapter 7 [Estlund, *Democratic Authority*]. This idea clearly aligns with the notion of procedural legitimacy that I have been suggesting. However, I do not hold that the epistemic value of adjudicative fact-finding procedures can, itself, fully support a framework for legitimate adjudicative fact-finding, as I noted in chapter 1, and outline further below. Though his ideas are developed in a different arena, Estlund's insights regarding the importance of epistemic value, and his steadfast insistence that legitimacy is located in the realm of process and not outcome, support my position that the legitimacy of fact-finding is to be found in procedural virtues.

ine effort toward factual accuracy, demonstrable through a fact-finding procedure that is authentically oriented toward accuracy.

One way to understand the significance of a factually reliable system of fact-finding is through Fuller's notion that the inner morality of law depends on congruence between the declared law and its administration through the courts.[49] With that in mind, consider a society that employs a coin toss as its process of fact-finding. Suppose that in such a society, the declared law is that a person is legally entitled to compensation for a negligently inflicted injury. But rather than relying on evidence to assess the relevant factual claims over the course of the litigation, the adjudicator tosses a coin to determine factual issues. For instance, heads means that the defendant's negligence was the factual cause of the injury; tails means that factual causation is not made out for legal purposes. In that society, there would be no genuine attempt at congruence between the law and its administration through the courts. There may be accidental congruence if the coin flipping happened to yield accurate facts, but whether or not there is congruence would be unpredictable, arbitrary, and irrational. That renders the law incapable of rationally guiding legal subjects. That, as Fuller notes, constitutes an unacceptable affront to the dignity of the legal subjects, and is unacceptable.[50] Even leaving aside the obvious affront to maintaining meaningful participation rights in respect of the factual determinations, this type of fact-finding process cannot be endorsed because it constitutes a wholly inauthentic and irrational attempt to ascertain the truth.

The general requirement for genuine truth-seeking is paralleled in Habermas's approach to adjudication as well.[51] For him, the rationality of a discourse aimed at assessing the truth of a claim breaks down if participants are insincere in their search for truth.[52] Since legitimate adjudicative processes should provide a structure for decisions to be made on the basis of the logic of rational discourse, it follows that adjudicative procedures of fact-finding must enable and manifest a genuine inquiry into the truth. David Dyzenhaus's comments on the

---

49 Fuller, *Morality of Law, above* note 2 at 81. See also chapter 2, Part 2.

50 *Ibid.*

51 See chapter 2, Part 2B.

52 For rationally motivated discourse to ensure "equal communication rights for participants, it requires sincerity and, it must diffuse any kind of force other than the forceless force of the better arguments." Habermas, "Between Facts and Norms: An Author's Reflections" (1999) 76 *Denver University Law Review* 937 at 940 [Habermas, "Author's Reflections"].

relationship between the procedures of rational discourse and a search for truth set out the point clearly. He recognizes that truth may not be attained in every instance, but the pragmatic reality is that a decision must be rendered in spite of uncertainty as to the truth of it. But that does not give rise to any necessary conclusion that truth does not or cannot have the reverence that it is owed in any theory of legal legitimacy, and in particular in a theory of legitimate factual determinations. He states:[53]

> We must in fact make decisions or accept closures which seem to cut off debate even in the face of disagreement, which we should expect to persist and even intensify as a result of the decision. But what can make such closures legitimate and thus not arbitrary is that they are based on an appropriate (though not ideal) process of inquiry and that the closure is temporary – it remains open to revision in the light of future experience. And these conditions, combined with the fact that the closure is based on the best evidence and arguments available, are what can give us reason to believe that we are at least on the right path to the truth.

In keeping with the theme expressed in Dyzenhaus's comments above, I maintain that an authentic attempt at ascertaining facts is not only laudable, but necessary within a legitimate adjudicative process. In so holding, I distance myself from those writers who suggest that the adjudicative system cannot be considered a search for truth at all.[54]

---

53   David Dyzenhaus, "The Legitimacy of Legality" (1996) 46 *University of Toronto Law Journal* 129 at 180 [Dyzenhaus, "The Legitimacy of Legality"].

54   See for example: Keith Kilback & Michael Tochor, "Searching for Truth but Missing the Point" (2002) 40 *Alberta Law Review* 333, argue that considering a trial as a "search for truth" is flawed for two reasons: first, because it is impossible for the trier of fact to know the truth, and second, since the concept of the "search for truth" has not been judicially defined, judges can pursue desired outcomes under its auspices; Note, "The Theoretical Foundations of the Hearsay Rules" (1980) 93 *Harvard Law Review* 1786 at 1787: "Since no evidence can provide more than a basis for inferences, which are by definition uncertain (by contrast to deductions, where conclusions follow with certainty from the premises), trials cannot discover absolute truth." In addition, while extraneous to my analysis, some epistemologist viewpoints hold that knowledge is fallibilist, so establishing truth is impossible whether in the context of a trial or otherwise. See for example, Michael Williams, *Problems of Knowledge - A Critical Introduction to Epistemology* (Oxford: Oxford University Press, 2001). For a discussion of the pros and cons of the debate around the nature of knowledge, see Simon Blackburn, *Truth – A Guide for the Perplexed* (London: Allen Lane, 2005), and for critical reactions to skepticism over the ascertainability of truth or "veriphobia," see Susan Haack, "Confessions of an Old-Fashioned Prig," in Susan Haack, *Manifesto of a Passionate Moderate:*

I aim to demonstrate that the tension between the importance of factual accuracy and the impossibility of guaranteeing it can be best reconciled by replacing the notion of outcome-accuracy as a necessary element of legitimacy with accuracy's procedural counterpart: a factually reliable process. A justifiable process must be factually reliable and, thereby, the outcomes that it yields are also factually reliable. This does not mean that the outcomes are necessarily accurate. Being products of a reliable procedure means that the outcomes are factually reliable, even though there is a risk that the outcome is not factually accurate, and irrespective of whether or not it is ever known if the outcome is factual.[55]

Shifting the value of accuracy away from the actual accuracy of the factual finding and into the realm of process is similar in form to my discussion of Raz's concept of legitimacy on the basis of outcomes that enable conformity to reason and its relation to Habermas's theory of adjudication as a rational discourse process. Elaborating that similarity helps to clarify my notion of factual reliability and how it can be assessed. Recall that in Raz's jurisprudence, law necessarily claims to have legitimate authority, in the sense that adherence to legal decrees best enable conformity to reason. Although legal institutions necessarily make this claim, they do not necessarily achieve it. I argued in chapter 2 that legal institutions can, nonetheless, maintain legitimacy on the basis of the *authenticity* of their claim of legitimate authority. That authenticity, I suggested, can be assessed by determining how well a legal system's law-making procedures coincide with Habermas's procedural principles of rational discourse, because those principles assure a genuine attempt at achieving a rational outcome.[56] Notably, this parallels Habermas's move discussed above of shifting the "rightness" of the outcome into the "rightness" of the process by suggesting that the "right" outcome is achieved through adherence to the "right" process.

Unfashionable Essays (Chicago: Chicago University Press, 1999), and Alvin I. Goldman, *Knowledge in a Social World* (Oxford: Oxford University Press, 1999).

55   Ho's explanation of the relation and significant difference between accuracy and reliability is helpful: "The reference to 'accuracy' when speaking of a finding of fact must be to the likelihood of its truth, and not how close it is to the truth. If this is right, we would arguably do better to speak of 'reliability' instead. . . . Reliability implies functional efficacy. . . . A verdict is more or less reliable depending on the reliability of the trial system which produced it Ho, *Philosophy of Evidence Law*, above note 47 at 66–67.

56   See chapter 2, Part 2B.

Adopting the same logic, an acceptable process of fact-finding is necessarily a system that claims to ascertain the relevant facts accurately. Even though adjudicative fact-finding cannot promise to invariably achieve that claim, it can maintain legitimacy, in part, on the basis of the authenticity of that claim. That authenticity can be evaluated by considering whether the fact-finding procedures enable a sincere search for truth, subject only to justifiable limitations. Accordingly, in my conception, assessing the factual reliability of the fact-finding process depends on assessing the genuineness or sincerity of an adjudicative system's claim of fact-finding through an objective evaluation of the fact-finding procedures.

By shifting the importance of actual outcome accuracy to a procedural concept of an ensured "best effort" at factual accuracy, I echo Fuller's observation that adjudication can be understood as a method of "imperfect realization of justice."[57] An authentic understanding of adjudication is contingent on accepting that imperfection.[58] With that in mind, I endorse Jerome Frank's view that we do not, because we cannot, demand perfection from the adjudicative process, but that we must demand a genuine effort.[59] And it is that "genuine effort" toward factual accuracy, as represented in its fact-finding procedures, which I use to assess the procedural concept of "factual reliability."[60] In the upcoming

---

57 Lon Fuller, "Needs of American Legal Philosophy," in *The Principles of Social Order: Selected Essays of Lon L Fuller* (Durham, NC: Duke University Press, 1981) at 263: "I have already expressed my conviction that adjudication, as a means for organizing human relations, can be discussed intelligently even though we are unable to define with precision its assumed end, namely, justice. I have also suggested that we can arrive at a better understanding of the aim we call justice if we discuss critically the various means by which it is imperfectly realized."

58 *Ibid.* For an analysis of epistemic limitations and the implications for legitimate outcomes in the criminal context, see Sarah Jane Summers, "The Epistemic Ambitions of the Criminal Trial: Truth, Proof, and Rights" (2023) 4 *Quaestio facti: Revista Internacional sobre Razonamiento Probatorio* 249.

59 Jerome Frank, *Courts on Trial – Myth and Reality in American Justice* (New Jersey: Princeton University Press, 1973) at 36: "Perfect justice lies beyond human reach. But the unattainability of the ideal is no excuse for shirking the effort to obtain the best available." Thomas Weigend, "Is the Criminal Process about Truth?: A German Perspective" (2003) 26 *Harvard Journal of Law & Public Policy* 157 at 173, arrives at a similar conclusion: "The public will accept whatever is presented as 'justice' only if justice is perceived to be based on an honest effort to find the 'truth.' There are no great expectations beyond that . . . .What then are the necessary ingredients of procedural truth? . . .The essential element is a visible, honest effort to collect and introduce facts on which the decision-maker can base a rationally defensible verdict" [Weigend, "Is the Criminal Process about Truth?"].

60 I note here that it is not my purpose to adopt a statistically grounded concept of assessing or quantifying reliability. Statistical reliability can only be assessed empirically

section, I have attempted to delineate the features that a factually reliable fact-finding system should have.

(2) How Should Reliability Be Reflected in the Adjudicative Process?

Assessing the reliability of a fact-finding process can bring many features of the civil litigation trial process under examination. While it is outside of my parameters to assess the merit of all relevant evidentiary doctrines, my aim in this section is to provide and endorse some overarching principles that should constitute the foundational features of fact-finding in a civil trial. Those basic elements would ensure that the fact-finding process demonstrably facilitates a genuine effort toward factual accuracy while maintaining an efficacious and fair adjudicative system.

First, the basic principle of enabling generous access to relevant evidence is key to maintaining a genuine fact-finding process. The Supreme Court of Canada has maintained that it is "a principle of fundamental justice that relevant evidence should be available . . . in the search for truth."[61] This principle is provided for within the basic rule of admissibility of evidence that stipulates that a trier of fact can consider any evidence that would tend to prove or disprove a fact in issue. In *R v Collins*, the Ontario Court of Appeal set out this principle as follows:[62]

---

by examining the percentage of errors that occur in a given fact-finding system. That approach to assessing reliability is impractical and potentially impossible, because confirming the truth of an outcome is often elusive. See for instance Shari Seidman Diamond, "Truth, Justice, and the Jury" (2003) 26 *Harvard Journal of Law & Public Policy* 143 at 150: "[W]e cannot compare . . . a verdict with some gold standard of truth because no such dependable standard exists." (This issue is particularly visible in the causal uncertainty cases that I discuss in chapter 4). I assess reliability by considering whether the fact-finding process is genuinely orientated toward factual accuracy. This does not depend on empirical precision, but on an authentic consideration of whether the features of a fact-finding process can be considered as committed to seeking truth within only justifiable limits.

61   *R v Jarvis* [2002] 3 SCR 757. See also David Paciocco and Lee Stuesser: "Given its role in serving the application of the substantive law, the law of evidence should ideally enable triers of fact to have orderly access to any information that could help them make an accurate determination about whether the substantive law applies." In David Paciocco & Lee Stuesser. *The Law of Evidence*, 7th ed (Toronto: Irwin Law, 2015) at 2 [Paciocco & Stuesser, *The Law of Evidence*].

62   *R v Collins* (2001) OJ No 3894 at para 18 (CA) [emphasis in original]. See also Doherty JA's discussion of relevance in *R v Watson* 1996 CarswellOnt 2884 (CA). At para 33, Doherty JA states: "Relevance . . . requires a determination of whether as a matter of human experience and logic the existence of 'Fact A' makes the existence or non-existence of 'Fact B' more probable than it would be without the existence of 'Fact A.' If it does then 'Fact A' is

> *Relevance* is established at law if, as a matter of logic and experience, the evidence tends to prove the proposition for which it is advanced. The evidence is *material* if it is directed at a matter in issue in the case. Hence, evidence that is relevant to an issue in the case will generally be admitted.

The concept of maintaining access to relevant evidence is in keeping with Habermas's ideal discourse condition of a full and free exchange of information. Any system that unjustifiably excludes relevant evidence can have the legitimacy of its claim of fact-finding questioned on the basis that its commitment to truthful fact-finding lacks sincerity. This brings to mind a potential development in Canadian civil procedure — the 2025 Ontario *Rules of Civil Procedure* reform proposal — which suggests that instead of demanding that parties disclose all relevant documentary evidence to one another before trial, the parties would be required to disclose only the relevant documentary evidence that they intend to rely on, and any known adverse documentary evidence. The underlying justification for this reform is access to justice via improving pre-trial procedural efficiency.[63] Can this be justified under the theory of procedural legitimacy being developed here?

I believe it can, because it cannot be said to unduly compromise the search for truth. It maintains that relevant evidence that will in fact be useful at trial, as well as any adverse evidence will be disclosed between the two sides in the litigation. This prevents parties from being buried in evidence that may have some tangential relevance but will not be relevant to the actual decision-making process because parties will not rely on it. As a procedural principle, this seems justifiable especially in a new age where electronic documents can be so numerous that their sheer volume may even hide the truth. Whether such a rule is susceptible to misuse, that is, parties failing to disclose adverse documentation or failing to even seek documentation that may be adverse because of fear of having to disclose it are best defined as problems of adversarialism that should be addressed through principles of ethical lawyering, which should orient lawyers toward discovery of truth while gathering evidence rather than winning a case.

---

relevant to 'Fact B'. As long as 'Fact B' is itself a material fact in issue or is relevant to a material fact in issue in the litigation then 'Fact A' is relevant and *prima facie* admissible."

63   The proposed changes to the Ontario *Rules of Civil Procedure* can be found online: https://www.ontariocourts.ca/scj/civil-rules-review/.

Besides such large-scale rule revisions proposals, there are a number of evidentiary doctrines in the Canadian legal system that necessarily and justifiably exclude relevant evidence from trial itself. Some such exclusionary rules further the goal of accurate fact-finding, like rules that purport to reduce unreliable evidence from the court process. For instance, preventing hearsay evidence for the purpose of proving the truth of a statement, or rules prohibiting prior consistent/self-serving statements, and rules requiring voluntariness for admissibility of confessions, are examples of evidentiary doctrines that are designed to prevent unreliable evidence from entering into the decision-making process. These rules can be understood as promoting (perhaps among other things) the commitment to accurate decision-making by preventing reliance on evidence that has a high risk of unreliability.[64]

Other exclusionary doctrines, however, may compromise the goal of factual accuracy in pursuit of other values.[65] Examples include privilege rules that prevent solicitor and client communications or spousal communications from being admitted at trial;[66] *Charter of Rights and Freedoms* principles that render improperly obtained evidence inadmissible;[67] or the principle of *res judicata*, which prevents reconsideration of issues that have already been adjudicated, even if there is an indication of a factual discrepancy in a previous decision.[68]

64　Sopinka, Lederman & Bryant, *The Law of Evidence in Canada*, 4th ed (Markham, ON: LexisNexis Canada, 2014) at 12–13.

65　See Weigend, "Is the Criminal Process about Truth?," above note 59 at 168, "[exclusionary rules] limits the pool of (relevant) information available to the decision-maker and thus reduce the chances that the verdict will be based upon a completely 'true' finding of fact."

66　For a discussion of the evidentiary principles of privilege, see Paciocco & Stuesser, *The Law of Evidence*, above note 61 at 7; and for a discussion focusing on procedural aspects of privilege principles, see Janet Walker & Lorne Sossin, *Civil Litigation* (Toronto: Irwin Law, 2010) at chapter 9.

67　*Canadian Charter of Rights and Freedoms*, Part I of the *Constitution Act, 1982*, being Schedule B to the *Canada Act 1982* (UK), 1982, c 11, s 24(2) [*Charter of Rights and Freedoms*]:

　　"Where, in proceedings under subsection (1), a court concludes that evidence was obtained in a manner that infringed or denied any rights or freedoms guaranteed by this *Charter*, the evidence shall be excluded if it is established that, having regard to all the circumstances, the admission of it in the proceedings would bring the administration of justice into disrepute." See also, Richard Fraser & Jennifer Addison, "What's Truth Got to Do With It?" (2004) 29 *Queen's Law Journal* 823 for an argument urging caution in excluding evidence under s 24(2) of the *Charter of Rights and Freedoms*.

68　Donald Lange, *The Doctrine of Res Judicata in Canada*, 2d ed (Markham, ON: LexisNexis Canada, 2004) [Lange, *Res Judicata in Canada*].

Inevitably, some doctrines that exclude probative evidence are necessary and justifiable despite their potential compromise to outcome accuracy. The existence and acceptance of these doctrines should not lead to the conclusion that the adjudicative process is not the business of seeking truth at all.[69] So long as the exclusionary doctrines are justifiable, a trial system can remain objectively genuine in its search for truth even though its commitment to factual accuracy cannot be absolute. In other words, we can still assess a system as factually reliable despite legally sanctioned doctrines that compromise accuracy by disallowing probative evidence. But on what basis?[70]

I maintain that the same values that give credence to law-making processes should also guide the necessary compromises to achieving factual accuracy. Assessing the justifiability of exclusionary doctrines on that basis has two dimensions. First, where ensuring respect for the agency of legal subjects requires exclusion of evidence, such exclusion can be considered justifiable. Exclusions of evidence on the basis of *Charter* violations, or exclusions for the purpose of protecting fundamental human liberties, are examples of evidence-exclusion principles that are justifiable on this basis.[71] Second, an exclusionary doctrine that is necessary to enable adjudicative efficacy can be justifiable as long as any associated affront to respecting human agency is minimized.[72] In

---

69   Weigend, "Is the Criminal Process About Truth?," above note 59, for example, gestures toward this when he says of the adversarial system that, "because the system excludes from the court's view everything that cannot be introduced as evidence on the day set for the trial, the 'truth' is based only on the relatively small array of materials then available, and valuable information will be ignored because one or both parties cannot present it at the right time in the legally prescribed manner. The adversarial system, at least in the form practiced in the Anglo-American world, therefore does not lead to the discovery of 'true' truth but of an artificially generated set of facts euphemistically called 'procedural truth'" at 160.

70   Recall that in chapter 1, I claimed that a viable proposal of procedural legitimacy will be equipped to assess when, and to what extent, epistemic concerns can be compromised in pursuit of other values. My discussion here is a demonstration of that aspect of the procedural legitimacy proposal.

71   It is outside my scope to engage in a more searching analysis into the underpinnings of *Charter* protections here, but I note that Lawrence Solum has made the point that compromises to accuracy on the basis of "ensur[ing] that the process of adjudication does not unfairly infringe on the substantive rights guaranteed by the basic liberties, such as rights of privacy and freedom of speech," must be considered acceptable. Lawrence Solum, "Procedural Justice" 78 *Southern California Law Review* 181 at 306 [Solum, "Procedural Justice"].

72   The idea that rules of fact-finding and evidentiary exclusions are underpinned by the value of respect for human agency is present in arguments from a number of scholars.

order to elaborate this further, below I demonstrate how the respect for agency justification scheme would apply to the doctrines of solicitor and client privilege, which illustrates the first dimension, and *res judicata*, which illustrates the second.

Solicitor and client privilege constitutes an assurance that communications between a lawyer and their client remain confidential, including preventing disclosure of such communications over the course of the litigation.[73] Surely, communications between a solicitor and a client could facilitate the accuracy of an adjudicative outcome, but

---

For example, Richard Peck has argued in "The Adversarial System: A Qualified Search for the Truth" (2001) 80 *Canadian Bar Review* 465, in the criminal trial context that: "evidence ought to be excluded where it has been obtained through state actions which violate human rights. This engages the central debate as to whether the value of the search for the truth, which must, of necessity, involve trustworthiness, is of a higher ordinate than the worth and dignity of the individual." Alex Stein has similarly explained a justification on the basis of respect for agency regarding the rule against drawing incriminating inferences based on past crimes: "By treating personality and action as causally interrelated, such inferences undermine the anti-deterministic postulate of free agency, epitomized by the famous precept, 'Judge the act, not the actor'. Free agency indeed serves as a pillar of the liberal theory of criminal liability. From this perspective, using the defendant's personality as incriminating evidence undermines his or her autonomy and degrades her individuality." *Foundations of Evidence Law* (Oxford, New York: Oxford University Press, 2005) at 32 [Stein, *Foundations of Evidence Law*]. See also Alex Stein, "The Refoundation of Evidence Law" (1996) 9 *Canadian Journal of Law & Jurisprudence* 279 at 293. In addition, David Wasserman, "The Morality of Statistical Proof and the Risk of Mistaken Liability" (1991) 13 *Cardozo Law Review* 935, argues for respect for individual autonomy as an underpinning moral value in fact-finding. On that basis, he argues, some statistical evidence is inadequate in establishing the requisite standard of proof because of its affront on treating people as part of a class rather than as individual agents. As Dworkin has held, "it is unjust to put someone in jail on the basis of a judgment about a class, however accurate, because that denies his claim to equal respect as an individual." Ronald Dworkin, *Taking Rights Seriously* (London: Duckworth, 1978) at 13.

73 See David Kaye (1947), David Bernstein, Jennifer Mnookin, Richard Friedman (1951), John Wigmore (1863–1943), *The New Wigmore: A Treatise on Evidence* (Austin, TX: Wolters Kluwer Law & Business, Aspen Publishers, 2011) at 2292: "Where legal advice of any kind is sought from a professional legal adviser in his capacity as such, the communications relating to that purpose, made in confidence by the client, are at his instance permanently protected from disclosure by himself or by the legal adviser, except the protection be waived." The Supreme Court of Canada stated in *Ontario (Public Safety and Security) v Criminal Lawyers' Association* [2010] 1 SCR 815 at para 53 that: "the only exceptions recognized to the privilege are the narrowly guarded public safety and right to make full answer and defence exceptions." But for a discussion of solicitor-client privilege doctrine in Canada, including comments on the changing state of recognized exclusions, see Adam Dodek, "Solicitor-Client Privilege in Canada: Challenges for the 21st Century," Canadian Bar Association Discussion Paper, 2011.

rendering those communications confidential is justified on the basis that it enables clients to frankly disclose relevant information in order to receive effective legal advice. Does this satisfy the notion that compromises to factual accuracy are justifiable if they are necessary to protect respect for human agency?

Upon closer consideration of the doctrine and its underlying commitments, I conclude that it clearly does. First, parties need legal representation because understanding the law and navigating through the legal processes is difficult. These complexities create a distance between community members and their legal system, and lawyers act as conduits to bridge that gap. The complexity of the legal system, which gives rise to the need for intermediaries, can render individuals unable to make fully informed, independent decisions in pursuit of their legal claims without the help of a third party. Needing an intermediary may require individuals to compromise their personal privacy in order to access legal knowledge and make decisions about their lives. This can be considered an affront to human agency.

Protecting the confidentiality of the communications between lawyers and clients helps to rectify this problem. When a client is assured that any communication with their lawyer is confidential, the compromise to personal privacy in order to access legal information is minimized, because the lawyer is bound never to disclose anything that the client reveals to them. That way, the client can gain access to the lawyer's legal knowledge, almost as if that knowledge were their own. Understood in this way, solicitor-client privilege exists for the protection of litigant agency. This interpretation of the solicitor-client privilege doctrine is consistent with Doherty JA's comments in a partially dissenting judgment in *General Accident Assurance Co v Chrusz*:

> The privilege is an expression of our commitment to both personal autonomy and access to justice. Personal autonomy depends in part on an individual's ability to control the dissemination of personal information and to maintain confidences. . . . The surrender of the former should not be the cost of obtaining the latter. By maintaining client-solicitor privilege, we promote both personal autonomy and access to justice.[74]

The commitment to respecting the personal autonomy of individuals, which grounds solicitor-client privilege, serves as a path to

---

74   *General Accident Assurance Co v Chrusz* (1999) 45 OR (3d) 321 at para 92 (CA).

justifying the potential increased risk of factual inaccuracy that comes with that evidentiary rule.

Now consider the doctrine of *res judicata*. *Res judicata* is a rule against relitigation of previously decided matters. As a rule of evidence, *res judicata* is an exclusionary principle.[75] It prevents proffering of evidence, as well as a new theory of the case, on an issue that has already been decided, even if a party has new evidence or argument that might negate the finding in the previous adjudication.[76] According to Lange, the Supreme Court of Canada gave its "best pronouncement" on the doctrine in its 1894 decision in *Farwell v R*:

> Where the parties (themselves or privies) are the same, and the cause of action is the same, the estoppel extends to all matters which were, or might properly have been, brought into litigation. Where the parties (themselves or their privies) are the same, but the cause of action is different, the estoppel is as to matters which, having been brought in issue, the finding upon them was material to the former decision.[77]

The rule of disallowing relitigation of issues already adjudicated is generally justified on the grounds that it protects the finality of adjudicative outcomes. That is a necessary worthwhile cause. For one, recognizing the finality of judicial disputes protects individuals from the expense of being "twice vexed by the same cause."[78] And more fundamentally, if adjudicative outcomes were not to be considered final, and previously decided issues could be relitigated, then judicial decision-making could not be considered authoritative at all. Absent their authoritative quality, adjudicative dispute resolution would lose relevance.[79]

The doctrine of *res judicata* suggests a preference for finality at the expense of a genuine commitment to factual accuracy. Recognizing finality is essential to an effective and useful adjudicative system, so *res judicata* seems acceptable. But can it be justified in light of

---

75 Donald Lange, *The Doctrine of Res Judicata in Canada*, 2d ed (Markham, ON: LexisNexis Canada, 2004) at 10.

76 *Ostapchuk v Ostapchuk* 1959 CarswellSask 13 at 180 (CA): "Assuming the requirements of the doctrine are met, the party against whom the issue was decided in the earlier litigation cannot proffer evidence to challenge that result."

77 *Farwell v R* (1894) 22 SCR 553 at 558. And Lange, *Res Judicata in Canada*, above note 68 at 2.

78 *Ibid* at 4.

79 See my discussion in chapter 1: A. Introducing the Fact-Finding Tension.

its compromise to outcome accuracy along with the impairment on allowing litigants to present evidence and argument of their choice?

The answer is yes. This becomes clear when the doctrine is considered in light of the test for how *res judicata* must be argued in order to successfully prevent presentation of evidence on a previously decided issue. A party alleging *res judicata* must show that the evidence or argument being proffered was available at the time of the previous hearing, and if due diligence had been exercised, it would have been proffered and considered at the earlier adjudication. Accordingly, the *res judicata* doctrine does not deprive a litigant of making a full argument and full presentation of evidence; it deprives a litigant of a *duplicative* right thereof. That being the case, given the value of protecting adjudicative finality, and the minimal impairment to litigant agency, it cannot be said that the *res judicata* renders the adjudicative process inauthentic in its commitment to factual accuracy.

Compromises to the goal of outcome accuracy can be accommodated within an adjudicative process that maintains a genuine commitment to factually accurate outcomes. The reality that adjudicative outcomes must be made on the basis of incomplete evidence does not suggest that the search for truth is not genuine. It does suggest, however, that there is a necessary risk of factual error owing to the unavoidable fact of evidentiary gaps. Given that the risk of error is unavoidable, adjudicative procedures must manage that risk in a justifiable way. In the next section, I endorse some general principles that would ensure a justifiable management of error risk while maintaining a reliable fact-finding system.

(3) Maintaining Reliability Alongside Fair Management of Risk of Error

The adjudicative system cannot feasibly guarantee factually accurate outcomes, so there is inevitable risk of erroneous outcomes. Adjudicative procedures must manage that risk fairly in order to maintain the legitimacy of outcomes.[80] Ronald Dworkin has provided what I view to be one of the most valuable proposals for what principled risk management would entail.[81]

---

80   In Alex Stein's words: "There is no escape from deciding how to allocate the risk of error in adjudicative fact-finding." Alex Stein, *Foundations of Evidence Law*, above note 72 at 3.

81   As Dworkin notes, the conundrums caused by the inevitability of inaccuracy in adjudicating claims has largely "been left to the simple formula that questions of evidence and

As I introduced in chapter 1, in "Principle, Policy, and Procedure,"[82] Dworkin explains that litigants have certain substantive rights, like the right not to be criminally convicted if not guilty, or the right to compensation if negligently injured, but since the adjudicative procedures cannot promise accurate outcomes every time, the vindication of those rights cannot be guaranteed. For Dworkin, the integrity of a legal system is nonetheless maintained through two procedural rights. Taken together, those procedural rights ensure appropriate recognition of the harm associated with factual errors, and a fair and consistent exposure to the inevitable risk of their occurrence.[83] As Dworkin puts it, community members should have:[84]

> The right to procedures that put a proper valuation on moral harm in the calculations that fix the risk of injustice that they will run; and the related and practically more important right to equal treatment with respect to that evaluation.

Dworkin's procedural rights proposal calls for two types of consistency, one substantive and one formal. Substantively, adjudicative procedures must tolerate a similar risk of error for similar types of error. That is what Dworkin means when he says the procedures must put a "proper valuation" on the risk of factual error.[85] Suppose, for example, that a community decides to criminalize tobacco consumption. In that society, there is a minimum sentence of a \$1,000 fine for consumption of illegal drugs, and the same goes for tobacco consumption. Suppose, though, that prosecuting for contravening all other illegal drug consumption requires proof beyond a reasonable doubt, but prosecuting for consumption of tobacco only requires proof on a balance of probabilities. That rule would violate Dworkin's first procedural right, because the harm associated with a factual error (i.e., being fined \$1,000 and

---

procedure must be decided by striking 'the right balance' between the interests of the individual and the interests of the community as a whole, which merely restates the problem." Dworkin, "Principle, Policy, and Procedure," in *A Matter of Principle* (Cambridge, MA: Harvard University Press, 1985) at 73 [Dworkin, "Principle, Policy, and Procedure"].

82 *Ibid.*

83 As I set out in chapter 1, I critiqued Dworkin's approach because of the suggestion that risk distribution alone maintains adjudicative integrity. For me, fair risk distribution is one among other necessary characteristics of procedural legitimacy. But Dworkin's approach to credible risk distribution is, for me, a wholly endorsable starting point.

84 Dworkin, "Principle, Policy, and Procedure," above note 81 at 92.

85 *Ibid.*

bearing a conviction for a crime not committed) is similar to other drugs, yet the risk of that harm manifesting is rendered higher for tobacco consumption.

Dworkin's second procedural right constitutes a demand for formal equality. The application of risk-allocating procedures must be applied consistently so that no party is arbitrarily visited with a different risk level. For instance, prosecuting violation of the tobacco prohibition should occur using the same standard of proof irrespective of whether the accused party is male or female, a Canadian born in Canada or abroad, has prior convictions or does not, and so on. That formal consistency, which promises non-arbitrary treatment of litigants is the backbone of procedural legitimacy.[86]

Dworkin's rights require internal coherence and consistency in application, but notably, they do not dictate the substance of the risk-allocating procedures. This suggests that in Dworkin's view, a society can legitimately allocate and tolerate risk of error in any way it deems appropriate, so long as its risk tolerance is internally coherent and is applied consistently to litigants. I generally agree. As Stein notes, "Moral considerations that inform risk-allocating decisions belong to the domain of politics,"[87] and there can be different reasons that lead to different levels of risk tolerance. For instance, in the Canadian legal system, we accept a greater risk of inaccurately imposing civil liability compared with criminal conviction. And we tolerate a greater risk of false acquittal compared with false conviction.[88]

How risk is allocated is substantively justified at the level of legislative law-making.[89] Within my narrower purpose of adjudicative

---

86   This basic element of procedural legitimacy was first articulated in chapter 1.

87   Stein, *Foundations of Evidence Law*, above note 72 at 13.

88   As David Paciocco has pointed out, "there is not the same virtue in a single-minded pursuit of truth about guilt, as there is in a singleminded pursuit of truth about innocence." David Paciocco, "Evidence About Guilt: Balancing the Rights of the Individual and Society" (2001) 80 *Canadian Bar Review* 433 at 435.

89   Relevant questions in that sphere could include questions of appropriate balancing between the different social costs of potential error, as presented in Erik Lillquist, "Recasting Reasonable Doubt: Decision Theory and The Virtues of Variability" (2002) 36 *UC Davis Law Review* 85; or Thomas J. Miceli, "Optimal Prosecution of Defendants Whose Guilt is Uncertain" (1990) 6 *Journal of Law, Economics & Organization* 189. Appropriate risk allocation could also be based on questions of optimal deterrence: As Mike Redmayne explains in "Standards of Proof in Civil Litigation" (1999) 62 *Modern Law Review* 167 at 172, a common argument about setting the standard of proof is that it "should be set at a level which will ensure optimal deterrence of tortious conduct (i.e. it should not under-deter, increasing

legitimacy, it is coherence and consistency in risk allocation that is paramount in an adjudicative system where error must be tolerated while maintaining respect for legal subjects who will be subject to potential error. Arbitrary and inconsistent risk allocating procedures would constitute irrational adjudication and impairment to respecting legal subjects as people capable and deserving of rational guidance through the legal system.

But internal and systemic consistency in risk allocation must be accompanied by two additional conditions in order to maintain an authentic commitment to factual accuracy. The first, simpler in nature, is a necessary restriction on the adjudicative standard of proof. The standard of proof is the clearest place where the state can control the extent of risk of error that will be tolerated and the distribution of that risk.[90] Conceivably, a society may have reason to adopt different standards of proof in some class of cases. For instance, perhaps a society seeks to dissuade litigation and adopts a 60 percent or 70 percent standard of proof instead of 50 percent. So long as the consistency requirements are met, this does not seem to *necessarily* compromise adjudicative legitimacy.[91] But can a 30 percent or a 20 percent standard of proof be tolerated, even if that standard of proof satisfies coherence and consistency requirements?

Given the claim that a legitimate fact-finding system must display a genuine orientation toward factual accuracy, a standard of proof that falls below the 50 percent threshold cannot be accepted. If the standard

---

the number of accidents, but nor should it over-deter, increasing the cost of safety measures and encouraging potential victims to be careless." Similarly, Dominique Demougin & Claude Fluet, "Preponderance of Evidence" (2006) 50 *European Economic Review* 963 at 963, argue "that a 'more-likely-than-not' decision rule provides maximal incentives for potential tort-feasors to exert care." For a similar analysis in the criminal context, see for example, Tone Ognedal, "Should the Standard of Proof be Lowered to Reduce Crime?" (2005) 25 *International Review of Law & Economics* 41 at 45. For one of the most comprehensive discussions of the burden of proof and factors to consider in setting it, see Louis Kaplow, "Burden of Proof" (2012) 121 *Yale Law Journal* 738.

90 As Louis Kaplow, above note 89 states at 741: "The stringency of the proof burden determines how error is allocated between mistakes of commission – improper assignment of liability – and mistakes of omission – improper exoneration."

91 This approach may not be acceptable to those who might justify the civil standard of proof on the basis that it treats litigants equally through a roughly equal distribution of the risk of error. In my view, the risk distribution is a substantive aspect of the proof of facts principles, and is within the legislator's jurisdiction to determine, subject to the qualification noted above.

of proof falls below 50 percent, then the fact-finding process cannot be genuinely oriented toward truth at all. That is because if the standard of proof falls below 50 percent then even facts that are not more likely to be true than false are accepted as true. Such a system would accept facts that are probably not true as true, resulting in a lack of reliability — it cannot be said that the commitment to factual accuracy in that system is genuine.

The second proviso is a stipulation of *how* the fact-finder should determine whether the standard of proof has been met. Picking up from Fuller's and Habermas's notions, rational decision-making is foundational to adjudication, and the same goes for the fact finder's determination about whether the standard of proof has been met. A fact-finding system is acceptable only if the standard of proof is applied *rationally*. For instance, if a judge concluded that an injured plaintiff established that the defendant caused their injury on a balance of probabilities on the basis that the plaintiff's expert witness has blue eyes, that factual conclusion is clearly irrational, even though the judge purported to apply the correct standard of proof. Similarly, if a judge decides to determine whether the standard of proof was met by considering only blue-eyed expert witnesses, their application of the standard of proof is irrational. Even if the ultimate finding of fact were correct in these examples, the process of concluding whether the burden of proof is discharged is irrational and unacceptable. The requirement for rationality in the application of the standard of proof finds well-stated support in Lock Hai Ho's account of acceptable fact-finding, as explained below.

(4) The Rationality Requirement

In *A Philosophy of Evidence Law*, Ho has argued that justifiable fact-finding depends not only on epistemic success, but also on ethical values. Those ethical values are, at least in part, represented in the process of arriving at factual conclusions. As he puts it, "it is not only the case that truth is needed to do justice; the court must do justice *in* finding the truth."[92] Whether justice is done in the process of finding the truth depends, Ho suggests, on the rationality of the fact-finding deliberation. If the deliberation process was irrational, then even if the

---

92   Ho, *Philosophy of Evidence Law*, above note 47 at 51.

ultimate outcome was accurate, one should conclude that an unjustifiable error occurred:

> A particular verdict may be correct even though it was produced by irrational reasoning. In such a case, one might say that no harm was done after all. But one should insist that something has gone wrong: the fact-finder has failed to discharge her duty properly in not deliberating as she ought to. It is wrong to find the defendant guilty by consulting [a] Ouija board or by the toss of a coin. It is wrong even if the verdict happens to be correct and even where rational support for belief in his fault exists on the evidence admitted in court. . . . Rationality is a demand in fact-finding that cannot be completely identified with the demand of reliability or accuracy.[93]

Ho's insistence on recognizing the value of rational fact-finding is grounded in the central value of being respectful of legal subjects' human agency. Picking up from Raimond Gaita's poetic conception of justice as humanity,[94] and Markus Dubber's[95] and Michael Slote's[96] accounts of justice as empathetic engagement, Ho notes that "the fact-finder ought to care to find the truth because she ought morally to respect and care for the person standing before the court. In this sense, the trial is not only about accuracy; it is, more importantly, about affirming a common humanity."[97] That common humanity can be expressed when "through reflection and the conceptualization of another person as a fellow moral being, someone with equal capacity for autonomy as oneself . . . one

---

93   *Ibid* at 73. Highlighting the significance of rational discharge of the standard of proof in the criminal context, Larry Lauden has posed the question, "If a juror feels doubtful about guilt but cannot even identify or formulate the reason for the doubt, then how can she possibly decide *whether* the doubt in question is rational or irrational?" Larry Lauden, *Truth, Error and Criminal Law – An Essay in Legal Epistemology* (Cambridge: Cambridge University Press, 2006) at 42.

94   Raimond Gaita, *A Common Humanity: Thinking about Love and Truth and Justice* (London: Routledge, 2000).

95   Markus Dirk Dubber, *The Sense of Justice – Empathy in Law and Punishment* (NY: NYU Press, 2006).

96   Michael Slote, *The Ethics of Care and Empathy* (London: Routledge, 2007); and Michael Slote, "Autonomy and Empathy" (2004) 21 *Social Philosophy and Policy* 293.

97   Ho, *Philosophy of Evidence Law*, above note 47 at 84. And also at 83: "In short, the trier of fact must appreciate, from the position of that person, the value of respect and concern. A verdict should be given against her only when it can be justified on grounds that she ought reasonably to accept. The standard of proof and evidential reasoning used in reaching the verdict must express adequate respect and concern."

comes to have respect for her and want to treat her in accordance with that respect."[98] Rational decision-making is foundational to maintaining that respect.[99]

Much of Ho's proposition resonates with my understanding of legitimate fact-finding. The requisite respect for the litigants that underpins the legitimacy of fact-finding is contingent on rational deliberation when arriving at factual conclusions.[100] But before closing the discussion of the rationality proviso, there are two related considerations left to discuss: First, whether legitimacy of fact-finding demands express

---

98   *Ibid* at 81.

99   A commitment to rational decision-making on the basis of the evidence presented suggests that judges must approach their fact-finding task with neutrality and impartiality. On its face, that is an uncontroversial requirement, and has been expressly endorsed by the Supreme Court of Canada (See *R v S (RD)* [1997] 3 SCR 484 and most recently in *Yukon Francophone School Board, Education Area #23 v Yukon (Attorney General)* 2015 SCC 25 [*Yukon Francophone School Board v Yukon*]. For example at para 22 of *Yukon Francophone School Board v Yukon*, Abella J notes: "Impartiality and the absence of bias have developed as both legal and ethical requirements. Judges are required — and expected — to approach every case with impartiality and an open mind" (reference removed). However, while I cannot offer a more thorough discussion here, the Supreme Court's application of the reasonable apprehension of bias test may suggest some dilution of the demand for judicial neutrality through commentary such as: "It is apparent, and a reasonable person would expect, that triers of fact will be properly influenced in their deliberations by their individual perspectives on the world in which the events in dispute in the courtroom took place. Indeed, judges must rely on their background knowledge in fulfilling their adjudicative function." (*R v S (RD)* at paras 38–39). If such a statement can be taken to suggest a compromise to the rationality requirement of judicial fact-finding, they are improper seen from the procedural legitimacy perspective that I am presenting here.

100 Micah Schwartzman has argued that adjudicative legitimacy requires judicial sincerity and public justification in order to provide those affected a reason to accept the decision. Micah Schwartzman, "Judicial Sincerity" (2008) 94 *Virginia Law Review* 987 [Schwartzman, "Judicial Sincerity"]. For me, a judge's sincerity, while laudable, cannot handle the same normative load as Ho's principle of rationality. Suppose that a judge believes in a magic coin and tosses it in order to make factual findings. They may be sincere in their subjective belief, but I, as a litigant, would not care about their sincerity; I do care, however, about their irrationality, particularly when it results in an outcome that is authoritative for me. As Martin Golding puts it, "It would be unfortunate if a judge's argument was mere rationalization and if the judge did not sincerely hold the reasons that he explicitly gives. But in an important respect, this fact, whenever it is a fact, is irrelevant to the justifiability of the decision. The justifiability of the decision depends on how well the decision is reasoned." Martin Golding, *Legal Reasoning* (New York: AA Knopf, 1984) at 8. My own references to "sincerity" or "authenticity" should not be confused with requiring a sincere judge. Rather, they should be understood as denoting objective procedural qualities. The rationality of a judge's deliberation can be considered a part of assessing how sincere (in an objective sense) a fact-finding process is.

reasons for factual finding. I explain below why I think it does. And second, the question of whether judicial deliberation is the only place where rationality is expressed in the adjudicative process. Adopting Habermas and Fuller as my starting point leads to my conclusion that this is a too narrow approach to adjudicative rationality. That is a point of divergence between Ho's position and mine, as I explain below.

The requirement for having rational reasons for factual conclusions in order to maintain adjudicative legitimacy is suggestive of a requirement for *giving* those reasons as well. Such a requirement for express reasons is supported within my theme of maintaining respect for human agency on the basis that public justification demonstrates an acknowledgement that community members can, and have a right to scrutinize the rationality of judicial decisions.[101] As William Richman and William Reynolds hold:

> When a judge makes no attempt to provide a satisfactory explanation of the reasons, neither the actual litigants nor subsequent readers of an opinion can know whether the judge paid careful attention to the case and decided the appeal according to the law or whether the judge relied on impermissible factors such as race, sex, political influence, or merely the flip of a coin.[102]

Providing express reasons for arriving at factual conclusions is an avenue for assessing the rationality of the deliberation process, and committing to providing those reasons contains an implicit respect for the litigants as rational, active players rather than mere passive receivers of authoritative decrees.[103] It sends a message that the community

---

101   Micah Schwartzman, "Judicial Sincerity," above note 100 at 1008.

102   William M. Richman & William L. Reynolds, "Elitism, Expediency, and the New Certiorari: Requiem for the Learned Hand Tradition" (1996) 81 *Cornell Law Review* 273 at 282–83. Fuller has also noted that, "By and large, it seems clear that the fairness and effectiveness of adjudication are promoted by reasoned opinions. Without such opinions the parties have to take it on faith that their participation in the decision has been real, that the arbiter has in fact understood and taken into account their proofs and arguments." Fuller, "Forms and Limits," above note 1 at 388. (Note that Fuller holds that while he supports a statement of reasons, he does not find them necessary for maintaining adjudicative integrity. His reasons for so holding are not particularly clear, but it seems that he finds that in some contexts like commercial arbitration, an absolute requirement for reasons may be too burdensome, particularly in the case of lay, volunteer arbitrators).

103   I noted in chapter 2 that David Dyzenhaus has also offered a compelling proposed addition to Habermas's theory by calling for a recognition of the importance of publicizing intelligible legal outcomes so that those outcomes can be subjected to further deliberation

member's assessment of its decisions *matters*. That is a message of respect. Jules Coleman has explained that the practice of giving reasons "presupposes the values of autonomy and equality" as follows:

> The commitment to equality flows from the fact that a practice of offering reasons and inviting criticism can arise only among people who believe that they owe it to others to justify their actions to others. . . . The commitment to autonomy is exemplified in the very idea that individuals can respond to reasons and arguments, that others' judgments are formed as a result of reflecting on the reasons offered. Anyone who offers reasons designed to convince or persuade others makes it clear that he treats others as autonomous and equal in the same way that one regards oneself, worthy of the respect a practice of offering reasons presupposes and as capable of being moved by reasons as only autonomous agents can be.[104]

On this basis, I maintain that giving full expression to respect for human agency within an adjudicative process requires that reasons for factual conclusions be expressed. This way, legal subjects are given a chance to discern the rationality of the deliberation that took place in the judge's mind, so far as that is reflected in the express reasons.[105]

My second question is whether adjudicative rationality is expressed only in the mind of a judge, as Ho's discussion suggests. In arriving at his argument for why rational deliberation matters, Ho starts by advocating for and adopting the "internal" point of view of the fact-finder. This is in contrast to the more common "external" point of view

---

by the public. This, as I understand, is akin to calling for public reasons to be given in the fact-finding context as well, so that judicial outcomes can be reviewed publicly. See chapter 2, and David Dyzenhaus, "The Legitimacy of Legality," above note 53.

104 Jules Coleman, "Authority and Reason," in *The Autonomy of Law Essays on Legal Positivism* (Robert George (ed) (Oxford: Clarendon Press, 1996) at 312–13.

105 Note that the Supreme Court of Canada has commented that defects in the reasons provided by judges can amount to procedural impropriety. See *Cojocaru v British Columbia Women's Hospital and Health Centre* [2013] 2 SCR 357. In that case, the appellants questioned the propriety of the trial judge's reasons due to extensive copying from the plaintiff's submissions. The Supreme Court of Canada held that the copying in the judge's reasons did not rebut the presumption of judicial impartiality, but noted that better practice is to refrain from extensive copying at (paras 73–75). A more extensive discussion of the adequacy of judicial reasons is outside of my scope, but see for example: H.L. Ho, "The Judicial Duty to Give Reasons" (2000) 20(1) *Legal Studies* 42; Richard Murphy, "Chenery Unmasked: Reasonable Limits on the Duty to Give Reasons" (2012) 80(3) *University of Cincinnati Law Review* 817.

which, if adopted, leads to the conclusion that the relevant criterion for acceptable adjudication is factual accuracy of the outcome, because if an outcome is correct, then justice is done.[106] Taking up the point of view of the trier of fact, Ho explains, this conclusion does not hold.[107] The judge, along with being concerned with what to believe, "must also be concerned about the morality of the process by which she reaches her verdict."[108] Given that Ho's operative perspective is that of the trier of fact, rationality or irrationality in arriving at a verdict is expressed entirely in their thought process. In other words, whether an outcome is rational depends exclusively on the fact-finder committing to being rational — she will rely on the evidence presented and weigh it fairly against the standard of proof.

Doubtless, the fact-finder's commitment to rationality is critical, but the judge's deliberations only tell part of the rationality story. Suppose that a litigant was coerced so as to prevent them from freely presenting her evidence and arguments. Even if a judge makes a reasoned decision on the basis of the evidence presented, the rationality of the outcome is questionable, at least in a sense that would be relevant to the coerced litigant.[109] Even if rationality motivates an adjudicator's conclusion, the outcome they arrive at may still be considered irrational. Encompassing rationality exclusively in the mind of the adjudicator misses this problem.

Adopting Fuller's and Habermas's approaches to adjudication provides an avenue to rectify this problem. They perceive the adjudicative process itself as an expression of rational decision-making, resulting in a more comprehensive understanding of rationality as a requisite feature of adjudicative legitimacy. Through the lens of Fuller's and Habermas's jurisprudence, it becomes clear that the adjudicative process itself must maintain a commitment to rational fact-finding, not just the fact-finder. The fact-finder's ultimate decision-making is part

---

106   Ho, *Philosophy of Evidence Law*, above note 47, chapter 2.

107   *Ibid* at 51: "From an external standpoint, the relevant criterion is the correctness of the verdict. There is a contingent connection, to which terms like 'accuracy' and 'reliability' refer, between the outcome of fact-finding and truth. Truth is needed so that justice (in the sense associated with 'rectitude of decision') can be done."

108   *Ibid.*

109   On the question of whose perspective is important: Solum, "Procedural Justice," above note 71 at 280: "When we seek to identify the conditions for the legitimacy of adjudication, we should assume the point of view of a citizen who is bound by a judgment that he or she has good reason to believe is in error and is adverse to the citizen's interests or wishes."

of that system. They must make a rational decision by considering the evidence and the argument presented by parties and applying the relevant standard of proof on the basis of that evidence and argument. But their mind is not the only place where adjudicative rationality is expressed. Rather, the entirety of the process should be conducive to rational decision-making.

As Fuller and Habermas both prescribe, ensuring rational adjudication involves ensuring that litigants have meaningful ability to participate. If a fact-finder makes an irrational decision in the sense that they improperly fail to take into account evidence presented by one party, as in the blue-eyed witness example given above, they erode the party's right to meaningful participation, because the right to participate through presentation of evidence is a façade if the evidence is not rationally relied on in concluding as to whether the standard of proof was satisfied.[110]

This leads to the final question on the nature of participation rights and the underlying value they protect. So far, participation rights have been discussed in relation to their role in maintaining rational outcomes. This elicits the question whether participation rights are *only* significant in relation to rationality, or if ensuring litigant participation protects other values as well. Answering this question is important because it influences the nature of the participation rights that should be maintained. I turn to this question below.

---

110   Given the significance that I am giving to the rationality of the decision-making process, it is worth noting important social science evidence that suggests that judges, like all decision-makers, adopt certain heuristics that may unconsciously bias their decisions. See Daniel Kahneman, Paul Slovic & Amos Tversky (eds), "Judgment Under Uncertainty: Heuristics and Bias" (1974) 185 *Science* 1124, and Daniel Kahneman, *Thinking Fast and Slow* (New York: Farrar Straus & Giroux, 2011); Stephen Porter & Leanne ten Brinke, "Dangerous Decisions: A Theoretical Framework for Understanding How Judges Assess Credibility in the Court Room" (2009) 14 *Legal and Criminal Psychology* 114; Eyal Peer & Eyal Gamliel, "Heuristics and Biases in Judicial Decisions" (2013) 49 *Court Review* 114; J. Rachlinski, "Heuristics and Biases in the Courts: Ignorance or Adaptation?" (2000) 79 *Oregon Law Review* 61; D. Langevoort, "Behavioral Theories of Judgment and Decision Making in Legal Scholarship: A Literature Review" (1998) 51 *Vanderbilt Law Review* 1499; Emma Cunliffe, "Judging, Fast and Slow: Using Decision Making Theory to Explore Judicial Fact Determination" (2014) 18 *International Journal of Evidence and Proof* 139. The best answer to this literature is, in my view, to recognize its significance and encourage further study on biases and cognitive difficulties in complex decision-making like trials, and continually make efforts through judicial education to maintain judges' awareness of decision-making pitfalls and provide tools to overcoming them to the best extent possible.

B. The Value of Participation Rights

Whether, and to what extent participation rights are valued in an adjudicative theory depends on the theorist's viewpoint as to the nature and purpose of adjudication. Theorists who place the ultimate value of the adjudicative system in its ability to produce accurate outcomes would conclude that a best effort toward accurate outcomes should wholly satisfy the requirements of legitimate adjudication.[111] It follows that for them, participation only matters so far as it affects outcome accuracy, and does not add any independent value of its own. Louis Kaplow, for instance, suggests in "The Value of Accuracy of Adjudication," that:

> One suspects that claimants who object to not being heard are those who are, for example, denied benefits. If only losers complain, however, one should be suspicious that the complaint is motivated by a concern for the result, and thus an objection to a lack of process may implicitly be an instrumental argument. An entirely plausible reason to object to not being heard is that one may believe (perhaps feel certain) that the decision was adverse precisely because the decision-maker was deprived of information one had to offer. Thus, the decision may have been inaccurate.[112]

In chapter 1, I explained why the starting point adopted by instrumental or outcome-accuracy focused authors is problematic. In summary, there are two issues that cannot be responded to if an instrumental approach to adjudicative fact-finding is adopted. First, it does not offer a response to the problem associated with achieving an accurate outcome *improperly*. If only accuracy mattered in adjudication, then problems associated with irrational, arbitrary, or otherwise improper decision-making would dissolve if the outcome turned out to be factually accurate.[113] Second, and even more fundamentally, an effective

---

111 I have already discussed that Dworkin is a proponent of an outcome-accuracy model of adjudication, and participation rights are notably missing from his procedural proposal. Similarly, even Ho, despite his commitment that outcome-accuracy must be accompanied by rationality, still maintains that outcome-accuracy is the paramount goal of adjudication, and as I have noted, participation rights do not find expression in his proposal.

112 Louis Kaplow, "The Value of Accuracy in Adjudication" (1994) 23 *Journal of Legal Studies* 307 at 390–91. And for Solum's treatment of Kaplow's argument, see Solum, "Procedural Justice," above note 71 at 291–95.

113 I discussed this problem in the introduction, Part 2C.

adjudicative system cannot guarantee outcome accuracy, yet it also requires that its outcomes are authoritative. That means that inevitably, some outcomes will be inaccurate yet authoritative, whether or not anyone is aware of inaccuracy. A theory that centralizes outcome accuracy cannot provide sufficient grounding for that authority. Making a "best effort to achieve accuracy" does not provide the full answer to a litigant who may accept that the adjudicative system rendered such a best effort, but ultimately failed in its task. Given the failure, why should they accept the authority of the outcome? As Lawrence Solum has expressed:

> How can we regard ourselves as obligated by legitimate authority to comply with a judgment that we believe (or even know) to be in error with respect to the substantive merits? The answer to this question cannot be accuracy – the hard question arises only when litigants have a warranted belief that the outcome was not accurate.[114]

As I have noted, it is legitimacy that grounds the authority of adjudicative outcomes *despite* its potential failure to achieve factual accuracy. Legitimacy does not, and cannot depend on outcome accuracy. Rather, drawing on Fuller's and Habermas's insights, legitimacy is achieved when legal procedures demonstrably respect human agency. In the adjudicative context, as I have elaborated above, that requires a demonstrable procedural commitment to genuine and rational effort toward achieving factual accuracy. Whether factual accuracy is ultimately achieved does not affect the legitimacy of the factual determination.

Given the normative foundations of legitimacy in my proposal, the relevant question for me is whether a genuine effort at accurate, rational fact-finding gives the fullest expression to respect for human agency in fact-finding procedures.[115] In terms of participation rights, my question is whether they are necessary only in relation to their impact on achieving a rational outcome as discussed above, or if they have a role in preserving respect for human agency independent of rationality as well.

I have already noted that rational decision-making presumes participation rights, because if some affected party's position is not permitted

---

114   Solum, "Procedural Justice," above note 71 at 274.

115   Robert Bone states in "Procedure, Participation, Rights" (2010) 90 *Boston University Law Review* 1011, "Anyone arguing for dignity or legitimacy as a basis for participation rights must be prepared to explain why dignity is not fully respected and legitimacy fully secured by an adjudicative system that does its best to produce an outcome for each individual that conforms to the substantive law." [Bone, "Procedure, Participation, Rights"].

or sincerely considered, then the rationality of the outcome is precarious. If enabling a rational outcome is the only value of participation rights, then the right to participate can be justifiably defined as a right to have one's interests represented in an adjudicative system. Owen Fiss has made the claim that representation of interests is key to grounding an authoritative outcome; a right of individual participation is not:

> What the Constitution guarantees is not a right of participation, but rather what I will call a "right of representation": not a day in court but the right to have one's interests adequately represented. The right of representation provides that no individual can be bound by an adjudication unless his or her interest is adequately represented in the proceeding.[116]

On the surface, Fiss's argument seems agreeable. If a litigant's interests were adequately represented in the decision-making process, then on what basis would they complain that they were not allowed to participate in the decision? They could not, for instance, complain that the rationality of the decision was compromised due to their inability to represent their interests. Solum's answer to Fiss's argument is persuasive and demonstrates why individual rights of participation are necessary in terms of respect for human agency. He explains that it is not "interests" in their own right that are the primary concern in the adjudication of a claim. Rather, the primary concern is the individuals who hold those interests. Solum provides:

> We are concerned about individual interests because we are concerned about individuals. Interests themselves have no moral standing. Individuals represent themselves, not because they are the best or most efficient representatives of their own interests; individuals represent themselves because they are human persons, who act on their own behalves, define their own interests, and speak for themselves.[117]

Given this response to Fiss's point, it is surprising that Solum does not clearly acknowledge that respect for human agency is at the heart of individual participation rights. According to Solum, "Dignity, equality, and autonomy are fundamental political values. The idea that they

---

116   Owen Fiss, "The Allure of Individualism" (1993) 78 *Iowa Law Review* 965 at 978; and Solum, "Procedural Justice," above note 71 at 301.

117   Solum, "Procedural Justice," above note 71 at 302–3.

connect in some way to the value of participation is sound."[118] He goes on to note, however, that "the error is to believe that any one of these values directly provides the value of participation – legitimacy plays that role."[119]

In Solum's account, however, the conception of legitimacy is unsubstantiated. He defines legitimacy in terms of its role and its significance, but not in terms of its requisite features. His account of legitimacy can be summarized as that which provides the grounding to adjudicative authority.[120] But he does not delineate any underlying normative commitments that could answer *on what basis* legitimacy provides that grounding. Without identifying the key normative features of legitimacy, Solum's statement that participation rights are underpinned by legitimacy remains hollow. Since it is an unsubstantiated notion of legitimacy that grounds the requirement for participation rights, the question of *why* participation rights are necessary within a legitimate adjudicative process cannot be answered beyond the answer, "because participation rights are necessary for legitimacy," which simply elicits the question.

The better approach, in my view, is to recognize that respect for the human agent is at the heart of legitimacy, and to preserve that fully, individuals must have a right to participate in their own adjudication. That right cannot be subsumed into the rationality requirement. That is because a system where representation of litigant interests is guaranteed, but individual participation rights were not protected, could preserve the rationality of the outcome while also failing to fully respect litigant agency.

---

118   *Ibid* at 289.

119   *Ibid*. And elsewhere [286–87] he notes: "The value of participation derives from the idea of legitimacy. Our focus on legitimacy contrasts with much of the prior literature, which has suggested three rival explanations – based on dignity, equality, and autonomy – for the irreducibly value of legitimacy. Each of these three rival explanations has a contribution to make, especially when considered in relationship to legitimacy. Considered in isolation, however, dignity, equality, and autonomy do not provide an adequate explanation of the value of participation."

120   See generally Solum, "Procedural Justice," above note 71 at 277–79. There, Solum explains the importance and role of legitimacy, but does not expound on its necessary features. For example at 277: "Why is legitimacy important? Citizens are not obligated to regard illegitimate laws as authoritative." And at 278: "The goodness of legitimacy flows from an intuitively appealing principle of political morality: each citizen, who is to be bound by an official proceeding for the resolution of a civil dispute should be able to regard the procedure as a legitimate source of binding authority creating a content independent obligation of morality for the parties to the dispute."

Despite the difficulty in Solum's approach, parts of his analysis support this notion. For one, he explains that participation rights are essential to legitimacy because denial would inflict a certain "moral harm" on citizens.[121] The very reason that this moral harm exists is because denying participation rights constitutes a denial of "a concern and respect for individual dignity."[122] He also relates a helpful hypothetical situation that elicits the intuition that representation of interests is not enough to ensure respect for human agency.[123] In his hypothetical, a fully competent adult is sued in a civil lawsuit, but is denied the ability to participate in the adjudication. Instead, the judge appoints a guardian ad litem to represent the person's interests. The guardian represents their interests well. But it still seems that the legitimacy of the proceeding can be denied. If I were that person, in the event of an unfavourable outcome, my intuition (shared by Solum) is that I have good reason to deny the authority assumed over me, because I was improperly denied the right to participate.[124]

A number of authors have picked up on this intuition to argue that participation rights in the litigation process are necessary, and are underpinned by respect for human dignity and autonomy of legal subjects.[125] For instance, Lawrence Tribe provides that:

> Both the right to be heard from, and the right to be told why, are analytically distinct from the right to secure a different outcome; these rights to interchange express the elementary idea that to be a person, rather than a thing, is at least to be consulted about what is done with one.[126]

---

121 *Ibid* at 298.

122 *Ibid.*

123 *Ibid* at 283–84.

124 *Ibid*

125 See for instance, Jerry Marshaw, *Due Process in the Administrative State* (New Haven, CT: Yale University Press, 1985); Richard Saphire, "Specifying Due Process Values: Towards a More Responsive Approach to Procedural Protection" (1978) 127 *University of Pennsylvania Law Review* 111, adopting a dignity-based approach to due process and arguing in favour of recognizing participation rights on that basis. Compare contrary position of Alex Stein, *Foundations of Evidence Law*, above note 72 at 33: "The right to be heard, and, indeed, the entire package of trial participation rights, are rights that ultimately derive from epistemic fallibility, not from moral virtuousness."

126 Laurence Tribe, *American Constitutional Law*, 2d ed (New York: Foundation Press, 1988) at 666–67.

In a similar vein, Robert Bone has noted that:

> I assume that the parties to mass tort cases have process-oriented participation rights that can trump utility and that those rights guarantee a robust form of individual control, including control over litigation of all significant issues relating to the determination of individual damages. I also assume that the intrinsic value of participation is historically tied to respect for individual autonomy: allowing a person to participate before subjecting him to the coercive power of the state respects his dignity as an autonomous moral agent.[127]

These contributions lend credence to the position that participation rights are necessary features in my conception of legitimacy.[128] On this basis, I endorse the conclusion that parties who will be substantially affected by the adjudication should have a right to participate in the sense of being allowed an equal and meaningful opportunity to present relevant evidence and arguments.[129] This is, of course, subject to justifiable admissibility rules discussed above.

---

127 Robert Bone, "Statistical Adjudication: Rights, Justice, and Utility in a World of Process Scarcity" (1993) 46 *Vanderbilt Law Review* 561 at 619. He also states at 625: "A strong participation right can be justified only by a normative theory of process value that grounds the value of participation in the conditions of adjudicative legitimacy, such as respect for a party's dignity or autonomy."

128 Some accounts hold that adjudicative legitimacy is tied exclusively to participation rights. That view overextends the normative value of participation rights at the cost of failing to recognize that factual reliability is also necessary to legitimate adjudication. Solum alludes to this problem in "Procedural Justice," above note 71 as well, at 272: "At this point, we can take stock of the participation model . . . [the interpretation which] emphasizes the dignity interest of litigants, at least gets off the ground, but the dignity-enhancing process is not sufficient for fairness in the face of skewed outcomes." Of course, my own approach to legitimacy does not suggest an exclusivity of participation rights, and includes a requirement for a genuine orientation to factual accuracy, as I have delineated above.

129 See Solum, "Procedural Justice," above note 71 at 305 for his statement of the "Participation Principle." I note that the requirement for participation rights is suggestive of a possible defect in the inquisitorial model of dispute resolution from the procedural legitimacy perspective, but a full discussion of the merits and pitfalls of inquisitorial dispute resolution is beyond the scope of this chapter. I briefly return to a comparison with inquisitorial models in the context of expert witnesses in chapter 4. In addition, I acknowledge that a call for participation rights would require further consideration and delineation, particularly in contexts beyond civil litigation. The question of who is substantially affected or directly affected can depend on the type of administrative decision at stake. Addressing the question of who could be affected in various instances goes beyond my scope in this project of

SUMMING UP: THE PROCEDURAL LEGITIMACY FRAMEWORK

My purpose in this chapter has been to uncover the general principles for how respecting legal subjects as autonomous agents can be reflected in the adjudicative fact-finding process. That leads to a substantiated procedural legitimacy proposal, and constitutes my suggestion for why, and on what basis, judicial fact-finding can be acceptable despite its unavoidable potential for factual inaccuracy.

The first part of the discussion centred on factual reliability. That is a central concern because of the underlying point that factual accuracy is an important goal in order to maintain congruence between the laws of a society and their administration through the courts. Incongruence between law and their administration constitutes an affront to the human agent. At the same time, factual accuracy cannot be guaranteed while maintaining an efficacious adjudicative system. Preserving the integrity of the judicial system, therefore, depends on maintaining a genuine best effort at getting the facts right. In my definition, considering whether fact-finding procedures manifest and facilitate a sincere effort at achieving accuracy is the relevant question to assess factual reliability. The authenticity of that effort can be presumed when:

1. In general, all relevant evidence is admissible.
2. Exclusions to relevant evidence are justified on the basis of respecting human autonomy.
3. The system ensures internally coherent and consistent error-risk management.
4. The standard of proof is, at minimum, a balance of probabilities.
5. The evidence presented is weighed rationally against the standard of proof, and the factual findings are accompanied by reasons.

In addition to factual reliability, participation rights also requisite features of legitimate fact-finding. A fact-finding system must not exclude an affected party from participating in the decision-making by presenting evidence and argument. The two elements of factual reliability and participation together provide the fullest expression of respect for human autonomy in adjudicative fact-finding procedures. When

providing guiding principles that may be used to assess fact-finding processes in the civil litigation context.

fact-finding procedures reflect those qualities, consistent application of those rules gives rise to legitimate factual determinations.

The implicit message of committing to consistent application of a procedural system that manifests these principles is that while we cannot guarantee factually accurate adjudicative outcomes, we can promise judicial outcomes that are right in a different sense: they are right in that they are a product of a valuable procedure that ensures respect for the human agent while simultaneously acknowledging the reality that factual findings occur in a context of uncertainty.

CHAPTER FOUR

Conclusion

A. INTRODUCTION

The starting point of this book, and its running theme, has been that determining "what happened?" is foundational to resolving any dispute. Judges are called on to resolve that question in most substantive disputes that reach them. It is a difficult question because of evidentiary gaps and complexities. No matter how difficult, however, the factual questions must be resolved in order for a legal claim to be decided. In this book, I have invited readers into an inquiry into why and, on what bases, we can accept the authority of a judicial decision that rests on factual conclusions that are made in a context of uncertainty.

Though I offer critiques of various judicial outcomes and scholarly approaches throughout, my inquiry did not arise out of a criticism of the legal system for its susceptibility to factual inaccuracy. My starting point, which remains central to my analysis, was the modest observation that we do not always know what happened, and we do not always know what the right answer is. That fallibility naturally manifests in the adjudicative system. Since knowing things *for sure* is not usually (if ever) possible, there is always a chance of arriving at an inaccurate conclusion. My effort has been to discover the legitimacy of the adjudicative system without rejecting, ignoring, or minimizing that frailty.

Acknowledging the unavoidable imperfection of the adjudicative system was soon coupled with the realization that an effective dispute resolution system requires outcomes that are authoritative by nature, and as such, the outcomes have to be legitimate.

Accordingly, I have been oriented toward finding the right balance between the judicial system's forgivable limitations and the uncompromisable demands that define legitimacy. That balance, I have suggested, is ascertainable through a concept of legitimacy that keeps procedural integrity at its heart. The preceding chapters were designed to uncover the concept of procedural legitimacy and its essential features.

My hope is that readers have enjoyed the intellectual journey through contemporary legal theory as applied to the foundational context of fact-finding. I hope also that you have been given enough food for thought to consider for yourself what makes the legal system valuable, and therefore what you see as your proper role within it. Given that I have offered a procedural paradigm for adjudicative legitimacy, my hope is that legal players will appreciate the weight of their responsibility in maintaining, upholding, making available, and improving civil justice procedures. Offering this book has been my attempt at taking my responsibility in this respect seriously.

B. SUMMARY

It is often helpful at the end of a long analysis to briefly sum up how the conclusions were drawn, and how one led to the next. I offer that here. In chapter 1, the inquiry into legitimate fact-finding led me to the notion that procedure is integral to legitimacy. That arose by observing how the adjudicative system resolves the above noted tension between the inevitability of factual uncertainty and the need for an authoritative resolution to the legal dispute. It is resolved by enabling facts to be found on a standard of proof that is less than certainty. In the civil litigation context, where I focus, a fact is proven if it can be shown to be more likely true than not. The implication contained within that method of fact-finding is that we accept the validity of outcomes that may be inaccurate — we accept up to a 49 percent risk of that. This means that the validity of an outcome does not depend on its substantive accuracy. The legal validity must, therefore, depend on the propriety of the process that gave rise to that outcome.

When an outcome has legal validity, it is authoritative and can be enforced. That authority requires justification, which I have referred to throughout this work as legitimacy. I reasoned that if procedural integrity is a necessary element of legal validity, and legal validity brings simultaneous implications of authority, then procedural integrity must underpin legitimacy as well. This led to my conclusion in chapter 1: consistent and appropriate adherence to legal processes is necessary for the legitimacy of an outcome.

That conclusion leads to the question of whether any process, applied consistently, would legitimize an outcome. For instance, can we have a process where fact-finding is based on a flip of a coin? Would outcomes that arise out of such a process have justifiable authority so long as the process was applied properly and consistently? Of course, the answer is no, and substantiating that response led to the jurisprudential inquiry that I undertook in chapter 2.

There, I began by unraveling some of the major themes in H.L.A Hart's and Joseph Raz's positivism. I noted that there are aspects of the separation thesis that must be accepted. The legal validity of a law, for instance, cannot depend on individual assessments of its moral acceptability. At the same time, I found the positivist commitment to an absolute separation of law and the justification of law to be limiting. Since legal validity brings with it authoritative implications, I suggest that legal validity must have some sort of in-built legitimacy. For me, that does not mean that an outcome that has legal validity must be correct in its outcome, but it must be justified in some way. That, again, prompted and reinforced my turn to process. Accordingly, in the second half of chapter 2, I turned to theorists who have offered proceduralist paradigms for law's validity *and* its legitimacy: Lon Fuller and Jürgen Habermas.

I noted stark similarities in Fuller's and Habermas's thinking. Both have offered unique accounts of legality and legitimacy, and the points at which their theories converge were the most significant for me. For both, legal processes must demonstrably embody respect for human autonomy. Consistent adherence to those procedures results in valid legal outcomes that are also legitimate. Fuller develops this concept by outlining eight rules that a monarch (King Rex), must follow when creating laws. These eight rules, which he calls the internal morality of law, all demonstrate that the lawmaker must respect the autonomy of their subjects.

Habermas offers a similar commitment to recognizing citizens as autonomous agents within lawmaking procedures, but in more familiar terrain: the democratic process. That process, for Habermas, is an expression of a rational discourse, and it is the rational discursive process that gives rise to the legitimacy of an outcome or claim. The fundamental feature of the rational discursive process is that everyone who is affected by the outcome of that process will have had an autonomous, non-coercive, and meaningful ability to participate. For both Fuller and Habermas, those who are under the authority of law deserve to be treated as free acting agents who cannot be treated arbitrarily.

In chapter 3, following Fuller's and Habermas's lead of centralizing respect for the autonomy of those affected by authoritative laws, I set out some general principles of fact-finding procedures that would ensure a demonstrable respect for litigants as free acting agents. The first part of chapter 3 required the most direct engagement with the role of factual accuracy in maintaining adjudicative legitimacy. My premise, as noted above, is that factual accuracy cannot be guaranteed, so adjudicative legitimacy cannot depend on it. This, as I have tried to reiterate throughout, does not mean that factual accuracy is irrelevant. An adjudicative procedure that disregards factual accuracy cannot be said to respect litigants as free-acting agents who should not be subject to arbitrary treatment. In chapter 3, I explained that factual accuracy is relevant in my proposal through a procedural conception of factual *reliability*. Fact-finding procedures are factually reliable, I suggested, when they demonstrate a genuine orientation toward achieving factual accuracy. As I noted in chapter 3, the authenticity of the fact-finding procedures can be presumed when:

1. In general, all relevant evidence is admissible.
2. Exclusions to relevant evidence are justified on the basis of respecting human autonomy.
3. The system ensures internally coherent and consistent error-risk management.
4. The standard of proof is, at minimum, a balance of probabilities.
5. The evidence presented is weighed rationally against the standard of proof, and the factual findings are accompanied by reasons.

Along with factual reliability, a legitimate fact-finding procedure will ensure full participation rights to those affected by the outcome. No affected party should be excluded from participating in the decision-making by presenting evidence and argument. Factual reliability and participation rights together provide the fullest expression of respect for human autonomy in adjudicative fact-finding procedures. This is what we must demand, absolutely, of our legal procedures. When fact-finding procedures embody those qualities, consistent application of those rules results in legitimate factual determinations. This is the substantiated procedural legitimacy proposal that constitutes my suggestion for why, and on what bases judicial fact-finding can be acceptable despite the unavoidable potential for factual inaccuracy.

C. LIMITATIONS

Before closing, it is important to reiterate the limitations of the ideas presented here. First, focusing on adjudicative legitimacy from the perspective of fact-finding means that I have only tangentially considered the legitimacy of judicial pronouncements on ambiguous laws. The propriety of these interpretations is clearly necessary for the legitimacy of judicial outcomes. Although the considerations around resolving both legal and factual indeterminacy in an adjudicative context can helpfully inform each other, I have presented my inquiry on adjudicative resolution of factual indeterminacy as one that is complementary to, and distinct from, questions about the how and when we can accept the authority of judicial resolution of legal indeterminacy. These questions, though I do not address them in this work, are no less valuable to the broader goal of maintaining a legitimate adjudicative system and outcomes.

Second, I have opted to illustrate procedural legitimacy mostly in the tortious injury context throughout the book. Its applicability extends, in my view, far beyond that limited scope. All of the conclusions presented regarding acceptable fact-finding here are applicable throughout civil litigation. I believe there is also significant transferability to the criminal context, because even there, factual uncertainty cannot be eradicated. Naturally, however, there are different concerns and values at stake in the criminal sphere compared with the civil sphere. I have not addressed those, nor have I addressed critiques of the ideas presented here that may especially arise in the criminal context. Wrongful conviction, for instance, is one of the most stirring examples of the impropriety of factual inaccuracy that surely cannot be made to seem "legitimate" no matter how laudable the procedure. I agree, and this project should not be taken as providing any justification for such an outcome.

Third, through this project I have contemplated adjudicative legitimacy through a jurisprudential lens, but there are practical and systemic realities that confront legal institutions and have very real impact on whether the adjudicative system really is legitimate, even if it may be in theory. These would not, I believe, detract from the thesis that procedural integrity is necessary for acceptable judicial decisions, but they are significant concerns for anyone interested in adjudicative legitimacy. I have not been able, in this work, to engage with the obviously important contributions that have arisen from critical scholarship shedding light on the practical realities of being a woman, or a racial minority, or a member of the LGBTQIA+ community, or a disabled person, for instance, trying to navigate within adjudicative procedures. These perspectives are critical to maintaining a legitimate adjudicative process that serves and centrally values human agency and dignity.

Somewhat related, my conclusion that the legitimacy of an adjudicative outcome depends, at least in part, on procedural propriety may give rise to questions around accessibility of those very processes in practical terms. Again, I have not engaged deeply in this element of the access to justice discourse here, but a concept of the necessary components of adjudicative legitimacy can surely contribute to that discourse.

D. FINAL REFLECTIONS

This project has enabled me to explore some of the most deeply held intuitions about what makes the adjudicative system acceptable and good. It has required me to come to terms with (and defend) the idea that fallibility does not equate to illegitimacy. At times that recognition has proven challenging, both intuitively and analytically. It is difficult, I have found, not to expect the legal system to be perfect, given the authority that it exerts, its role in maintaining societal stability, and its symbolic significance as a representation of the unity of a community. But I have learned that it is analytically unsound to impose a standard of perfection to assess anything.

That lesson applies to this book. The analysis contained here is, of course, not perfect. As noted, there are certain discussions and perspectives that I have had to leave unaddressed, and there will be places where my analysis will not have gone far enough or will have fallen short of covering every possible counterposition. But this book represents my best attempt to understand and make use of the often brilliant insights of others, and to try to reconcile and explain the disagreements among some of the most influential thinkers in contemporary legal philosophy. I do not assume that this book offers an end point, and rather hope that it will serve as a starting point for those who believe in the goodness of law despite its (and our) fallibility, and who may be developing their own voice in defence of that belief.

In final conclusion, I note that my broadest running commitment in this book has been to expressly advocate for consistent application of procedures that manifest respect for human dignity via recognition of individuals as autonomous, free agents. This can be understood as promoting the foundational principle of rule of law — good legal procedures (and the outcomes that emerge from them) must be applied consistently and equally to all in order to preserve legal legitimacy and ensure that the authority that the legal system and its actors assert is justified. At one time, this may have seemed trite or too obvious to need expression. But in 2025, as we gawk at the global rise of authoritarianism and degradation of democratic values, pleas for preserving the rule of law must become louder and more frequent, as well as accessible and analytically crisp. I hope that this book contributes to that.

Table of Statutes

Table of Cases

Index

About the Author

Nayha Acharya is an associate professor at the Schulich School of Law, Dalhousie University. She teaches in the areas of civil procedure, dispute resolution, tort law, and legal ethics. Her primary research interests are civil procedure including alternative dispute resolution. She also researches, writes, and speaks on legal education, emphasizing holistic teaching and learning.